WISE
IRISH
WOMEN

WISE
IRISH
WOMEN

A Journey of Love, Loyalty, and
Friendship to Inspire the Irish Spirit

Patricia Connorton Kagerer
and
Laura Prendergast Gordon

Wise Irish Women
A Journey of Love, Loyalty, and Friendship to Inspire the Irish Spirit

ISBN 978-1-612548-06-7
Library of Congress Control Number 2011944983

Printed in China by Global PSD
10 9 8 7 6 5 4 3 2

Author contact information: www.WiseIrishWomen.com

With love and gratitude this book is dedicated
to women who face the challenges of life and meet
them with dignity, passion, and endurance.

We want you to know that we see you.
May these stories inspire and touch your souls.

We also dedicate this book to the
Prendergast, Dalton, and Connorton families.

To our grandmother Peggy Dalton Prendergast and
grandfather Tom Prendergast.

To their daughter Pat Prendergast Connorton
and son Thomas Aidan Prendergast.

Each of you gave us the extraordinary gifts
of unconditional love, faith, and hope.

We love you more than you will ever know.

One day we will meet again.

Contents

Acknowledgments

We would like to give special thanks to our editor, Kim Pearson of Primary Sources (www.primary-sources.com), our assistant, Natalie Eckberg, and our book coach, Jan King (www.janbking.com). We are grateful to Cynthia Stillar-Wang, director of The Small Press (www.brownbooks.com), the first person to encourage the writing of this book, for her guidance and encouragement to bring it to life.

Thanks to our family members, Pat, Patrick, and Aidan Gordon, and Markus, Tommy, and Annie Kagerer and all the Connortons, Prendergasts, and Kagerers for your love, laughter, patience, encouragement, and excitement.

Heart Elated

a poem by Laney DeJesus

(I) .....wave and smile at YOU.... my heart sent soaring from across the way......

(And SHE)..... your past stands outstretched like a wall blocking....

(YOU).... shadowed from your future... ME.... bright and sunny....

(And I) ......look on hopelessly as YOU.... bump over and over into that barrier....

(As WE)...... question what WE say.....and where this road is going?

(Try)..... so hard to understand where you've been .....as I tenderly protect and caress your heart carrier.....

(To make you SEE ME) .... and how I feel when YOU can't even see YOU.....

(A battle to reach out and grab YOU)..... embrace YOU.... fight the storm of hurt together YOU & I side by side....

(So I can give this love of mine that's YOURS) .....YOU frozen in time...... please melt for ME and forget your foolish pride! YOU over there.......

(already)...... in my eyes on this side with ME here....

(LOOK AT ME as I see YOU).... Not SHE who has moved on over and over.... Dear man YOU are so near! See YOU facing ME......

(our eyes locked) .... YOU see YOU......I see ME.....we've just erased that fear.....My love....tearing down that wall taking gently your hand.... YOU feeling my warm sun spread across your lonely island. YOU.... finally wave and smile back at ME......

(OUR heart wide open elated as I welcome YOU home).....

About Laney DeJesus

Laney DeJesus is a poet, social media expert, entrepreneur, and a die-hard fan of everything Irish. Laney loves Ireland so much she has a tattoo of the country on her chest.

In an effort to share this love, Laney partnered with her cousin James Hayes. Utilizing her social networking talent, America-based Laney and Ireland-based James created the Irish Social Networking group "Friends of Ireland," one of the largest Irish social networks on LinkedIn. "We recently ranked 12 out of 2,430 in group searches for 'Ireland' and 3 out of 1,040 in group searches for 'Irish'," says Laney. "We're also on Facebook, Twitter, and technically YouTube. I record Friends Of Ireland meet-up events under LaneyOfLimerick. I love the fact that we are global and reach out to all those who are Irish everywhere and those who have a love of the Irish or Ireland. It's been an incredible journey and one where I have met some amazing and wonderful people!"

Laney lives her life by the Irish Claddagh, which symbolizes love, loyalty, and friendship. She loves her home country of America and her Irish connection. Laney is loyal to her Irish roots and through her work and poetry has shared it with thousands of people. Laney's passion for Ireland has opened the door to long-lasting friendships that span the globe.

Laney loves to travel and considers Glin, County Limerick, Ireland her second home. Much of her family still lives there. Laney is proud of her dual citizenship with the USA and Ireland, giving her the opportunity to celebrate the best of both worlds. For the last thirty years Laney has owned a fudge business, Chocolate Moose Fudge (www.facebook.com/chocolatemoosefudge). In her spare time Laney writes poetry and records music. Laney's poem "Heart Elated" is a fitting beginning to *Wise Irish Women*. When we explore our hearts, our heritage, and our dreams, we find ourselves.

In the Beginning

Ireland is arguably the most beautiful country on earth. Rolling green hills, rainbows, glorious oceans, castles, and crosses—it is without doubt a magical place. Everywhere you look you see the Hand of God. The people are a heartwarming, funny, welcoming group who love to celebrate and share stories, people who have never met a stranger. Ireland could be considered perfect in almost all respects.

Yet underneath the lush green appearance and behind the magical stories, Ireland has a dark and turbulent story. Its history has been scarred by sadness, war, and human struggle. There is a reason that millions of Irish emigrants left their homeland and migrated around the world for a chance at a better life. Some left looking for adventure. Others left for survival. The harsh reality is that Irish people left because as beautiful and wonderful as Ireland was, it did not offer many of its people a future. Family farms were given to the first-born son, leaving other sons and daughters without a means for earning a living. Children had to grow up fast with the understanding that they had to fend for themselves and find their own path. However, whatever their reason for leaving, the connection to the country and the culture was rarely lost.

Our grandparents, Thomas Aidan Prendergast and Margaret "Peggy" Dalton Prendergast, referred to Ireland as "home" despite having lived in the United States for over forty years. They spoke fondly of where they came from, told stories about the old country, and remained intimately connected to family members back home. Although the Internet did not exist and phone calls were astronomically expensive, they continued their connection to the place they came from. As they shared fond memories and Irish wisdom, they passed their beliefs and values down to their grandchildren so that we too can share them with our children and apply them to our lives.

Chapter One

Irish Love of Family

*I*rish women are known for the strength of their motherly love. An Irish mother is proud of her children to the point of defiance. She is selfless and generous, quick to defend and just as quick to prod her children toward the good. She possesses an uncanny ability to inspire children to do more, go further, and try harder than they believed possible.

An Irish mother's love is the foundation for the family and the source of her children's successes; she instills in them the knowledge that they are the equal of everyone, but also that everyone is equal to them. The Irish mother's love does not depend on financial status, educational level, or other outward trappings of success. An Irish child can be assured that his or her Irish mother will share in the pains of life's challenges as well as the joys of its successes.

Bask in the warmth of the following stories of Irish mothers, from Jane Treacy, who credits her career on QVC in large part to her mother's support and insight; to Judy Daly, her mother's alanna, who learned that families are built on love as well as blood; to Peggy Prendergast, the authors' own grandmother, whose joie de vivre *and love of adventure made her an exciting companion well into her nineties; to Pat Prendergast Connorton, Peggy's daughter, who taught her children that even when life is sorrowful, goodness will always prevail.*

Patricia "Pat" Prendergast Connorton

It is no surprise that the Irish trait of "family first" was deeply ingrained in Pat Prendergast Connorton—after all, she was raised by her mother, Peggy. Pat grew up in the Bronx, New York, along with her big brother, Tom, whose relentless but good-hearted teasing helped her become one tough lady. Like her mother, Pat was practical, never complained, and accepted life's challenges with dignity.

She married another first generation Irish American who grew up in the Bronx, Frank Connorton, in the old and beautiful Lady of Mercy Church in their neighborhood. Their forty-six years of marriage were ones of deep love and commitment—to each other, their children and grandchildren, their parents, and the Irish traditions of their families.

When Pat's mother and father moved to El Paso, Texas, to be near her brother Tom, Frank and Pat followed them a few years later, embracing the move just like Peggy did—as a new adventure. Also like her mother, Pat's dedication to experiencing life to the fullest never wavered—she became an entrepreneur in her sixties.

Pat is no longer here to write her own story, but the strong bond between her and her daughter Tricia, one of the authors of this book, is evident in the following stories.

Pat's Story, as told by her daughter Patricia: Love and Work

My mom had a strong work ethic that she passed down to all her children. After working dozens of years as a well-respected nurse, at the age of sixty-five she became an entrepreneur by opening her own consulting business providing nursing services to various clients, including the US Department of Labor. She loved her profession. I often asked her if she would retire soon and she would always respond, "What for? I love what I do."

Mom relished her independence and was grateful that she had choices her own mother did not have. She wanted her daughters to be independent, too. On her death bed I promised Mom that I would not wait until I was sixty-five to start my own business.

"I love you more than you will ever know." That is what my mom and my grandmother used to say to me. I know in my bones that this was true. Although she was a matter-of-fact person, the love Mom had for me, my brother, Peter, and my sister, Peggy, ran deep. We know how lucky we are to have had that love. I used to say that a fear of God was not what kept me grounded in high school; it was a fear of Mother. I was not afraid of her anger or that she would take her love away from me. I just respected her so much that I did not want to disappoint her.

Mom had a knack for seeing the best in people and accepting us for who we were without judgment. Her children's friends came to her for advice, listened to her wisdom, and were encouraged by her strength. My friend Charlene attributes surviving her high school years to the peace and acceptance she found in my home. Mom encouraged all of us to live life to the fullest without fear. She let us know she was praying and supporting us every step of the way.

When I was a child, I would often hold hands with my mom while we sat in church. Sometimes I would study her hand and play with her wedding ring, hoping that it would make the time go by faster. I was fascinated by the fact that we had the same hands. Mine were smaller, but they were the same. My middle finger curved slightly to the left just like my mom's. Today when I go to church with my own kids they sometimes hold my hands and play with my rings. I feel the same sense of calm that I felt as a child, knowing where I belong and where I come from.

Understanding Grief

One of my mother's most lasting lessons was given to me in the time of her greatest challenge. In May of 1971 I was in third grade at Mesita School in El Paso, Texas. The school was three houses down the alleyway from my Grandma's house. My favorite things were my dogs, my grandmother, my Barbie collection, and my future little sister, who was due "any day now." She was all the family talked about, and all I did after school was to plan for "Maureen" to finally be born and come home and be my sister. I spent hours sorting and organizing my best things so that I could put them away for my new sister to play with one day. I dressed the dolls in my Barbie collection in their original outfits and placed their additional outfits and accessories neatly on hangers in my pink Barbie wardrobe trunk. I folded up my Brownie uniform in tissue paper in a white box with a pink ribbon—sock holders, beanie, sash and all. I picked out my best stuffed animals and put them in a special trunk for Maureen so she would have something of her own to play with.

At the dinner table each night we would talk about the baby coming. "Mom, what room will Maureen sleep in? Why can't she sleep with me?"

"First of all, Tricia, we don't know if it is a girl or not," Mom patiently replied. "What if you end up with another brother? Second, it will be a long time before the baby can play with you. Little girls need lots of sleep and babies stay up at night and cry. You will see. It wouldn't be long before you would not want the crib in your room. But you can be my big helper for a while."

Mom set up the bassinet both my brother, Peter, and I had used beside her bed. The baby was due any day. As a matter of fact the baby should have been here already. Mom grew bigger by the day and she was more uncomfortable than ever but she never complained and she never missed work.

Mom worked as a nurse in the operating room at Hotel Dieu Hospital next to Saint Patrick's Cathedral in downtown El Paso. She was saving up her time off for after the baby so she continued to work. Mom wore funny clothes to work: blue scrubs and an ugly blue net on her hair and comfortable white nursing shoes. Mom was really good at being a nurse and all the doctors requested to have Pat as their nurse. She worked a lot of hours. She was up before us and gone well before the sun came up. When she met us at Grandma's house after school we spent time having a cup of tea and talking about the events of the day.

Being Irish, we had a cup of tea for everything: celebration tea, afternoon tea, after dinner tea, tragedy tea, bad weather tea, sickness tea. My grandma put on the kettle for any occasion. I had an orange cup with frogs on it that Grandma and I got at Walgreens. My tea was always served in that cup with lots of milk and sugar—and lots of love.

Finally the day came. Dad dropped us off at school just like any other day. I hoped Mom would have the baby during the day so I would get out of school early. Around 1:00 p.m. I was in class working on my Spanish ditto sheet when the loud speaker came on. "Please send Peter and Patricia Connorton to the front office." I jumped up from my seat and shrilled, "My baby sister finally came. I am going to meet her." My teacher said, "I know you are excited, Tricia. Please gather your things quietly and do not disrupt the rest of your class. Bring a Polaroid picture of your new baby sister tomorrow to share with everyone. Good luck."

I gathered my things as quietly as I could and darted down the hall to the office. My brother and I met my dad in the hall and he took us out to the parking lot. I kept asking him, "Is it a girl? Tell me, is it a girl?"

But something was wrong. I looked up at my dad and saw his eyes were full of tears. One tear streaked down his cheek. "What is wrong, Dad? Tell us!"

As we approached the car he looked at Peter and me and said, "The baby did not make it."

We got in the car and I began screaming, "That can't be! How could that happen? Babies don't die before they live—I don't understand!" Dad was crying out loud by this time and he drove us straight to my grandma's house.

Grandma was waiting at the door and she hugged us both tight and told us the horrible news. She tried her best to explain. "The baby was very big because she was late. The umbilical cord was in the wrong place and caused the baby to lose oxygen while she was being born. She died at birth and is in heaven. Your mom and dad named her Maureen. Tricia, put on the kettle and we will make a cup of tea and I will answer all your questions. We will say prayers for your mom and your sister."

We sat at the little kitchen table for a long time, praying and not really comprehending what just happened. I hurt all over. I had no idea that a baby could die at birth.

I wanted to see my mom but she was in the hospital and too sick for visitors. *What if Mom died too?* I thought. I was scared of the future for the first time in my life. How had the best day of my life suddenly become my family's worst day ever?

Going Through the Pain

Grandma came to stay with us. My dad planned a little funeral at the chapel at Hotel Dieu Hospital. Dad told me Mom was still too sick to come to the funeral. It was the only time I saw Maureen. True to the Irish Catholic tradition, the little baby's white casket was open. She was beautiful with red hair like me and purple, lifeless lips. If it had not been for the lips I would have thought she was just a sleeping baby. She was wearing the christening gown my mom and I had picked out for her just a few weeks before on one of our Saturday shopping days.

As I got older I realized my mother could not be there because of her grief. At the time I figured that giving birth to a baby that died made you very sick.

After several days it was time for Mom to come home. She was wearing her same cream-colored silky blouse and navy-blue slacks that she had packed in her little overnight case preparing for the happy day. Despite the familiar clothes, I had never seen my mom look like that before. Her eyes were distant and her gestures slow. She gave Peter and me a hug then lay down on our orange plaid couch and fell asleep. She lay there for hours. I did the only thing I knew to do—I made a cup of tea. She thanked me and left it sitting on the tray table next to her as she slept all afternoon.

The next day Mom was on the couch again. I covered her in the pink and green afghan my grandma had made for me and put my best stuffed animals beside her. I sat with her and held her hand. Her dark eyes were still distant. She looked like Mom, but Mom was not in there anymore.

After four days Mom got up, got dressed, and went back to work. After school that day Mom met us at Grandma's house and we had tea. Mom was back. She asked Peter and me, "How was your day? What did you pack for lunch? Show me your homework." That night we said our prayers and added Maureen to the long list of people we prayed for. Mom tucked us in and kissed our heads good night.

Year later when I was an adult, over a cup of tea at the kitchen table, Mom tried to put into words what she went through when Maureen passed away. "I felt responsible. I was a nurse and I knew the baby was late. I knew better. I failed my baby. The baby was so big that the umbilical cord wrapped around her tiny neck in the birth canal and she had no oxygen. God bless her, she never had a chance to live. I questioned everything I knew. I questioned God. I questioned my faith."

At the hospital they gave Mom pain and anxiety medication. "I could have taken those pills the rest of my life," she said. "There is nothing better than to feel nothing when all you have been feeling is pain. For three days at home that is what I did. I felt nothing. I took my medication and I lay on the couch, wishing to never feel again. Then I looked at you. I saw you bringing me tea. Caring for me. The fear and pain in your eyes. I knew I had to get up. Tricia, no matter what happens in life, you have to go through it. You cannot go through life expecting to deal with tough things in limbo. The only way through the challenges is to go through them. That applies to everything. Happiness, sorrow, joy, and anger. You have to feel it. Taking pills, drinking; they only prolong the agony. You will have to go through it sometime so you might as well go through it as quickly as possible and move on."

Over the years, I have learned that this advice is contradictory to the way we often live our lives. It is easier to have a few cocktails, take a pill, repress our emotions, and feel nothing. We are not supposed to cry or get angry or lose control. Yet the journey of life has always been a difficult one. Life is a cycle and there are good times and bad. No matter what our society teaches us to expect, stability and perfection do not exist.

The Unbreakable Bond

Some of Mom's best days were when she became a grandmother. She bought a big SUV so we could take family trips together, and we had adventures seeing the Grand Canyon and the mountains of New Mexico. Like my relationship with my own grandmother, Mom created a bond of unconditional love with her grandkids and made them feel welcome and special. My son, Tommy, spoke to her every night before he went to sleep until the day she died. My daughter, Annie, wanted to live at Grandma's house. She liked it better there than in her own room at home.

In November of 2007 Mom suddenly got very sick and had difficulty breathing. Within a few short weeks, my mother, the rock of our family, my best friend, my confidant, my biggest fan and cheerleader, passed away. I held her hand as she took her last breath. I found myself in the same boat that Mom was in when Maureen suddenly died. There I was, left behind. My two children left without Grandma. Me left without my everything.

My feelings were so big and awful that for a few months I didn't feel at all. I wouldn't allow myself to feel. I got up every day, got dressed in pretty clothes, did all the things that I was supposed to do, and felt nothing. Three months after the funeral I woke up at three in the morning from dreaming about my mom. She came to me and for a brief moment I thought she was alive. The nightmare of losing her and living without her the last three months was the dream. She was back.

Then I actually woke up. I went to the bathroom to splash water on my face and get myself together. I sat down on the edge of the bathtub and put my head in my hands. I started to cry. The crying became weeping and the weeping turned to sobbing. I felt like the pain of losing Mom was coming out of my pores. My arms ached and my hands were sweating pain. All the pain I had carried around for months was finally coming out.

It is a normal part of life to grieve. Society may not agree and our culture prescribes pills and placebos to help us numb ourselves. Yet living a life on autopilot is not worth living. Spending your time on earth self-medicating just to avoid the pain does not work. Like my mom said, we all must go through it. It is an important process in the human condition. Our children need to learn that life is not perfect. We take the good with the bad. What is important is to live it all, feel it all, and know that you come out the other side stronger and better for having gone through it.

That's what Irish wisdom is all about. The Irish have had strife, trials, and tribulations throughout the history of their beautiful and tragic country. You can't just give up. You cannot just pretend that everything is perfect. You are not truly living if you only acknowledge the surface.

Faith in a higher purpose and belief that my loved ones are still with me gets me through each day. I talk to my mother every day. A spirit as strong as my mother could never simply fade away. She is with me and my children, watching over us, guiding us.

Margaret "Peggy" Dalton Prendergast

For her ninety-five years of vibrant living, Peggy Prendergast was the beating heart of her family. Daughter, sister, wife, mother, grandmother—these are the words she loved to hear, to her the greatest honors she could know. From Ireland to New York to El Paso, Texas, Peggy's love of adventure and all the quirks and curves of life spread her lively spirit throughout her family. Her example bestowed upon them the joy of life and the strength to live it well.

Peggy died in 1995 so she cannot tell her own story here. But her spirit lives on in her grandchildren, two of whom are the authors of this book. They have heard Peggy's story many times and have retold it to their own children. Now you get to hear it too.

Peggy's Story, as Told by Her Granddaughter Laura: An Adventurous Spirit

My grandmother, Margaret "Peggy" Dalton Prendergast, was born

April 13, 1900, in Gorey, County Wexford, Ireland, the youngest of six children. Peggy was unlike most Irish girls of her era, being possessed of a love of adventure and dreams beyond her station in life. She spent her young years taking care of the animals on her family's farm, going to school, and waiting for her brother to take her on a ride on his motorcycle, a new-fangled innovation that was the ultimate in adventure and excitement. It didn't happen often, but when it did Peggy was in her element, her abundant strawberry-blonde hair flowing freely behind her as they sped over the Irish countryside.

In school and in her spare time, Peggy read as many books as she could get her hands on, especially those set in far-away lands, and dreamed of how someday she would go and see the world. She grew to be a beautiful Irish lass with sparkling green eyes to go with her red-blond hair, and many suitors came calling. But the idea of being a wife and living on a farm just down the way from her family farm did not appeal to her, and she resisted the local lads and their charms. While her brothers and sisters either married or joined the convent, Peggy wanted something different and waited for adventure to appear. She was not willing to settle for less—or to settle down.

By 1925, Peggy's father began to worry. "You're not getting any younger, Peg," he frequently reminded her. To which Peggy replied, "I'm not joining the convent and I won't marry only because I receive an invitation."

Eventually Peggy's only remaining suitor was a nice young man who faithfully visited every Friday. He was slow in proposing, though, which was fine with her. She had no burning desire to stay in Ireland, but no viable plan for how to get out either. She knew she wanted more than the quiet life of a village farmer's wife, but what else was there in Ireland? Her sisters had joined the convent, but Peggy had no real interest in the religious life.

She was adrift, waiting for more, until one day her sister Kieran told Peggy about how the Church was taking a group of nuns to Australia for study and missionary work. Kieran was one of them, passage to

Australia paid in full by the Church.

This gave Peggy an idea. If she promised to become a nun, the Church would take her along to do missionary work. Peggy figured she could always change her mind about becoming a nun at the last minute, but by then she'd be in Australia, launched on her adventure. What a perfect idea.

Peggy visited the convent with her sister Kieran and went about the process of signing up to become a nun. They seemed happy to have her, and she packed and planned for the big trip.

Parties and blessings were given; the town folk came by to wish her well. Shortly before her planned departure, she made the mistake of confiding in her sister Mary, revealing her intentions. Mary put her loyalty to the Church above her loyalty to Peggy, and before Peggy could board the ship, the Sisters were on to her. Since the nuns knew she was only signing up to get out of Ireland, she was barred from the trip.

Disappointed but not defeated, Peggy was more determined than ever to find a way to emigrate. She wrote to her brother Pat, who had immigrated to America and was living in New York: "I want to leave the farm and move to America. To do so I need two things: a sponsor and a job. Can you help me?" After what seemed like an eternity Peggy received Pat's reply: he found her a job as a nanny for a family in the city, and he would sponsor her.

A New Life

It took over a year of scrimping for Peggy to save the money for her passage and make arrangements to meet Pat in New York. She told her reliable suitor, "I am moving to America." He showed up with a ring the day before she was leaving. "Thank you for your offer," Peggy told him politely. "My mind is set and you waited too long. If things don't work out for me I'll let you know—you can wait or not as you choose."

She said good-bye to her family, not knowing when, if ever, she would see them again. Though her heart was a little heavy, she did not look back. She boarded the ship with one suitcase that held every possession she had, spent two weeks at sea, and arrived in New York via Ellis Island on July 4, 1928. The trip was grueling, boring, and tough—little company, little to do, and a lot of sea sickness.

As Peggy walked through New York City the first time, confused thoughts swirled through her head. *I have never seen so many people in my life. Where is everyone running to? What happened to the sky? You can't see it for the buildings!* Despite her apprehension, Peggy set out to make New York her new home. "I had more guts than sense," she said later.

"My job required me to look after two young boys every day. One had a breathing condition so we took long walks in Central Park for the fresh air. The family was nice enough but the homesickness weighed heavy on my heart. I was always quite the talker back home and the first year in America without my sisters and family was a lonely one.

"Even so, the Irish in New York looked out for one another and we all did what we could to make a bit of extra cash on the side and to support one another," she recalled. "A distant cousin who lived in my apartment building made 'hooch' in the bathtub of her tiny apartment every night. That's what illegal homemade liquor was called during those Prohibition days. I helped take care of her little one or stirred the concoction from time to time. We took our batch out to the streets and sold it right out of the baby carriage. One night luck was against us and the bathtub ingredients caught fire. We loaded up the baby carriage with the baby and the hooch and ran out of the apartment building. We passed the firemen in the hall with a friendly 'how do you do' as they made their way to put out the fire. That was the official end of my bootlegging days. I thought I would have a heart attack with all the commotion!"

Peggy's homesickness was still there after she'd been in New York for a year—until the evening that everything changed. "My brother Pat was meeting an insurance salesman at our apartment one evening," she told us. "I opened the door when I heard a knock, and there stood Thomas Aidan Prendergast. He had jet black hair and was over six feet tall—that man was a looker, all right. I politely invited him in. As good looking as he was, he was quiet as a mouse. When he did speak he mustered up the courage to say, 'May I take you out to dinner?' I looked up into his dark brown eyes and said, 'I thought you'd never ask!' Tom grabbed his hat and we left the apartment together. He never even mentioned the word insurance."

Three months later Tom proposed to Peggy. Not only did they fall in love, they discovered they were both from Gorey, County Wexford, in Ireland. Their families were acquainted and they had grown up within five miles of each other. In yet another twist of fate, Tom's brother and Peggy's sister in Ireland met and married around the same time. Two Dalton sisters married two Prendergast brothers—on opposite sides of the world.

Marriage is an Adventure Too

Tom and Peggy went on to have two children, Thomas Jr. and Patricia. Due to the Depression, things were always tight and money did not come easily. Tom was a generous man and helped everyone he could, often to his own detriment. Many a Friday found Peggy dealing with an empty pay envelope after Tom felt compelled to help out some neighbor or friend. Still, their tiny apartment on 194th Street in the Bronx was always full of love and laughter.

Hard work and persistence assured that both their children were able to attend private Catholic school and go on to obtain college degrees. Thomas Jr. attended Regis High School and Fordham University, both on scholarship, and Patricia attended Mesachordia School of Nursing. Peggy was most proud of the fact that both of her children were college educated. She told her children and her grandchildren, "Education is your inheritance. It is a gift you give yourself and lasts a lifetime. No matter what life presents to you, with an education you can take care of yourself."

Tom and Peggy loved their life in New York, but as they got older and Tom retired, they thought it was time to start another new adventure. My father, Tom Jr., had moved to Texas, and they decided to join him. They were ready to enjoy the easy lifestyle and sunny weather in El Paso. I clearly remember the feeling of excitement that permeated our home when we heard Grandma Peggy and Grandpa Tom were moving from New York. Though we had seen them often, the thousands of miles between us made regular visits difficult. We were thrilled they were going to be living nearby.

Both in their sixties, they bought a small house with a large yard so my grandfather could get back to his Irish roots and enjoy gardening. Within a few years, my aunt, their daughter, Pat, and her family followed them to El Paso, so their whole family was again living within a few miles of each other.

Grandma's House

Their home was a few blocks down the alley from our elementary school. It was a special treat to be allowed go to Grandma and Grandpa's after school for a visit. One of them would walk down the alley to the school's back gate and wait for us to leave school. After a short walk home, we grandchildren took seats around the kitchen table for tea and an after-school snack. My grandmother made the hottest, strongest tea and served it in a beautiful Irish teapot. It was real tea, made the old-fashioned way with boiling water from a kettle and loose tea steeped in a preheated pot. No easy teabags for Grandma Peggy. I was amazed that she was able to drink the hot liquid without burning her lips—you could almost see it boiling as she drank. I took my tea with lots of sugar and milk; to this day I take comfort from a nice cup of tea when I am stressed or worried.

Grandma made us grandchildren feel special, important, and loved. She was always thrilled to see us and fussed over us, making sure we had a treat or more tea while we did our homework. If you were lucky enough not to have homework, you could curl up on her sofa, wrap up in one of her homemade afghans, and watch TV.

As I grew older and went away to college and law school, I always knew my grandmother was at home praying for me and waiting to hear about my adventures. She sent cards and letters and stayed in touch. I knew she was there for me, waiting patiently at home.

Going Home

Peggy was a proud American citizen but she had a love of the old country that was deeply embedded in her soul. Despite living in the US for over sixty years, she never lost her soft brogue. Her voice was a wonderful reminder of the ties we shared with the home country. She and my grandfather travelled back to Ireland for an extended visit every few years, usually spending four to six weeks traveling around the country and reconnecting with relatives. Since they both had large extended families living in and around Gorey, a trip home involved a lot of visiting.

Grandpa Tom was fond of saying, "I want to die in Ireland." He got his wish, for it was on one of those trips to Ireland that he became ill, "took to his bed," as they say in Ireland, and died. According to his wishes, he was buried in the family graveyard at the church in Oulart, so he could stay in Ireland forever.

I was almost twelve years old in 1969 when my mother, sister, and I were traveling in Europe and got the news that my grandfather was ill. We had intended to end our vacation with a family reunion in Ireland, but suddenly our plans changed and we frantically tried to get to Ireland before he passed. My father traveled from the States and was able to get to his father's bedside just in time. I vividly remember everything about the traditional Irish funeral that followed. Most of all, I remember my grandmother. She was devastated but she was strong. She dealt with the tragedy with quiet dignity and never lost her composure. "Loved ones are on loan from God," she said. "God never promised we could keep them." After a few days, we left Ireland and returned home to El Paso. As so many Irish men and women have learned, life goes on in spite of grief.

Peggy came back to America alone and went about figuring out how to be a widow. She was lonely and sad, but as she said, "I had to go on and I did that by surrounding myself with my two children and my five grandchildren—and with lots of prayer. I always knew Tom and I would be together again in heaven. He left before me but I still had plenty of life left to live."

Travels with Grandma Peggy

About fifteen years after Grandpa Tom's death, I had just finished four years of college and three years of law school, and I was ready to take a break. I had a month free before my first job began and an idea popped into my head. Grandma Peggy had just passed her eighty-third birthday and was still in excellent health. She had not been home to Ireland since my grandfather's death, and one of her beloved sisters was still alive, though in declining health. Why not go to Ireland and visit the relatives?

Why not indeed? Peggy eagerly agreed, and we made arrangements and headed to Ireland.

My grandmother was a wonderful traveler. She was the consummate good sport, never complaining and never cross. But she could be tough, even pushy if necessary. She was not willing to put up with bad manners or poor service. She spoke her mind but she never lost control.

Watching her assert her wishes reminded me of a subway trip I took with Grandma when I was a child and visiting her in New York. It was rush hour and she had me firmly by the hand. She was meticulously dressed in a wool coat and pillbox hat, and she was also armed with a hat pin. It was a wonderful tool for clearing a path through a crowded subway car. "Stay with me," she ordered and I watched wide-eyed as people jumped out of her way. In a flash we were across the car and seated in the last available seat, me on her lap. Some poor man was shocked to find that he almost planted himself on us when he started to sit and before realizing the space was taken.

Grandma smiled sweetly. "Sorry, occupied," she said, and the man, looking bewildered, moved on. "Never hesitate when making a decision," she advised.

Travel from El Paso to Europe can be an exhausting challenge. El Paso is in far west Texas and requires a minimum of two plane trips before even beginning to cross the Atlantic. My grandmother did not bat an eye or utter a word of complaint. She clutched her pocketbook, which held a paperback novel and some knitting and was set for the duration. Although I knew she was old, I kept forgetting it. She didn't act old.

Arriving in Dublin, we rented a car so that we would be free to travel around at will and visit with everyone who was available. By this time, my grandmother was used to some of the creature comforts of the American lifestyle. She was not impressed that we had to "wind down the windows" to get a breath of air. Still she was happily willing to play the role of navigator and back seat driver. As we maneuvered our way around Dublin and across the Irish countryside, she was frequently heard to mutter about the lack of signs or clear directions. Of course, if we found ourselves too lost, we merely stopped and asked for instructions and someone was always more than happy to help.

Our first stop in Dublin was for lunch with Peggy's sister, my Great Aunt Sister Kieran, who had lived most of her life as a cloistered nun at the Convent at Cabra outside of Dublin. She was retired, as only nuns can be, living a serene life of prayer and introspection and living in a beautiful old convent, cared for by other equally elderly nuns. We were greeted with great celebration, and a scrumptious lunch was prepared for us. The sandwiches, sweets, and tea were served on a magnificent, paper-thin Belleek china tea service. I cringed each time the nun who was acting as our server banged the pot down on the tray, certain it would smash into a million pieces.

They fussed and catered to us and were genuinely thrilled at the visit. Everyone smiled and exclaimed and hugged and kissed us with expressions of joy. We were treated like royalty. Sister Kieran was not able to walk well or maneuver the many stairs in the convent. But no worries—whenever she needed to be moved from one room to the next, a bevy of nuns appeared from nowhere and whisked her up the steps as she perched gingerly on a wooden chair.

The Irish love to visit and American relatives coming home is one of the best excuses for a party. As word of our visit spread, invitations poured in. The good thing was we never had to plan a meal; the bad thing was we were expected to eat a feast at least five or maybe six times a day—breakfast, mid-morning tea, lunch, mid-afternoon tea, dinner and often, after-dinner tea. The Irish are magicians when it comes to laying a table. Even when arriving with no notice we were presented with baskets of freshly baked bread and muffins, cakes and pies baked from wonderful fresh fruits. Each feast was supplemented with a family favorite and frequently involved a ham or turkey ready for carving.

A challenge came when we were offered—no, presented—a ceremonial glass of the hard stuff. Being Americans, we were expected to be able to hold our whiskey. But I was small of stature and a nondrinker, with the exception of the occasional mild Piña colada. I was in no shape to sip, much less finish, a glass full of straight, warm Irish whiskey. I did not like the stuff, and I had to drive us around the countryside.

My grandmother, seeing my dismay, whispered loudly, "Just dump it in a plant!"

I couldn't do that; it would have meant the death of the plant and a waste of good whiskey. I finally just had to say, "No, thank you! I really, really cannot drink this and drive us home." I am sure they were disappointed about the teetotaler American relative who could not hold her whiskey.

The month in Ireland flew by. We left after a wonderful experience with amazing memories. Best of all, I spent memorable hours just enjoying my grandmother.

Let Me Get My Pocketbook

Peggy was as feisty, tenacious, and as strong at the age of ninety-five as she was at twenty-five. She went back to Ireland again and again to visit her family there. In 1994 she was the oldest person to fly on Delta Airlines and was proud to receive a 20 percent discount on her ticket.

As I became an adult and married and started a career, my opportunities to spend time with my grandmother were limited by some of my other obligations. She was never one to complain, however. She was always willing to go along, no matter how trivial the errand or how boring the activity. Even though she lived by herself until she died, she was rarely alone. There was always someone coming or going from her house. Any moment of time that was spent with someone she loved was a treasure. Whether it was a trip to the grocery store or going on a weekend getaway, Peggy never turned down an invitation to get out of the house. She always said, "Let me get my pocketbook! Off we go!"

She lived every day to the fullest, enjoying her family, never complaining, and looking forward to any activity as yet another adventure. She died peacefully on a beautiful spring morning shortly after her ninety-fifth birthday, while sitting in her favorite chair waiting for her morning tea. Without a sound, she was gone. We still miss her and remember her every day. We always will.

Jane Treacy

In the early days of cable television, a fledgling industry was born. Direct merchandise sales to a market of millions of television viewers around the world was being explored. The industry experimented with providing consumers with detailed information about products that were unusual or difficult to obtain, at a good price, for sale from the convenience of their own home. It has proven to be a winning formula.

A young Jane Rudolph applied for a job as host for the home shopping program on a whim. Though armed with a broadcasting degree and intending to pursue a career in a more "serious" journalism arena, she responded to a want ad in the paper with virtually no idea of what would be expected of her.

On the day of her interview, she was full of misgivings and the weather was bad. She almost cancelled her interview. After talking it over with her mother, she followed her advice and went ahead and met with the producers. Two weeks later she was hired and has since enjoyed a career spanning over twenty years. She is widely regarded as one of the most successful celebrity hosts on the extremely popular television shopping network, QVC. Despite her success and celebrity, she has never forgotten her Irish roots and has incorporated her love of Ireland and respect for her beloved mother into the programming and products that are sold on QVC.

Jane's Story:
My Mother, Virginia Cahill Unsinn

I am Irish both by luck and by birth. My mother, Virginia Cahill Unsinn—Ginny as she was called—was half Irish and half German. Her family immigrated to the United States from County Kerry during the dreaded Potato Famine over a century ago. My mom grew up in an Irish community in upstate Pennsylvania's coal mining country.

My mother's Irish looks—red hair and green eyes—matched her love of all things Irish. But she wasn't a traditional lass; Mom was a twenty-first century woman living in the mid-twentieth century. Educated with a degree in home economics, she moved on her own from upstate Pennsylvania to Philadelphia for a high-powered career as head dietician at what was then Fitzgerald Mercy Hospital. There was only one thing wrong. According to the social rules of the 1940s, she was supposed to be married.

Mom often thought of following in the footsteps of her two sisters, Frances (Sr. Regina Therese) and Theresa (Sr. Mary Joan), and joining the Immaculate Heart of Mary convent. She was religious and still had not met a man who could hold her interest. The life of a nun could be adventurous; Theresa had gone to Peru, teaching poverty-stricken children at the convent school. In those days when you went abroad to serve, you usually went for life and no one came to visit.

In the spring of 1947, missing Theresa and searching for a plan for her life, Mom took a leave of absence from work. All by herself she journeyed to Peru to visit Theresa—and she had to change planes several times to get there. While in Peru, Theresa took Mom to meet a local legend, a wise woman who made predictions and read the future. Theresa spoke in Spanish to the wise woman. "This is my sister, Virginia. We think she's going to be a nun like me." The old woman looked Mom in the eye for a long moment. When she finally spoke she said in Spanish, "No, she has the eyes of a bride."

By the time her trip ended and she was on her way back to America, Mom felt more confused than ever. Was the wise old woman in Peru right about her future? What were the odds of a twenty-seven-year-old business woman meeting a man and settling down? But Mom had figured out something else. She did not have a call to a religious life.

At home, Mom began delivering the letters and Peruvian gifts sent from the sisters to their relatives. She made plans to meet a group of friends for dinner. Unbeknownst to Mom, her friends invited a young man named Sylvester Rudolph. When Mom walked into her friend's house, Sylvester Rudolph fell in love. He thought Mom must be straight from Ireland because of her creamy skin, red curls, and green eyes, and was surprised to find out that she was American. Mom was equally impressed with Sylvester, who was handsome with a kind smile and warm eyes. She did not hesitate to say yes when he invited her out for dinner the following weekend.

My parents' official first date was to the "Knife and Fork Inn" in Atlantic City. Mom was resplendent in a dress with matching hat, purse, and gloves; and Dad wore a suit, tie, and wing-tipped shoes. Only four months later they were married. They stayed together for more than forty years and had five children. Even after all those years and children, Dad still wrote Mom love letters. She never shared them with anyone, not even me. After my parents died—Dad the last in 2008—I found the letters carefully hidden away in a shoe box, and read them for the first time.

Even though she married, Mom did not give up her ambitions for a career. She went back to college and obtained her master's degree while raising five children. We all went on to great careers and all of us regard Mom as the best mother in the world.

Love of Ireland

My mother always had a strong love for Ireland, which she passed down to me. In the spring of 1988 Mom and I took our first trip together to Ireland. We both fell in love with the country. The Irish people saw Mom on the street and would say, "So you've come home?" I'd answer, "Yeah, she really has come home." I was so enamored with Ireland that as we stood on the ring of Kerry I looked at Mom and said, "I'm going to go home and I'm going to marry someone Irish so that I can always have ties to Ireland." Mom just smiled and said, "OK, Janie!"

Back at work at QVC after our Ireland vacation, a young man named Sean Treacy, who worked at QVC but whom I'd never met, came up to me and said, "Oh, I heard you went to Ireland. I've just got back from Ireland myself. My dad is from there." This piqued my interest—especially after what I had said to Mom. Unfortunately I had two rules about dating. I never dated anyone in the TV business and I never, ever dated anyone I worked with. So I hesitated over having much to do with him until one day Sean said, "My cousin Pat is here from Cork. Would you like to get together for lunch?"

Well, I could certainly go to lunch to meet Sean's cousin. That night after work I told my mother, "Mom, my future husband and I are getting together. This guy at work, Sean, has a cousin named Pat from Cork and we are going to lunch. This is the man I was telling you about. This is the rest of my life!" Mom just smiled and said, "OK, Janie!"

A few days later I met Sean for lunch. But somehow the cousin from Cork never showed up. The lunch lasted about five hours. Sean and I talked about our mutual love of Ireland and we certainly had our work in common. When I got home Mom said, "Hmm. Quite a lunch you had, wasn't it?" Sean and I were engaged four months later and we've been married for twenty-one years. Over those years we've traveled to Ireland together many times. Sean has many relatives still living there. I am happily surrounded by a huge Irish clan on both sides of the Atlantic.

Broadcasting as a Career

As I was growing up I loved school and dancing. I studied ballet with the full intention of becoming a professional dancer. I was one of those kids who left early every day for school, my hair in a bun and prepared to dance four or five hours that day. It was not until the end of my senior year that the thought occurred to me: *I think there might be more to life than just the ballet barre!* A guidance counselor noticed that I had not listed any colleges on my plan. When he asked why, I told him, "I'm not going to college. I want to be a dancer." But then he asked me, "What you are going to do when you're thirty?"

That question really stumped me. I went back to the counselor for guidance. "What do you want to do?" he asked.

"I don't want to do anything else. I want to be a dancer," I said again.

He sighed. "Well, if you did go to college for something, what would it be?"

"I don't know," I said, after thinking a moment.

He persevered. "So what else do you like besides ballet?"

"Baseball."

"Baseball," he muttered. "Great. These kids are really killing me." But then, bless his heart, he said, "OK. What is it about baseball that you like?"

"Oh, I could be the first female broadcaster for the Phillies!"

Finally he smiled, saying, "OK. Broadcasting. Great." Much to his and my parents' relief, it was with that intention that I applied for college and eventually got my degree in broadcasting from Kutztown University. Talk about an angel in my path.

QVC

My mother played a big role in how I got my job at QVC—and ultimately in my success. In the early days of my career if I wanted to work in front of the camera, I was expected to jump from job to job very quickly. I had just returned home to Philadelphia to host a public affairs show for a local station as a freelance assignment. One day I saw a want ad in the paper for a new shopping channel host. I had no idea what a shopping channel was and didn't even have cable TV at the time. I thought it might be an interesting way to spend a few months and earn a little money until I landed another broadcasting job. Many of my friends in the "business" urged me not to go to the audition, saying it would ruin my career. But at twenty-four, I had all the confidence in the world, although my goal was to make it in news and to work for a shopping program would be a little strange. But hey, I had a car payment to make.

The day of the audition I had second thoughts and almost didn't go. I was sitting in my mom's kitchen and said, "I'm not going."

"Why not?" Mom asked.

"I've never sold anything in my life," I said. "I never even had a job at the mall. I can't sell anything. I'm not a salesperson. I'm a broadcasting major! You know that's what I do."

"Oh, you're a natural-born salesperson," she shot back. "Here, sell me this pencil." She tossed me a pencil.

I took the pencil in my hand and looked across the kitchen table at my mom. Without thinking too much, I said, "A pencil is really great because an artist can draw a picture, an architect can design a home, a husband can write a love letter, and a child can get an 'A' on their test."

"Go to the audition!" Mom said.

It was a rainy night, and as I drove to Westchester, Pennsylvania, the doubts flooding my thoughts were as heavy as the rain. I walked into the half-built studio, and the man who ended up being my boss came up to me and said, "Hi, welcome! This is going to be really easy so you don't have to be nervous. We just want you to sell us this pencil."

I looked at him and he looked at me and I think he thought, *Oh, this one is freezing up.* I took a deep breath, looked at the camera, and said, "A pencil is a really great thing because . . ." I repeated exactly what I said to my mother in her kitchen just an hour before. When I was finished he said, "OK. This is usually where we say, 'Don't call us. We'll call you.' But, can you come back tomorrow?" Two weeks later I was on the air at QVC.

Truthfully, I would have been the worst news person in the world. Who knows where I would be right now if I had not gone to that interview. When I talk to young people in high school or college I always tell them, "Don't miss your yacht while you are waiting for your ship to come in." After all, I had no plans to work in the television shopping industry because it didn't even exist when I was in school. But the industry has evolved and grown and I have a new job every day.

I am blessed to have created a life that I truly love with a career that inspires me. When my daughter Cara had to write a story for school about whom she admires most she wrote that she admired her parents. What she said about us floored me because I thought she would have said, "Because they care for me. They're always there for me." Instead she said, "I admire my parents because they've chosen careers that they truly love."

The year after Sean and I were married, the buyers on QVC thought of doing a show for Saint Patrick's Day that featured goods from Ireland. Sean and I had a ski trip planned that we were looking forward to when the CEO at the time, Doug Briggs, called and said, "What are you and Sean doing this weekend?" I said, "Oh, we're going to Killington, Vermont, to ski." He said, "Do you want to go to Ireland?"

"Sure, why not?" I said and called my husband. "Can we cancel the reservations for skiing? We're going to Ireland."

Sean, videographer Bill Martin, and I got on a plane, flew over to Dublin, and met some of the early vendors who are still on QVC today. We went on a whirlwind tour around Ireland with a camcorder and went on air with the products. It was a four-hour program and everything sold out. The program is now an annual tradition and one of my favorite programs to host. Our Saint Patrick's Day program was so successful that QVC wanted to start another event closer to the holidays. I got out my book of Irish celebrations and festivals. We looked at the Galway Races, the Galway Oyster Festival, and a couple of other things. Then someone said, "What about Rose of Tralee? That's so romantic." And that's where that program came from. The date varies each year but is around September. Everyone at QVC is so excited for our Irish guests. They are wonderfully special.

My mother instilled in me the mantra "To thine own self be true." I found a bracelet with the inscription and gave it to my daughter Cara when she became a teenager. I will do the same for Deidre when she enters her teen years. This is what young women need to know. Today our culture tells as to look a certain way, be a certain size, and change our faces to look younger. I'm forty-eight years old in a business that worships youth. I now work in front of HD cameras. (Where were they when I was twenty-five and ready for them?) But this is me and I don't want to look like somebody else. I'm not knocking anyone who feels that surgery is right for them. I just have to be true to me. When I start trying to be someone else, I don't care where I am or what I am doing—TV or no TV—then I'm not successful.

So many times women worry about what they don't have or what they can't do. This will eat you up inside. So I get on my knees every day and I thank God. I thank God for my husband, my two amazing daughters, my family, my friends, and my career. I don't ask for anything unless something really difficult is going on in my life. My mother had a great saying. "Too much human energy is wasted upon worrying about things that never happen." Gratitude and faith keep me grounded in who I am. Worrying is simply wasting time.

One Sunday several years ago I was visiting my dad and went down to the basement to do the laundry. I noticed a little jar on the ledge above the washing machine. It had probably been there for ages but for some reason that day I took it down and opened it. Inside was my maternal grandmother, Cahill's, antique pink pearl rosary coil bracelet from Ireland, perfectly preserved in the little box above the dryer for so many years. The bracelet was another symbol of the love between my mother and my grandmother and their strong connection to Ireland and to their Catholic faith. The rosary bracelet is a tribute to the Blessed Mother and the strength and courage of a mother's love.

At that moment I decided to show it to my good friend Stephen Walsh, owner of JC Walsh & Sons Ltd. He designs jewelry every year for the Saint Patrick's Day QVC show and we have become good friends over the years. Stephen's family has been in the jewelry business for years, since his father started the company. Stephen took the bracelet to show to his father, and promised to redesign a new version out of Connemara marble. When Stephen unwrapped the bracelet to show it to his father John Walsh, John took one look and said, "Stephen, I made this bracelet back in the fifties." The bracelet found its way home back to its original maker after all these years. My grandmother now lives on in each Connemara marble rosary bead bracelet many own from QVC.

My mother lives on in the QVC Irish shows also. While attending Immaculata College one of the sisters gave my mom a beautiful pendant of the Blessed Mother. Once again, I trusted Stephen to take this precious piece of jewelry back to Ireland for their company to recreate for the QVC customer. The Mother's Love pendant is now a popular seller each year. I show my mom's picture on the air from her days at Immaculata and I feel her still with me. These are the ways that the Irish spirit is kept alive. It is so resilient and it just never dies.

Like most Irish parents, my parents encouraged us to study hard, learn everything we could and go freely wherever our lives take us. All my brothers and sisters have at one time studied or settled thousands of miles away from home. I remember my mother saying good-bye to my brother John when he lived in Vancouver and she could only see him once a year. I could see the sadness in her eyes just saying good-bye to him. Recently, someone in the family came across a picture of my father-in-law taken in the 1950s in Mullaslin, Ireland. It was the day he left for America; the day he left his mom. Even on that day all of the family is all smiles. They were happy for him that he was going to follow his dream to have a better life. I often imagine how so many Irish mothers felt when they were saying good-bye to their children embarking on the journey to America, knowing they would possibly never see them again. These circumstances created a need for love to fly back and forth and for connections to endure the test of time and distance.

That's probably why I feel so close to my mother even though she has been gone for twenty years. The love just doesn't end. I often counsel QVC viewers who reach out to me when they are going through the loss of a loved one. QVC has an online community and I've heard from countless women over the past eighteen years who have lost their mothers. I often think of the Irish saying, "Your tears are a gift." Had I not had the connection to my mother, had I not experienced the gift of unconditional love that she gave me, I would have avoided the tears. I also would have missed out on the best gift I was ever given—the gift of a mother's love. I received it fully from my own mother and I pass it on completely every moment to my two daughters, Deirdre and Cara. A mother's love is endless and the love flies back and forth.

Judy Daly

A common trait shared among many Irish families is the love that allows them to embrace those who are not family by blood but family by choice. Nearly anyone who has spent time with people of Irish heritage will comment upon their warmth and friendliness. No one is a stranger. No one need feel lonely if they know an Irish man or woman. This is what connects Irish families across oceans. It is what lets Irish mothers encourage their children to follow their dreams no matter how far away.

Now sixty-five, Judy Daly has not forgotten her Irish upbringing on a dairy farm in Ireland's Midlands. "I believe that in my adult life I have been true to the kind heart that nurtured me in childhood— my mother," she says. While traveling the world in her career with the Monet Jewelry Company, Judy shared love with everyone she met. Judy's story is a testimony to her mission in life, which she states as, "I enjoy life's journey and remind myself every day that I am only passing through." Love and friendship opened the door for Judy to create an unlikely connection with a child from South America.

Judy's Story: Fairymount

I was blessed to be one of Brigid Kelly Daly's seven children. My mother gave me the gift of unconditional love. In her presence it was easy to believe in God and the goodness in human beings. Because of her, I believe that the greatest force in the world is love.

We grew up on a dairy farm called Fairymount; a beautiful place high on a hill in Ireland's Midlands. My family was the first Catholic family to live in Fairymount House. My father would sometimes mention that with pride, I suspect because he was part of the old IRA and fought for Irish independence.

On school days we walked the half-mile to the two-room schoolhouse and played with our friends as we walked. Our school days began and ended with prayer. The milestones of childhood were tied to religion, making first communion and confirmation. The four girls helped with housework and the lads helped with the farm work. The girls also had "yard jobs" feeding the calves and hens and washing up in the dairy. We did not have a lot of stuff to play with other than some board games and a ring board. We skipped rope and played hopscotch. We had a swing and created a seesaw by placing a plank across a tar barrel.

The land itself was a magical playground and a source of comfort and joy. Spring brought newborn lambs to the fields and wild bluebells and primroses to every wood and ditch. In summer we carried tea in a bucket to the men making hay in the field; the smell of that new hay is with me still. We made necklaces from the daisies in the meadow, then lay on our backs and looked at airplanes high in the sky heading for America. And we talked about one day going there. In autumn, corn was cut and stacked then brought to the barn for the thrashing. Thrashing day brought all the neighbors to the farmyard to help; the kitchen was a busy place, feeding round after round of men. In autumn we climbed trees to collect hazelnuts and searched the fields for mushrooms. In winter we longed for snow and sometimes got it; then a snowball fight and making a snowman caused loads of excitement. The sounds, smells, and scenes from my childhood filled my soul with beauty and helped me connect with the divine. Growing up in the Irish countryside gave me deep roots and a feeling of belonging that has sustained me throughout my life.

Of course, life had its share of challenges too. Dairy farming is hard work and it must be done every day of the year. My mother worked inside and outside. She was a good cook; she fed my father, seven children, and several workmen three meals a day, every single day. She worked from early morning to late at night but it was not her style to complain about things such as "too much work." Like all good Irish mothers, she understood her children were born to live their own lives—that you give your children "roots and wings" then set them free to live their life, wherever fate takes them.

I do not have children of my own but my seventeen nieces and nephews and the twenty-six children in the next generation give me ample opportunity to pass along love, as do my many godchildren and the children of friends.

My mother was a devout Catholic and truly lived her faith. Yet she was not consumed by the rules of the Catholic Church. Her faith was far bigger than that. Back in the 1970s when my sister Mary was marrying a non-Christian she thought our mother might be upset. Mary thought she was reassuring her by telling her, "My children will be raised Catholic," but it was our mother who reassured Mary when she said, "Raise them to be good people, alanna. That is what matters."

Alanna

The Irish word "alanna" means "darling"; it is often used as a term of endearment for a female child. The phrase *alannamochroi* means "darling of my heart." Although the Irish language was not spoken by many people from my mother's generation, due to the 'ban' imposed during centuries of English rule, Irish words and phrases such as this survived and are commonly used. So my mother rarely called her four girls by our given names; she always used the word alanna instead. Because of the comfort I felt when my mother called me "alanna" I took to using that word and phrase myself.

Best friends meet in unlikely places. My girlfriend Barbara and I met at an Al-Anon meeting in New York City. Barbara was of Italian descent and like most of us had experienced her fair share of heartache in life. It was the early 1980s and Barbara was working hard on becoming a healthy person in mind, body, and soul, having left her marriage to a "problem drinker" behind. It was during this time that Barbara's mother was diagnosed with cancer and became gravely ill.

Barbara would visit her mother in the hospital and call me for support. I would comfort Barbara the way my mother comforted me. I told her, "It is in God's hands, alanna," and I prayed for both of them to find peace. Sometimes that is all a good friend can do.

Barbara's Dream

Barbara's dream was to have a baby and she had applied to be an adoptive parent. She wanted to bring a baby girl to America and give her the chance of a better life. The process, especially for a divorced woman at that time, took forever. As she waited she worked on herself, her job and her relationships. She was in a long distance relationship, not her dream situation, but he was a good man and Barbara hoped they would one day raise her daughter together.

The day finally came when Barbara received a phone call telling her there was a baby girl from Colombia who needed a home. Barbara was over the moon with excitement. After all these years she would finally be a mother. We met for tea and she asked me if I would be her daughter's godmother. I was thrilled and excited at the possibility. I knew Barbara was passing along the gift of love to me. Barbara also told me she was going to name her daughter Alanna. From me she knew the word as an endearment and when she found Alanna in her book of baby names she told herself, "That will be my daughter's name."

Alanna was born in Curiti, a city in Colombia, South America, on October 17, 1989. I felt an immediate bond because my birthday is also October 17. Barbara flew to Colombia to meet her daughter and bring her home to America. When I saw Barbara hold Alanna for the first time she had a look of happiness on her face that I had never seen before.

Alanna was a beautiful, strong, sweet-tempered baby. For the next two years Barbara lived the life she had dreamed of and planned for: that of a working single mother. That's not an easy life: but Alanna was an easy child to care for and Barbara was never happier. Yet this was to be a short-lived experience. In October of 1991, when Alanna was only two years old, Barbara was diagnosed with lung cancer. I spent as much of my spare time as I could with Barbara and Alanna from October of 1991 to September of 1992, helping look after Alanna while Barbara battled her illness.

It was during this time that my mother's health was failing. She was living in a nursing home back in Ireland. In April of 1990 my mother's artificial hip had dislocated, leaving her unable to stand or walk; she entered a nursing home in June of 1991. It was in that nursing home, during a visit home in late September of 1992, that I received a phone call telling me that Barbara had only a few months to live. I remember sitting on the bed next to my mother as I told her the news about Barbara. My mother knew very well that her own death was fast approaching, yet she took my hands and held them tight and said, "Go to them, alanna—they need you." That was her way.

Taking her advice, I returned to New York to be there for Barbara. We spent the next three months preparing for Barbara's death. Barbara made a video message for Alanna and wrote her letters. She wanted to be sure that although they were only together for three years, Alanna could comprehend the love and commitment Barbara had to her. She also wanted Alanna to know the joy she had brought her.

Good-bye

During those three months my mother's health was also rapidly failing. I had booked a ticket to go visit her for Christmas 1992. But when I spoke to her on the phone during the second week of that December she sounded very weak. I told her, "I'll be there soon, Mom." She asked, "Can you come now, alanna?" The next day I was on a flight to Ireland. My sisters, Mary and Joan, who also live in New York, followed soon after. All six living children got to say good-bye to her and she died peacefully on December 18. One month and one day later, on January 19, 1993, I held Barbara's hand when she died at Sloan Kettering Hospital in New York. That was a difficult time in my life, but I am grateful that I was able to be with both of them in spite of the vast ocean between them. I still sometimes think of that "circle of love" of how Alanna got her name and how love gets passed down.

Alanna was readopted by her legal guardians, Barbara's brother Vinnie and his wife, Stephanie. They have been wonderful, loving parents to Alanna, and she gained two lovely big sisters when she went to live with them. Alanna is now an independent, beautiful young woman, working and living a full life.

I'm thankful she was a big part of my life too. She spent every third weekend with me while she was growing up and we visited Ireland together a few times so she could share my homeland with me.

I love the USA, my adopted land. It has been my home for over forty years now. Yet Ireland has an almost magical hold on me. I love the Irish landscape and its culture, and I love its generous, spirited people. Going back and walking in the fields where I grew up is a spiritual experience. From being raised on a farm I understand that death is a natural part of life. I believe that those who pass over are not gone but are simply serving a different role as a spiritual guide in my life. Most of all I know that my time on earth is short and I must try every day, in some small way, to pass along the love that was given to me by my Irish mother.

Chapter Two

Irish Roots

*N**o matter how far an Irish man or woman may roam, each feels a strong and unbreakable tie to "home." They may find a new place to make a life, have a family, follow a dream, but always in the back of their mind is a pull, a tie to the old country. Some Irish left because of adversity at home, some left out of necessity, some left to court adventure. But wherever they roam, the call of Ireland remains a constant.*

Being from Ireland is being of Ireland. Each emigrant takes a piece of Ireland with them but also leaves a bit of their heart behind. Across the world, the common bond of being Irish will open doors and create opportunities.

Knowing where you come from and recognizing how that personal history has impacted your life allows you to embrace the new and move forward toward your dreams. The Irish are adept at respecting their past but moving toward the future. It does not matter how hard the past or how trying the challenges, the Irish embrace their roots, draw strength from adversity, and emerge better and stronger. Through it all they remain part of their homeland.

Explore the roots of the fascinating women in this chapter, from Mary McAuliffe, who teaches Ireland's past in order to improve the present; to Janet Stephenson, who loves being part of the Irish community because for ninety-three years it's been so much fun; to Karen Rankin, whose connection to her Irish roots taught her the meaning of winning; and to Nannette Rundle Carroll, who grew up hearing her ancestors' stories of sacrifice and hardship in pursuit of the greatest gift—freedom.

Mary McAuliffe

The people of Ireland have always cherished and respected their history. Even before they preserved the past in writing, they enjoyed a rich oral tradition of passing on the old ways through vivid and colorful stories. Despite its struggles to maintain a national identity and preserve its traditions, Ireland is now actively reclaiming its treasures from the past. A respect for the past is evident in the careful preserving of family folklore and traditions. Irish architecture, arts, and even the landscape are full of symbols and meanings related to her strong and colorful past. Ireland is rich with stories of war, famine, and grief, although Irish stories also embrace fairies, religion, and an undying faith that things will get better.

The story of Ireland's past is still being explored and discovered. Her story is evolving with the resurgence of an interest in preserving the identity of the past in arts, language, and culture. Ireland is also surfacing much of its darker past and bringing it to the forefront to create a better future. It is no wonder that Mary McAuliffe, department member of social justice at the University College in Dublin has made history her life's work, focusing on aspects of social justice.

Mary's Story: Knowing the Past

I grew up in the small village of Daugh in North Kerry, where every field has a name. Stones in the fields often have some historic association as place or boundary markers. The castles and abbeys throughout the area were my playgrounds.

My dad, Dan McAuliffe, was a lover of politics and history. He was a great sportsman, a footballer, a farmer, and a businessman. He was also an avid reader. He owned The Elm Bar, one of the four pubs in the small village. The bar was named for the gigantic elm tree that stood next to the pub until it died in the 1970s with the spread of Dutch elm disease. Attached to the pub to this day stands the house I grew up in. The Elm Pub is a lively town pub and still in our family today.

I spent many a weekend with my grandparents Bridie and Tim Kennelly just a few miles up the road from Daugh, in the village of Ballylongford. My brothers and sisters and I were especially fond of climbing to the top of my favorite castle Carrigafoyle, built in the 1490s by the O'Conor Kerry clan. It was our castle where we would reenact the many battles and sieges that happened there.

There was no place I would rather be than at my grandparents' house. I was enveloped in love there. My mother, Nancy, and my grandparents believed that we could do whatever we wanted in our lives as long as we worked and studied hard. I had loving, hard-working, supportive parents and grandparents. I was encouraged to live my life on my own terms and to make a difference in the process. I also benefited greatly from my parents' commitment to education.

From the age of twelve to seventeen I attended boarding school at the Convent of Mercy, Doon, County Limerick, along with my sister Bridget. It was about sixty miles from home. Long study hours, lifelong friendships, independence, and a strong self-belief all came from this experience. My parents sacrificed for us to attend boarding school and it was an investment that changed my life. Education and history became my passions and I went on to obtain a PhD from the School of History and Humanities of Trinity College in Dublin.

I have devoted my life to making a difference in the lives of women through the study of history. When you educate a child, you educate a village and you educate a nation. Our past has an influence on our future. When we speak and learn about history, when we remember our past mistakes, we can only do better for the future.

Ireland has experienced a long, continuous, and often fractious relationship with our neighboring island and therefore shares a history of the same spirituality, religion, ideas and ideologies as those who occupied our lands. We also have a long history of conflict, rebellion, and revolution. During the seventeenth and eighteenth centuries, under the laws known as the Penal Laws, if you were Irish Catholic you were not allowed to practice your religion. You were not allowed to obtain an education to any degree or any higher standard, unless your family could afford to send you abroad to France. During a period lasting several centuries, most native Irish people were disinherited from their land. With this came an underlying sense of injustice. Yet that very injustice is what connects the Irish people so strongly to the land. We fought for our land. We fought for justice and social justice. We suffered though famines created by economic situations and aggravated by natural conditions—but we came through it all and hopefully we will again come through these modern hard times.

The Great Famine of the 1840s left a strong imprint on the Irish people. This tragedy gave the Irish a deep sense of compassion for those elsewhere in the world affected by horrific circumstances. Whether it is famine or flood, the Irish want to help others because we have our own memory of suffering. Despite the suffering from the past, the people maintain a sense of great joy and pride in their heritage. The Irish have a long history of literary wonders and a deep and colorful cultural history.

The women's story in Ireland has often been that of struggle. In the second decade of the twentieth century, when Ireland was still governed by England, women were given a guarantee of equal rights and equal citizenship as reward for their participation in the nationalist struggle against English rule. They were told that once Ireland was free, once there was a Republic of Ireland, women's issues would be dealt with. When Ireland became the Irish Free State in 1922, women's issues were neglected. The powerful Church and the government of the day—mostly made up of men—eventually wrote the 1937 Constitution of Ireland, where women were positioned in the home and not granted the freedoms and protections promised. One specific article of the Constitution said that a woman, by economic necessity, should not be obliged to work outside the home—even though the State would not provide for her.

Even though women were actively involved in the fight for Irish freedom between 1916 and 1922, the fight for women's equality was forgotten. My own grandmother was in *Cumann na mBan* and told me stories of gun running during the War of Independence. She described women who bravely took up arms and actually joined the conflict. Once she attended the large funeral for a local man who had been shot dead by the Black and Tans. My grandmother hid a rifle up her skirt and at the appropriate time took it out and fired a volley of shots over the coffin. Then she immediately hid the rifle under her skirt again. In fact, most of my female ancestors were involved in the war but the men weren't. The men stayed home and farmed while the women were off gun running.

The women of Ireland also struggled under the control of the British; they spent their lives and spilled their blood for their rights. So when the British left, they expected to be provided with a reward of their rights and freedoms as they had been promised. The reality was very different. Women were not allowed to work in certain jobs. They could not work in certain professions. They were forced to give up their jobs when they got married. These provisions were written into law, and were the end of the promise of equal citizenship. To this day, women in Ireland still live under strict laws regarding abortion and reproductive rights that have a disproportionate impact on women.

Things are changing, slowly, and we've made some strides. It's easy to forget that women's rights can be threatened anywhere. Women must never forget the progress we have made and to work consistently and diligently to protect it. Ireland's history illustrates how women were on the verge of receiving true equality under the law, but since then those rights have been slowly chipped at and eroded. Since the 1970s Irish feminists of the second wave have achieved much in the way of full equality for Irish women, but there are still many issues, such as accessible and affordable childcare, to be dealt with.

Most have heard of the worldwide scandal of sexual abuse of children at the hands of trusted, revered priests in the Catholic Church. This scandal became public in the 1990s and rocked the solid foundation of the Catholic Church. Ireland, with its strong and powerful commitment to the Catholic Church, suffered irreparable damage. The scandal left many questioning how a country and a people could put so much faith and trust into a church only to be so wounded and abused in the process. Recently after a long struggle by many brave, tenacious advocates, restitution for the victims in Ireland has finally come.

A long-hidden and little-known history is the story of thousands of Ireland's women, judged to be "sinners" by the Catholic Church-driven society of the twentieth century and even beyond. Irish Girls who were considered flirtatious or promiscuous were sentenced to lives of penance. Their crime? Bearing children out of wedlock, leaving abusive husbands, or simply being in the wrong place at the wrong time. The punishment? A lifetime of "penitence" spent in the service of the Sisters of Charity, Mercy, Good Shepherd, and other orders. They performed harsh, thankless chores such as laundering prison uniforms, clerical washing, and caring for elderly nuns or their aging peers, while forever trapped behind the walls of Ireland's numerous convent laundries.

These women are now called the "Magdalenes," named after Mary the Magdalene, who served her Jesus loyally and was rewarded with his forgiveness and love. Unfortunately no reward existed for these "penitents." They were told to forever hide their shame inside convent walls, work under harsh conditions, and be often mistreated by the sisters. It is a story of which many Irish are ashamed, which is perhaps why it has only come to light recently.

In 1993, property held by the Sisters of Our Lady of Charity of Refuge in Dublin, which once served as a convent laundry, was to be sold to a developer for public use. It was known at that time that some 133 graves existed, unmarked, in a cemetery on the convent grounds. The graves belonged to women who had worked in the service of the convent all their lives and were buried there without a memorial stone or the names over them—graves totally unmarked, women completely unremembered.

When knowledge of the graves became public, there was public outrage and some families came forth to identify and claim some of the women as their long-lost daughters, mothers, grandmothers, and sisters. Yet many remained unidentified. At the time of the 1993 discovery, a memorial was established and the remaining unclaimed bodies were to be cremated and reinterred in the Glasnevin cemetery in Dublin. But a problem arose: an initial exhumation order was given for 133 bodies. Only seventy-five death certificates existed. The exhumation revealed another twenty-two bodies. The 155 bodies were quietly cremated.

Even in death these women suffered callous, inhumane treatment and were robbed of their dignity. In addition to graves gone unmarked, women in their fifties, sixties, and seventies now still go "unmarked," languishing today inside the convent walls. Many of them were given new names and ages upon admittance. Most had no contact with their families, making their true identification enormously difficult.

I have adopted the Justice for Magdalene Committee as my most recent activist work and I serve on the Advisory Committee of JFM. JFM campaigns for justice for the Magdalene women. These women worked as slaves. They received no compensation. They were abused. Now they are trying to survive without a pension, without education and without support. Justice for Magdalenes's mission is to create a voice for the Magdalene women. We respectfully seek justice for the victims. We seek redress and an apology from the Catholic Church of Ireland and from the Irish government, as it was also complicit in sending women to the Magdalene laundries. We hope to help establish advisory and reintegration services for the survivors so they have a chance now, finally, for a better life.

The issue of women's rights is greater than the boundaries of Ireland. There are women all over the world who are still suffering and are still not free. In some countries females suffer horrible atrocities in the name of laws or religion, which delegates them to second-class citizens. As women of today, we must never forget where we have come from and guard our rights so we do not lose what we have gained. Being one of the lucky ones given a loving home, solid upbringing, an education, and a strong family foundation, I must use that strength to tell the stories of others. I want to leave the world a better place for the next generation. Bringing to light the stories and history of the wrongs of the past is my way of improving the future.

Janet Stephenson

Kansas City native Janet Stephenson knows firsthand about the cultural influence of Ireland. Embracing her Irish roots to provide a foundation for her life, she is an example to her friends and family of how to live for faith and family. Taking great pleasure in the little things in life, she makes every day a celebration and enjoys the simple pleasures of life—like a cold Coca-Cola and cookies for breakfast. Janet is an example of a woman living life on her own terms, even at the age of ninety-three.

Janet's Story: Secret to a Long Life

The secret to living to be ninety-three is not in what you eat, how much you exercise, or what possessions you accumulate over the years. The secret is in faith and family.

I've lived a charmed life. I am the youngest daughter of Thomas Sylvester Cauley and Mary Ann Kelly Cauley, and I was born in Rushville, Indiana, on April 14, 1918. Being the last of six brothers and sisters was a great advantage since I always had them to look out for me. I was also blessed to be born Irish Catholic with wonderful parents. My dad was a hard worker. He had a construction job building bridges in Indiana. When we moved to thirty third Street in Kansas City, he got a job as a plasterer, which is what he did for most of my childhood.

My mother only had a sixth grade education, yet everything she did, she did to perfection. She could do it all. She was an excellent cook. She could sew beautifully; the inside of her clothes looked just as good as the outside. She not only made all of my clothes for many years, but after I married and had children of my own, she made clothes for them too. In our old home movies, everyone looks like we're going to a party because the clothes she made us just to play in were so gorgeous. My mother paid attention to detail and took pride in her work. Back then women didn't have careers. But if she had wanted to go down that path, she would have been amazing at anything she set her mind to doing—and she would have worn a hat and gloves while she did it.

I guess we were poor, but no one ever bothered to tell me and I never noticed. I grew up during the Great Depression, yet I always had enough food to eat and clothes to wear. My house was a happy one. We celebrated so much that my dad would tell my mother, "You celebrate the first of the month!" Valentine's Day, Saint Patrick's Day, Mother's Day, one of our birthdays—there was always a reason to have a little event.

I have kept that tradition going and love to decorate for the holidays—every holiday. I have a window that faces the street, and you know what the occasion is by the decorations in it. Whether it's a new great-grandbaby, a birthday, or Christmas, I decorate the window. I also still dress up for Halloween and have been seen driving around town and even visiting the halls at Rockhurst High School in my dog costume.

I grew up in Kansas City, Missouri, in Redemptorist Parish. The parish has been under the care of the Redemptorist priests and brothers since 1878. The church there now was dedicated in 1912 and was completely renovated in 2000. It's one of the most beautiful churches in Kansas City. I went to school there from kindergarten through high school. Everything centered on the church, and our whole neighborhood was Irish Catholic. That was all I knew, and I wouldn't have it any other way. I'm grateful and proud to be Irish. The Irish can manage to have a good time no matter what is going on around them. I can't imagine being anything else.

A Sense of Community

Being Irish Catholic gave me a strong sense of community. There was a large group of Irish Catholic kids that I have been friends with for life. We started kindergarten together, celebrated First Communion and Confirmation together, married and had children about the same time—all with a deep connection to the church and the community. It was a way of life. The priests often came over for dinner. My mom made cakes for the nuns.

One of those kids I grew up with was Tom Stephenson, who became my husband when I was twenty years old. Tom and I had known each other our whole lives. When asked how we met, he would always say, "Janet is like Jesus. She just always was!" I cannot think back far enough to when he wasn't a part of my life. We had a great group of friends who did everything together. Of course most of them, including Tom, are gone now.

Tom died when he was fifty-two. All of my siblings died in their fifties. I guess you could say I have planned to die since I was in my fifties too. I'm really surprised and happy that I have made it this far because being ninety-three is amazing. Everyone pampers you.

Tom was an amateur golfer and had gone to Dallas for a golf tournament. He died of a heart attack in his hotel room. It was a complete shock. We had a printing business that I suddenly had to think of, and my kids to raise on my own. My top priority was for them to be able to finish college and support themselves. I was fortunate that my son, Tom, who was a freshman in college at the time, had a football scholarship to Missouri and paid his own way through college. My oldest daughters, Judie and Sue, were finished with school. But Sallie was just 18, and Jan, my baby, was only 15. My brother, John, who was the Washington bureau chief for the *Kansas City Star*, was a tremendous help to me and to my kids. After Tom died, he was there for us. That's what family does.

When I was seven years old, I made my First Holy Communion. We celebrated by stopping at the Irish grocery store called Browne's and getting a nickel bag of cookies and a Coke. That has been my favorite breakfast for my whole life. Browne's and I are both still here, though I really don't have any business making it to ninety-three years old. I really do drink Coke and eat Vanilla Fingers cookies for breakfast. I never drink water, and I don't eat vegetables. It's all in your attitude. Sometimes I think, "Enough is enough!" But I'm still very independent. I drive. I travel. I play golf. I go where I want to go. As long as I'm still having fun, I guess I'll hang around.

I'm lucky to have lived in the same house for sixty years. Tom and I bought it when we were a young married couple. It had been his family home and just happened to be on the market when we were looking for a house for our growing family. We went to see it, and I fell in love with it. We added on two rooms and raised our five children there—with only one full bathroom. As my granddaughter Caitlin, who lives with me, says, everything in it is "original."

Living Life

I do have a lot more than Coca-Cola to keep me going. I love sports and am a diehard football fan. I learned the game from watching it with my dad. When I was about ten years old, my dad and I would take the streetcar to see Rockhurst High School football games. I still go to Rockhurst games. They have made more state championship appearances than any team in Missouri, and I have seen many of those games, including when they won it in 2010. I get so worked up over the Kansas City Chiefs that I will not hold a great-grandchild during a game because I'm afraid I'd forget and throw him across the room in the excitement. Football is one area of my life where I lose all reason and control.

I'm a little calmer playing golf. I never played when Tom was alive. I tried it out a few times with him, but it was a disaster. About ten years after he died, I decided that I would learn to play and have really enjoyed it. Most of the women I play with, including my daughters, are much younger than I am. I was going to quit last year, but then I got a birdie one day playing with my daughters, so I'm back for another season. I used to always walk the course, but about four years ago I started using a cart.

Another thing that keeps me going is Saint Patrick's Day. It starts early in the morning at Browne's and continues all day long from party to party. And I don't even drink. I send out Saint Patrick's Day cards like most people send out Christmas cards. I have never missed the Brookside Saint Patrick's Day parade in my neighborhood, which is held the weekend before the big downtown parade. My kids, grandkids, and great-grandkids have all walked with me in that parade.

Faith and Family

My faith and my family have gotten me through all the rough spots in life. Knowing that God is in my life is the best gift I've been given. I may not understand all that happens but I have faith that things will improve. I worry that younger people may not have that kind of faith. Without it, I don't know how they will make it through all the challenges that life will certainly throw their way.

Family is all-important to me. You don't choose your family, but it always has been and always will be. Having a close relationship with each of my children and knowing that they all turned out all right and have good lives is the best accomplishment possible. With five children, sixteen grandchildren and twenty-seven great-grandchildren, family is all around me. I have had two granddaughters live with me: Sarah when she was starting her business, Tippi Toes Dance Company, and Caitlin while she was in law school and now while she's working as a public defender. I still go to basketball games and birthday parties for my great-grandchildren. They stop by and visit me all the time. My son flies me to Dallas for visits and enters me in every football pool he can find around the country to keep me entertained. We all love to tell our family stories to make each other laugh. We laugh a lot. We love each other. What else could you possibly want in life?

Karen Rankin

As a business development executive working with C-Suite executives, Karen Rankin defines success as the completion of an action item or a goal.

Through a desire to make a difference and a connection with a little girl named Elizabeth fighting to survive cancer, Karen dedicated much of her time to the Leukemia & Lymphoma Society (LLS) and Team in Training. Team in Training provides athletes with the skills, camaraderie, and support to complete a marathon. In exchange for training and support, the athletes help raise money toward cures for blood cancers like leukemia—the number one disease killer of children—lymphoma, and myeloma. All the money raised by Team in Training participants goes to support the LLS. Little did Karen know that her work to help families with cancer would prepare her for one of the biggest challenges in her life: facing the loss of her own father to cancer.

Over the years Karen learned that true success is not about being crowned the victor. It is about completing the race. Karen runs marathons, and she knows that marathon runners succeed when they simply cross the finish line. She lives by the words she heard from her Irish upbringing: "To finish is to win."

Karen's Story: Core Values

People know I am Irish with a single glance. My red hair, freckles, blue-green eyes, and warm smile tend to give it away. Aside from the outward signs that I am Irish, I have a deep sense of pride and strong core values that go back to my Irish roots.

Growing up we were taught to take pride in our Irish heritage. That included a strong work ethic, honesty, always lending a helping hand, and being true to ourselves. These core values were the keys to my great-great-grandparents' success in Canada, after having left Ireland for a better life. They give our family tree its roots of strength, courage, and passion.

My mother, Paula Rundle Rankin's, family came from Ireland. She was a first-generation American born in the United States. My dad, Bob Rankin, was adopted and grew up in New Jersey. He was adopted by a United States ambassador, a single man who traveled all over the world. One of the qualities that attracted Dad to my mother was her strong connection with her Irish Catholic roots. My father took on the Irish Catholic connection as his own.

Dad never met a stranger and he was known for checking in on people he had not seen in years. We bounced across the country as Dad coached at the University of Illinois, the University of Rhode Island, Michigan State University, the University of Tennessee, and others.

Sports were my refuge in every move we made. I joined the swim team and I made friends. Mom made every house a home. The cities changed but the Irish traditions stayed the same. We celebrated Saint Patrick's Day with frenzy. We listened to Irish music. We said our prayers. Family meant everything to us. Mom took shifts at work so she was home when Dad was working. As two working parents with no family to help, they did not want us to become part of the American latchkey kid population.

Running for the Cure

Always looking for opportunities to give back and make a difference was another Irish trait that took me down a path that changed my life. In 1997 I joined the volunteer staff at Children's Medical Center in Dallas. In my role as lead volunteer I taught a class for the parents of children with cancer. The class was designed to provide guidance and support to the parents who were dealing with a child with cancer while raising other healthy children at home.

Every twelve weeks we started with a new group of families. I remember specifically one little girl who connected with me from the moment I laid eyes on her. Elizabeth was eight years old, with big blue eyes and a sparkling smile. She had leukemia. She joined her parents and the group after her chemotherapy treatment on Thursdays. My heart was touched by her strength and spirit.

In an effort to bring her some small comfort, when class was over, I would air rub her legs after her treatment. I had to be very careful for my hands not to get too close to her legs and I had to control the speed of my movements. If it was not just right I could see the pain on her face. I could only imagine how much pain little Elizabeth endured. I thought to myself, *Wow, cancer sucks. There has to be more I can do.*

Rise to the Occasion

It was Saturday morning and time for my manicure. Nothing like a little "me time" after a loaded work week. I had a regular appointment with Nancy and I looked forward to seeing her tucked away in the little corner of the salon. I loved going to the salon. It reminded me of the movie *Steel Magnolias.* As I turned the doorknob to enter I heard all the ladies chattering about their lives. No topic was off limits and most focused on their children, their in-laws, or their bosses they loved to hate. When I closed my eyes I expected to see the characters Ouiser, Annelle, Trudy, and M'Lynn to appear. It was just like a scene in the movie.

This particular Saturday as Nancy was trimming and polishing, she could not contain her excitement about a half marathon she just signed up to do in Disney World. She explained that she was involved in a program called Team in Training and it supported the Leukemia and Lymphoma Society (LLS). Having heard all about my time and connection with Elizabeth, Nancy still had a little trouble convincing me to accompany her to an informational meeting about the group the following day.

Sunday I found myself reluctantly driving to the Galleria Mall to rendezvous with Nancy at the meeting. I convinced myself I was going only to support Nancy and there was no way I was going to get roped into running a marathon and spending time and money going to Disney World. Regardless of the noble cause, I knew this just wasn't for me.

I arrived at the large gym swarming with over a thousand people— standing room only. This was a much bigger deal than I had thought. The program began with a motivational speaker sharing a story of how LLS changed her life and her family's life for the better. Next up on the stage was a group of cancer survivors and people going through cancer treatment. Each one spoke about how LLS saved their lives. They thanked the people who devoted their time to run to support cancer research and encouraged those of us who were not yet involved to use our health and our voices to make a difference.

The final presentation was done by no other than Elizabeth and her mom from my Thursday night class. As I heard Elizabeth's mother tell their story, my eyes were glued to Elizabeth. Here was this little girl up on a stage in front of a thousand people, brave and strong, fighting for her life. As her mom finished her presentation Elizabeth looked out at the crowd, flashing her adorable heartfelt smile and gave a little wave as she walked off the stage to a roaring crowd in front of her.

The program was over and I realized that in spite of its power I was still dead set against signing up. I had some serious limiting beliefs and doubts about how I could ever run 13.1 miles and the daunting task of raising $3,000 from sponsors. It was just not something I thought I could do.

I was making my escape without signing up when Nancy and I spotted Elizabeth. Nancy suggested we go say hello. Elizabeth and her mom saw me approaching and Elizabeth's mom excitedly said, "Karen, I am so proud that you are taking on this challenge to help Elizabeth and so many others! We are so grateful to people like you, willing to make a difference."

I was hooked. I signed my forms and turned them in. For the last ten years I have been running and fighting for a cure for cancer. In the process I have raised over $100,000 for LLS. Every step I run, I think of Elizabeth. Ironically, my work with the LLS provided preparation and knowledge that I had no idea I would need—until the day my father was suddenly diagnosed with cancer.

Cancer Hits Home

As a football coach my dad had a strong and enduring presence about him. He ran six miles a day and played golf. So his cancer diagnosis at only sixty-six came as a shock to us all.

Two tumors were found in Dad's brain on April 1, 2008. He had surgery two days later, and they tried to remove as much of the tumors as possible. He was diagnosed with a grade 4 glioblastoma multiforme, a cancer that continues to multiply. The area of the brain in which the cancer was found was the motor area of the brain, thus the cancer was affecting all of Dad's motor reactions, and all the drugs made him very weak. On August 3, 2008, just four months after his original diagnosis, Dad's new journey with God began as Jesus came down to carry him to heaven.

Surviving the loss of my dad and helping my mother get through it has been the biggest challenge in my life. I find comfort in the fact that he is now my angel watching over me.

I would have been ill-equipped to cope with any of this, much less to be a rock of strength for my mother, had it not been through my work with LLS. Over the years I had seen families struggle with diagnoses of cancer. I recognized how it could turn a family upside down. My training and education and all the hours in class, running with other families, and earning money to find a cure somehow brought me comfort.

My father's cancer was quick and relentless. We had little time to prepare, little time for hope, little time for good-byes.

As my work with LLS continues I realize that I may not have saved my father but I may one day make a small difference in the future of a child and save a life. Perhaps I will help a family in need with comforting words and actions. Maybe one day the dollars I have raised will find the cure. This is what life is all about. Hope and giving.

I have learned that the Irish Catholic core values my mom and dad taught me are what matters most. Growing up and being active in sports provided me with the strength to know that I can do anything. I can survive and even thrive. I participate for the love of the sport and I am able to give back to the community through fund-raising and sponsorships. It is a way to visibly confirm to me that while I never win at the events, I have won these races by being out there and competing. I win every time someone makes a donation to Team in Training and I contribute to cancer research.

When my great-great-grandparents left the farm in Ireland in hopes of a better life, they did not have a map or a plan. They simply knew that they had to try. They had to live for the moment and live their core values. I now build on their strength. I will live my core values, make a difference and give back. If that is not winning I do not know what is.

Nannette Rundle Carroll

Nannette Rundle Carroll is a popular speaker, management trainer, and author of *The Communication Problem Solver*. She is also a top-rated faculty member with the American Management Association. Nannette does not take her success for granted. She remembers her parents and grandparents and how hard they worked and the sacrifices they made so Nannette would have the best gifts of all—faith and an education. These gifts enabled her to design a career around her passion for writing and communicating, which would not have been possible without the lessons they taught her.

Nannette's Story: Ancestor Stories

My father's grandfather was James O'Neill from County Wicklow, Ireland. He and his wife, Ann Murphy, were tenants on a farm. They were proud of being farmers until the English landowner demoted them to laborers. They had to move to a tiny cabin and work hard just to survive. My Irish ancestry runs long and deep and so do the struggles my family faced in search of a better life. These stories made me a proud Irish American.

My dad was born in 1905 in Streetsville, Ontario, and was regularly forced to run through a lineup of boys who threw snowballs at him because he was Irish Catholic. The boys figured he must be hiding guns under the altar of the church. The irony is that his surname, Rundle, is a British name. However, he always identified as Irish because of his love for his mother, who died when he was only twelve, and for his grandmothers, Bridget and Elizabeth. They kept the flame alive in him of his Irish ancestry and how they never gave up. My father often spoke of his grandmother Elizabeth O'Neill, who emigrated on a "leaky boat" with her parents. He narrated the story of a family, cold, sick, and frightened, in the bowels of the boat, clinging to their rosary beads and reciting the Hail Mary over and over.

My family survived their journey and thanked God every day for delivering them to safety and freedom. Elizabeth walked to church and back every Sunday, even during the coldest days of Ontario winters. They only stopped once for a warm cup of tea at a relative's home on the eight-mile trek to Mass.

My mother, Loretto, whose maiden name was Haffey, may have had her family name "anglicized" when her ancestors landed in North America. Her Auntie Bridget Haffey Carney, a family oral historian, told her that if the customs officers did not understand your name, they would shorten it and write the name the way it made sense to them. Auntie Bridget said that the Haffeys original surname could have been the O'Haugheys.

In the 1930s, my mother had difficulty finding placement as a teacher. Signs were posted saying "Irish need not apply." She told me she had to work in the country because of her heritage. Although there was freedom to worship in Canada, it still fell under the jurisdiction of the British crown and prejudice ran rampant.

My parents told stories so we knew where we came from and would never forget to be grateful for our Irish heritage and our faith in God. They wanted us to understand how much our ancestors had invested sweat and tears to make a better life for themselves and their progeny. My parents moved to the United States where Irish could get good work. They wanted us to experience the American dream—that if you set goals and worked hard enough to attain them, you could do anything you wanted. Most of all, they wanted their children and grandchildren to have better lives than they did.

My mother believed in manners and kindness. She was heavily influenced by Emily Post and Amy Vanderbilt. We were taught that because we were Irish, we had "culture" even if we did not have money. Culture meant good breeding, education, musical education, and excellent manners. It meant treating others well. She often said, "Before you say anything about anyone, let it pass through three gates: Is it true, is it kind, and is it necessary?" Simple sayings and principles like this have guided me through my life. Mom had an adage for almost every day to guide us in our behaviors and culture.

I had a magical childhood. Music, singing, dancing the Irish jig, and storytelling were a big part of my family's life. Saint Patrick's Day was a great event in our home. Every year we hosted a party. Ginger ale and beer were turned to green. Mom played the piano and everyone sang Irish songs like "Danny Boy" and "An Irish Lullaby" (better known to us as "Too-Ra-Loo-Ra-Loo-Ral"). We danced and sang well into the night. It was my favorite night of the year. I carried on these traditions with our own daughter. She learned the Irish favorite songs. Also, on Saint Patrick's Day morning, she would find evidence that our own leprechaun had come in the night. "Mr. O'Carroll" wrote notes to her in tiny little handwriting. He also left pennies on the floor from his pot of gold.

Storytelling was a rich and important part of my childhood and adulthood. I studied English literature in college in addition to minoring in art. Family storytelling may have been where my love of writing came from. My mother had journals from various trips she'd taken over the years. She documented important events in her life.

I started writing stories at the age of six. I found my hiding place in my sisters' closet under the eaves. There I could have a private, quiet space amidst the hubbub of a family of eight. My desk was a cardboard box since it was a storage closet. I took the milk glass lamp from my sisters' dresser and stretched the cord into my "office." My older sisters each had a red metal little kid chair with their name on it. I'd haul one of those into my secret hideout and spend hours writing short stories. One day my father bought a used typewriter, so I began to type up my stories. Both parents always encouraged me to write.

Later, my husband and I compiled and published a book of my parents' stories. The content came from recorded interviews that many of us did with my parents. Various family members of all ages also wrote their memories of events with our parents. We are a family of writers.

Communication

As a young child, I yearned for people to communicate better. I decided that when I grew up, I would be an expert communicator and have peaceful relationships with people. I even decided that my goal was to meet every person in the world. I was convinced I could do this (although the farthest I'd ever traveled was about a hundred miles to Canada to visit relatives.) In the world I would create, by meeting everyone there would be no misunderstandings that couldn't be worked out amicably. People would enjoy relationships with everyone.

As an adult, my professional work always involved communication. We worked in cross-functional teams across the corporations before the term was invented. We had to use influence and interviewing skills with professionals from the bottom to the top of the corporate ladders. From my first job as admissions counselor for my college to my last corporate position as director of management development and training for the worldwide division of a Fortune 100 corporation, communication and understanding various cultures was essential. I was in charge of setting up international training and development. I dealt with cultures from around the world and helped set up succession planning.

Through my consulting and management training work, I realized that communication is the foundation of all management functions. Whether a manager is delegating, setting goals, coaching, or setting a comfortable, productive work environment, what they say and how they say it is the real bottom line. Getting work done is all about being collaborative—especially in tough situations. Outside of work, being a successful communication problem solver also makes us happier human beings.

My ancestors worked hard to survive. In Ireland many had been teachers—what I eventually became in my consulting practice. Many ancestors worked on the Panama, Erie, and Welland Canals. Some were machinists. My grandfather was the manager of a dredging company that dug part of the Welland Canal in Canada. Another grandfather worked on the railroad as a carpenter. As my dad put it, "You didn't think about what you *wanted* to do, like people do today. You did the work that was available." Yet my parents didn't want their children to have to live that difficult life. My mom continued teaching in the US My dad was treasury manager for Univac—his name was the corporate signature on the payroll checks. He did this without benefit of a high level education. My parents ensured that all their children got a good college education so that we would have professional options.

The Impact on Me

I was raised to be a hard worker and always do my best. We were taught personal responsibility and took pride in working for whatever we got. No handouts. From the time we were little, we worked for any "extras." As young teenagers, if we wanted special Breck shampoo (rather than the Castille shampoo that came out of the gallon jug), we had to babysit to earn the money. We learned the ethic of earning our own way. My parents were excellent role models, valuing hard work and effort. They shared their values through example and by telling us our ancestors' stories. Most of all, I learned the importance of keeping the Irish tradition of storytelling alive.

Sadly, three of my grandparents died well before I was born. I did not have the luxury of knowing them personally. I knew them only through the legacy they gave my storytelling parents. I am grateful my parents cared enough to share their stories with me. I continue to remember the difficulties they and their Irish ancestors faced. I appreciate their struggles and how they succeeded by persistence, faith, and hard work. I never take my ability to design my own life and my own career for granted.

Chapter Three

Irish Passion

*T*he Irish are known for loving, laughing, working, and even fighting with great exuberance. Several of the women interviewed for this book shared the same core maxim for making them the fulfilled and happy women they are today: "Do what you love and you will never work a day in your life!"

How magical to rise each day and know you will spend it doing something you love—something that challenges you, feeds your soul, and lights a passionate fire that will never go out. Here are three women who do just that—Mary Higgins Clark, the famous author who even in her eighties is still fueled by a passion for storytelling that has enthralled millions of readers worldwide; Elaine Ni Bhraonain, who took her love of Gaelic and made it into a unique career that has enabled thousands of Irish people to revel in their linguistic heritage; and Corinne Dillon, whose passion for finding the connections between seemingly disparate cultures, such as Irish, American, and Chinese, has enriched them all.

Perhaps reading about these passionate women will light your own fire.

Mary Higgins Clark

Serving as grand marshall of the 2011 Saint Patrick's Day Parade in New York City is only one of the most recent tributes paid to one of America's favorite novelists, Mary Higgins Clark. She celebrated her eighty-fourth birthday on December 24, 2011, and she shows no signs of slowing down. Her latest novel, *I'll Walk Alone,* was published in April 2011, the forty-first of her suspense novels to appear on the best seller list.

What keeps her going? It's not the money or the fame. She keeps writing because of one thing: she loves to tell a story. Fascinated by stories and storytelling since childhood, she never once doubted that she would make this passion her career. Fortified in her belief by her Irish parents' support and strong Catholic upbringing, she did just that. She continues to write stories today because this passion is still very much alive.

Mary's Story: Once Upon a Time

My story begins on December 24, 1927 in the Bronx, New York, as the second of three children born to Nora and Luke Higgins. My parents enjoyed a typical Irish courtship, having "kept company" for almost seven years before finally marrying. My father came to America in 1905 at the age of twenty-one with just five pounds in his pocket, and he had his living to make before marrying. My mother, the child of Irish immigrants, was close to forty and Daddy had just turned 42. My brother Joseph was born within a year of their marriage and I followed almost two years later. Johnny was born in time to celebrate Mother's forty-fifth birthday.

During my early childhood, my brothers and I enjoyed the relative prosperity of being the children of a successful pub owner. My parents had even purchased a six-room brick and stucco semi-detached house. My mother loved her home and carefully furnished it with furniture and bric-a-brac, some of which I still have.

Like nearly everyone in America, as the Depression deepened, our family felt its effects. In those days people relied on credit from local merchants; there were no credit or debit cards. My father's customers expected that he allow them to run a tab for their drinks and dinners. But soon many of them couldn't pay their tabs so my father began to carry losses. If he refused his customers credit, they simply went elsewhere. So the money situation got tighter and tighter, and my father had to lay off people who helped run his bar and grill. Soon he was working longer and longer hours, until one Friday he felt so tired and sick he did not go into work at all.

That next Saturday morning I was attending a 7:00 a.m. Mass in honor of the Blessed Virgin, like a good Catholic girl. Returning home, I turned the corner on Tenbroeck Avenue to see a police car outside our house. My beloved father was dead. He had died in his sleep.

My mother was convinced it was the terrible stress of his business that killed him. Just before his death, a judgment had been issued against him for non-payment of his bill from the wholesale liquor dealer and he was scheduled to go to court on Monday morning to answer for the debt. The shame and anxiety of the whole thing was just too much.

His death was devastating. I had been a "Daddy's girl" so I missed him terribly. But that was only the beginning of our problems. Mother tried to get a job but she was told she was out of luck, even though before her marriage she had attended Hunter College and worked for B. Altman & Company department Store, where many Irish were employed, and worked her way up to a position as a bridal buyer. But during the Depression, college-educated professional people were on the streets begging for work. So she decided that the only solution was to rent rooms in the house. We all moved downstairs so she could rent the two big rooms upstairs and my little one.

My mother never gave up. She planned and plotted for ways to make ends meet and stretch the $2,000 in insurance money that she received upon my father's death. Joe, who had turned thirteen the week after my father died, took a newspaper route. Mother and I took babysitting jobs. We struggled for several years before it all became too much and we eventually lost the house. We moved into a three-room apartment near the trolley line and Mother moved the full contents of our home—all six rooms of furniture—into the small space. She was certain that our fortunes would change and someday we would get the Tenbroeck house back.

Of course, I was young and when you're young you don't know how bad things are. I was sure I would be a successful writer someday. All I had to do was work hard. I was raised on the stories of my parents and their parents, and how hard they had to work to make it in America. My mother was the second child of nine, and she defied her family's expectations to get married early—she waited until she was nearly forty, and had worked her way up at B. Altman & Company, and when she did get married she had the children she wanted. My father made "Higgins Bar and Grill" a success. I also never forgot the story of my grandmother, who wanted to be a writer but instead raised nine kids and went to her grave at sixty-two, saying, "I know I could have written a book."

In the Irish culture, if you work hard you will make it. Yes, you will have hardships, but if you do not give up, if you love what you do, you will make it. Of course I was naïve but I believed that, I really did. When I was fifteen, I worked after school at the Shelton Hotel downtown. It was my job to answer the phone and say, "Hotel Shelton, good afternoon." If I got downtown early, I'd walk along Fifth Avenue and window shop for the clothes that I would have when I was a successful writer.

My faith in my eventual success wasn't dashed even when I got rejected. When I was fourteen, I sent some of my poems to the Saint Joseph's Orphan Home in Jersey City and got the most beautiful rejection letter it's possible to get. I've kept it all these years and now it's framed and hanging in my home.

November 24, 1942

Dear Mary,

We are very grateful to you, dear, for your kindness in sending us your poems, but just now we have enough poetry for several future issues of *The Orphans' Messenger,* and we never like to hold copy, as we always feel that our generous contibutors (sic) might have an opportunity of getting their stories or poems published elsewhere before we could use them.

Your ideas are lovely. If you study and work God will bless your efforts and who knows but what you may one day be the FAMOUS Mary Higgins, whose poems are all so beautiful. Why not make it a practice to say a Hail Mary before you begin any composition, as a petition for our Blessed Mother's aid? I always do, even before I begin to acknowledge letters, and She always does help me —She will help you too.

With a prayer to our Lady to bless you, I remain

Sincerely yours in Christ,
Mother M. Evangelista

Grown Up

Tragedy continued to shadow our lives. Just a few years after my father's death we were forced to face the untimely death of my beloved brother Joe. He graduated from high school in 1944 and immediately enlisted in the navy. The war had broken out three years earlier and even though my mother could have claimed him as her sole means of support, she let him enlist. Six months later she received an urgent call. Joe was gravely ill, having contracted spinal meningitis while in training school. She made the longest trip of her life while she traveled across the country to be at his death bed. He was eighteen.

Joe was the light of my mother's life. It's said that the firstborn child of an Irish mother is the Christ child. Joey was a preemie, and Mother kept a journal from the time he was born. She wrote, "I never left Joseph once that first year. I was so afraid he'd slip away." Later she also wrote, "He was the most beautiful baby. The other two had allergies." But she would have thrown herself across the train tracks for any of us.

The tragedy had a lot to do with the decisions I made in my life. Shortly after Joe's death, I graduated from high school. I made up my mind to go to secretarial school rather than college. I wanted to grow up, earn money, marry, have children—and write. I wanted to get on with my life as quickly as possible. As I had seen, life was unpredictable and could be short.

A year later, I was ready to head out for an office job. I was fortunate and landed a position with Remington Rand, the typewriter and office equipment producer. I liked my job and was actually being given some professional writing assignments writing catalog copy. But I didn't want to write catalog copy; I wanted to write short stories, so I began to study the market and attempt to write. I knew my mother was behind me every step of the way—she told me and everyone she knew what a wonderful writer I was and how I'd someday be famous—but I needed other people to agree with her. I sensed I needed to know more about life and the world around me. I knew something was missing from the tales I struggled to write.

One afternoon, my friend Joan invited me to have a glass of wine with a friend who was a Pan American Airlines stewardess. That meeting set me on the path for my next career. I spent the year after I turned twenty-one traveling the world as a Pan Am stewardess.

Love, Marriage, and Writing

I was sad to leave my job at Remington Rand but excited to face this new opportunity. To celebrate my departure, my boss and his wife invited me to dinner at his home. He instructed me to bring a date.

I had developed a crush on a young man from our neighborhood, Warren Clark. I saw him every week at church and made it my business to greet his mother each Sunday. His younger brother Ken was a close friend of my brother Johnny. Even though he was nine years older than me, I was determined to get him to notice me.

I thought about whom to invite as my date and decided that it was time to make a move toward Warren Clark. After all, what did I have to lose? Getting up my courage, I called him and invited him to dinner.

He agreed mainly because he could not think of a reason to refuse. He told his cousin later that he was afraid he was robbing the cradle.

We met my boss and his wife for dinner. After we left, Warren invited me for a nightcap at an after dinner spot nearby. A comedian came out and started a routine which was a little raunchy and a bit beyond me. I struggled to appear sophisticated so I could impress Warren, trying to laugh at the right times by taking my cue from the audience. Warren was jotting down something on a napkin. "What's that?" I asked.

"The people we'll have at our wedding," he said in a matter-of-fact tone.

I just looked at him. "Fly for year and get it out of your system," he said. "We'll get married next Christmas—people are more generous then." He added, "I'll take my mother to drive-in movies while you're away."

Well, I did as he suggested. I flew all over the world for a year and then married my Warren on December 26, 1949. And for the next fourteen years and nine months we lived happily ever after.

My desire to write was still as strong as ever. Immediately upon our return from our honeymoon, I signed up for a course at NYU in short story writing. I told Warren, "I have to learn how to be a professional writer—I must. It's leaping inside me." I learned a lot from that class, plus as a result of that course I found a writers' group that met for nearly forty years and gave me the encouragement, support—and criticism—that helped me become the writer I am today.

Around this time I joyfully realized that I was pregnant with our first child, our daughter Marilyn. My dreams were being fulfilled. Four more children followed during the next several years. All the while I was writing, short stories mainly of the romance, boy-meets-girl genre. I wrote constantly, while the children were napping, while they were playing in the sandbox, everywhere. Warren was supportive but realistic. He considered this my hobby which he was happy to assist, but he didn't want me to be hurt. He was concerned that I would be devastated by the growing pile of rejection notices.

I was disappointed by the rejections but never devastated. When I got a rejection slip, I'd just type another cover letter and send the story out again. Sometimes the editor would put a personal note on the rejection in handwriting, usually something like, "This isn't right for us, but try us again." I took heart from those. Of course, there were others that weren't so kind—I remember one from Redbook that said, "Mrs. Clark, your stories are light, slight, and trite." That one made me think, *I'll show you, baby.* I did, too. Years later when magazines asked me to send a story to them, I told my agent, "Make them pay."

The moral is never to quit. Keep going and trying. I always had the sense that I was going to make it. Shortly after moving into our first house, with three small children at home and six years' worth of rejection letters, I received the news I had been waiting for. I sold my first short story, "Stowaway," about a stewardess who finds a stowaway from Czechoslovakia on her plane, for $100 to *Extension* magazine. I framed that letter too.

Changing Tides

The tide had changed. I soon began selling short stories and even acquired an agent. I was writing and caring for my family. Warren had a good job working for Northwest Orient Airways. Everything seemed perfect except for one small worry. I had begun to be concerned about Warren's health. My concern was well-placed. His heart was failing. He suffered three heart attacks in the five years before he left us. He died on September 26, 1964. He was only forty-three.

Grief seemed to be overwhelming us. I was blessed with a mother-in-law whom I admired, respected, and loved. She was visiting us the night that Warren died. She had told one of her friends that she did not want to outlive her sons. The night he suffered his fatal heart attack, she collapsed at his bedside and was gone with him.

I did not have much time to mourn. Because of Warren's poor health, we had not been able to purchase much insurance. As I sat in our living room, alone and thinking, I knew that I had to find a way to support my family.

The short story market had dried up and I had only earned a total of fifty dollars during the first nine months of 1964. Still, I had a friend who was making a living as a writer, so I knew it was possible.

More important, I was determined, just as my mother had not taken her grief over my father's death out on us, not to take my grief out on my children. I would try and give them a happy home and childhood, no matter what.

Five days after Warren's funeral, I signed an agreement to write sixty-five four-minute programs to be aired on the "Portrait of a Patriot" radio series. I began my professional writing career in earnest. It was no longer a hobby.

I was making a living as a writer, working long hours writing the scripts for the radio series and then I was asked to work in the office, call on clients, and make sales calls. I was commuting into New York every day and not getting home until 6:30 at night. Still, I felt like I didn't have a choice. I was making good money and I did not want my kids to do without.

I was so lucky to have my mother. Although she had to take three busses from her cramped apartment (because she refused to get rid of her furniture) in the Bronx, she came to my home nearly every week, nearly all week, to help me care for the kids. But she refused to move in with us, because after taking care of five kids, she needed to crawl home and rest on the weekends.

But even with my mother, working and taking care of five kids was a high-wire balancing act. At that time, mothers with a career were a rarity. But you do what you have to do. The trick was to balance the time and effort between my work and theirs, which was school and basketball practice or whatever their interests were at the time. Because the truth is that one minute they're all underfoot driving you crazy, and the next minute they're grown up and gone. I didn't want to miss anything.

Immediately after Warren's death I resolved that I would not marry while my children were growing up. I loved my children above everything and I was determined to give them the best life possible.

I knew that I did not want to risk their happiness by letting another man into our family—what if he did not like one of them? What if he resented me spending time and money on them? What if he wanted me to stay home and bake cookies? That just wasn't me. Warren knew that; he understood and valued my independence. But Warren was special. I would put my personal life on the back burner for a while.

George, Martha, and Alice

I still had a burning desire to write and tell my own stories. Warren had been dead a little over a year when I started thinking about writing a novel in earnest. I had an idea to write about the love story between George and Martha Washington. So many people have the wrong ideas about them, and I was so tired of hearing about that cherry tree. But when would I have the time to do it? I would have to get up at 5:00 a.m. and write until it was time to get the kids up at a quarter to seven. It was difficult but it was something I had to do—so I just did it. I didn't want to wait for "someday." Anyone who says they can't make the time *won't* make the time. If you want it, you make it.

Three years later, in 1968, I finally finished my book. I called it *Aspire to the Heavens*. When it was published in 1969 I was thrilled to see it on the bookshelf of a local bookstore. I received a total of $1,500 less 10 percent commission for three years work, but I was officially a published novelist.

My mother, my greatest fan, died on June 3, 1969, four months after *Aspire to the Heavens* was published. Through it all, she was there for me with an undying spirit and tremendous support. She had given us all the gift of her constant devotion and unfailing love. When her body began to fail her and she could no longer take care of us, she left us. She never wanted anyone to have to take care of her. I miss her still.

Aspire to the Heavens did not sell. I was proud to be published, but I thought I'd like to write a book that somebody might buy. So I looked at my own bookshelves and saw that they were full of books by Agatha Christie, Mignon Eberhart, and other authors who wrote suspense. I realized that I had loved reading suspense since I was a child. I always wanted to be the first to know "whodunit." Who better to know first than the author? By reading those suspense books, I had taught myself to write suspense without knowing I was doing it. One of my professors had said, "Take a true situation and turn it into fiction." So that's exactly what I did in my first suspense novel, *Where Are the Children?* I took the true story from the 1960s and 70s of Alice Crimmins, who went on trial for the murder of her two children, and I used it as a springboard for a fictional story.

When I'm asked about what to write, I give the same advice I was given. Write what you know, or write what you like to read. Or take a true situation, one that intrigues you, and ask yourself "Suppose," "What if?" or "Why?" Look around you. Or just read page three of the *Post*.

Making It

As I was working on *Where Are the Children?* I was convinced I was writing a pretty good story. Finally, after many months, I was finished. I spent another year retyping and editing but when I was finally through, I knew it was good. In September of 1973 I dropped a copy of the manuscript off with my good friend and agent, Pat Myer. I was delighted when she thought it was good enough to send on to the publishers.

I waited. Finally on April 4, 1974, I received the call that Simon & Schuster wanted to buy the novel for $3,000. The kids and I called our friends and we celebrated. I knew that $3,000 was not a lot of money but my book had *sold*. Then a few short months later, on July 18, I got another call from Pat. The paperback rights to the novel had sold for $100,000. Of course I was thrilled—especially since that sale finally helped ease our money worries.

I continued to write and finally, the really big break came a year later. I had written another manuscript called *Crossroads,* which was published under the title *A Stranger is Watching.* I had been working with Pat and she had sent it on to Simon & Schuster, who had an option on it. This time I wasn't just thrilled; I was stunned. Simon &

Schuster offered $500,000 for the hardback rights and Dell offered $1 million dollars for the paperback rights.

From $3,000 to $1 million—now that was a big raise.

A Stranger is Watching is in its seventy-fifth publication now. It has never gone out of print. And my little Cinderella story, *Aspire to the Heavens,* became a best seller ten years after its first publication. It went nowhere back in 1969, but in 1979 the Mount Vernon Historical Association came after me—one of their members, a direct descendant of George Washington's brother, happened to read it. She told me it was an accurate account of George and Martha's relationship, based on the letters they had in their family. The Historical Association offered to buy it for $1,000 and reprint it. So I joked with my editor at Simon & Schuster, "Simon & Schuster may not have been interested in my first book, but I'll have you know certain people are." He said, "Mary, I never read that book."

He got a copy, read it, and the next day he called me. "This is wonderful," he said. "We can get portraits from Mount Vernon and intersperse them in the book. We'd love to publish it—will you take $1 million?"

That's how Cinderella married the prince. Even today I still sign about eight hundred bookplates a month for the Mount Vernon Historical Association, because they sell the book in their gift shop. It just sells and sells and sells. People who know me as a suspense author are often surprised when they buy this book and find it is a historical romance.

Happily Ever After

The years passed and I continued to write. I came to realize I needed more room, so I bought my home in Saddle River, New Jersey. Happily it has become a gathering place for all my children and grandchildren.

Most important, I share it with the second love of my life, my husband, John Conheeney. I had thought that I would never again enjoy the wonderful relationship that could exist between a man and woman. My daughter Patty encouraged me to invite John to a party

I was hosting in celebration of the publication of one of my novels. "Have I got a hunk for you," she told me, and I laughed. He came, and, as they say, the rest is history. We started dating on Saint Patrick's Day, and in June he asked, "Mary, would you like to get married in a couple of years?" I said, "John, how old do you think we are?" So we were married eight months later on November 30, 1996. "I had to find a gown that goes with gray roots," I said.

As I look back on my life, I feel blessed by the opportunity to tell my tales. There is a wonderful saying that I have tried to live by: "If you want to be happy for a year, win the lottery. If you want to be happy for life, love what you do." I love being a storyteller.

I know that whatever writing success I have enjoyed is intertwined with the fact that my genes, sense of self, spirit, and intellect have been formed and identified by my Irish ancestry. My Irish roots gave me my tenacity, and my desire to make the best of things came from my mother. I never heard her complain and I knew she was there for me and my children.

I would like to share some advice with parents and teachers if you have an aspiring writer. Encourage them. Don't look at the spelling or the grammar. Look at the creative thought. It's like a little candle flame—be careful not to snuff it out. Nurture it and protect it. Let it grow. You never know when you will have a writer who will be able to grow up and write what they love.

The joy of doing what you love goes on and on. I still love what I do. If I felt that I could no longer tell a good story or I was getting repetitious, then I wouldn't do it. But I still have stories I want to write. I'd like to write another historical love story. Go right outside the suspense genre, just to see if I could make it without the Mary Higgins Clark name. I'd use my grandmother's name, the one who died at sixty-two still wanting to write a book. The author will be Bridget Kennedy Durkin, my grandmother's name, and the dedication will read: *To my beloved granddaughter MHC.*

Elaine Ní Bhraonáin

Nelson Mandela famously said: "If you talk to a man in a language he understands, that goes to his head. If you talk to him in his language, that goes to his heart."

Elaine Ní Bhraonáin is an ambassador of this philosophy, making it her life's work to reconnect people of Irish ancestry to their native tongue, Irish Gaelic. Through the language classes she teaches in New York, she hopes to increase not just the fluency level of her students, but cultural pride as well.

For decades, the Gaelic language teetered on the brink of destruction as the ruling English class sought to suppress all elements of the Irish culture. Teachers punished Gaelic-speaking students by hanging sticks from students' necks and notching them every time they spoke Irish. Every notch represented a future beating.

Now, the culture and language are enjoying a revival, thanks to Elaine and others like her. The history of oppression and the fight to reclaim their culture goes hand in hand with the lessons of vowels and consonants, subjects and verbs. They are aligned.

It's a labor of love for Elaine, who understands that language is about much more than communicating. It's about knowing who you are, where you came from and who you want to be. For her, the answer is always, proudly: Irish.

Elaine's Story: The Irish Language

I grew up in Dublin, Ireland, and was raised bilingually. My Dad spoke Irish Gaelic to me while my mother spoke English. I completed all my education through the medium of the Irish language by attending all-Irish speaking primary (elementary) and secondary (high) schools.

Dad was interested in all things Irish, especially the language, and passed this down to me. Although not a linguist, he was an enthusiast; he did not get bogged down with the grammar and the baggage that comes along with it. He just enjoyed speaking Irish and used it at any opportunity. I simply accepted that Irish was my paternal language and

English my maternal, but when I was a teenager and Dad spoke Irish to me, I answered him in English just to be rebellious. At that age the last thing I wanted to be was different; I wanted to speak English to both my parents just like all the other kids in my housing estate.

When I was eighteen and it was time to make decisions about what I wanted to study, I was confused as many adolescents are. One day I wanted to be a veterinarian and the next day I wanted to be an interior designer. Dad sat me down and discussed my choices. He first asked me, "What are you good at? And then he asked, "More importantly Elaine, what do you really enjoy?"

"That would be Irish," I answered. "My teacher told me I have a flair for it."

"Go with something you enjoy," said Dad.

Dad explained that "the secret is to find a profession you enjoy and are passionate about and you'll never have to work a day in your life as it will be a pleasure to work."

That conversation changed my life. Dad's words are the ones I live by. My Irish language has opened doors for me and taken me on a journey I never would have imagined for myself.

New York

I obtained my degree and master's in the Irish language at University College Dublin. After college I moved to New York to teach Irish. Some back home in Ireland could not understand how I was going to find a job teaching Irish in New York. They said, "Are you crazy? Who in New York would want to learn Irish?" Luckily I never listen to naysayers; I choose instead to listen to those who support me, like my grandmother and my mum. My grandmother always gives me an honest opinion and my mum is a typical Irish woman, always jolly but grounded; she knows what she wants out of life and how to get it.

After many years teaching and networking in New York, one connection led to another and I now am a teacher at several different Irish-based organizations in New York; I am an Irish language newspaper columnist; and I also do some work as a correspondent based in New

York for Irish television channels such as RTÉ and TG4, and radio stations Radio Na Gaeltachta, News Talk BBC, and Radio and Life.

When I first came to New York I worked harder than ever before to make a name for myself. Any connection or opportunity that appeared in my path I grabbed. My dad always said, "The harder I work, the luckier I get," and I believe this to be so true. The more you are willing to do to achieve your dreams, the closer they come to you.

One of the hardest things about moving to New York was leaving my grandmother, whom I love and respect so much. My Nana, Rose Brennan, is 104 years old and still lives in her own home in Ballina, County Mayo. When I left for America in 2003 I went to say good-bye to her. It was the hardest thing I ever did because I thought I would never see her again as she was then almost ninety-six. Each year that she is still with us is a gift. She is the most positive and perhaps stubborn person I know. I hope I am like her.

Born in 1907 and having lived through economic revival, recession, war, the industrial revolutions, and no less than four Irish currencies, Nana has a different take on the economy and our current "recession" in Ireland. In her mind and experience this is nothing. Nana said, "I have lived through many a recession and this is far from one." Nothing stops her from thinking positive about the current economy and the future.

After being in New York for a few years, I realized that to really make a career out of my interest in Irish culture and history, I needed to obtain my PhD, so I enrolled in a PhD program at the Institute for Irish Studies at the Queens University in Belfast. My research is focused on "The Negotiation of Irish Identity in New York." I want to prove to Irish-born people that second generation or third generations, even fourth generation Irish Americans, are just as Irish as Irish-born people. When I moved to America I was a bit skeptical about how "Irish" these self-proclaimed "Irish Americans" could be. Yet as I have gotten to know so many Irish Americans I have become aware of the pride they have in their roots. They are still connected to family and land in Ireland. They are knowledgeable about Ireland and want their children to realize that Ireland is an important part of their heritage. Embracing families who left Ireland but never forgot it will create unity for both our countries.

American Connection to Ireland

Ireland has lost so many of its people to emigration and Ireland should now open its gates and welcome our Irish people back home. It is about more than filling up tour buses and kissing the Blarney Stone. It is about reconnecting families and understanding our cultural heritage. We must recognize that the Irish who left did their part in preserving Irish culture across the Atlantic. They passed it down from generation to generation. In my PhD work I will examine whether "Irishness" in America is more authentically Irish than "Irishness" back home, and I will explain how Irish Americans respect, promote and nurture "Irishness."

I am interested in exploring why some traits create a stronger Irish identity than others. I have friends who are half American and half Irish and travel on their Irish passport. They tell me it is because the Irish pose no threat; Ireland is seen as a neutral country. "The Irish are trusted all over the world," they say. Compared to other ethnicities, the Irish also excel at socialization. We are friendly and fun-loving and these traits help promote our culture and gain trust all around the world.

When my PhD is completed, one of my dreams is to establish an Irish elementary (primary) school in Manhattan where students can study, learn, and experience everything Irish; from Irish history, music, and sports (such as Hurling), to Irish language, Irish literature, folklore, and culture. Many people consider the Catholic schools in America to be as close to Irish as you can get but I want to take it one step further. If someone immigrates to America from Spain, France, Japan, or Germany, they can find schools for their children to attend that promote their native language and culture. That is not the case for Irish children and it is my intention to change that.

By carving out a niche for myself, I have designed my own career on my own terms. I am able to promote the Irish language in New York while writing my doctorate at the same time. My definition of success is the feeling I get when I hear my adult students converse in the Irish language in Manhattan or when a young child in my Irish kindergarten class recites a poem in Irish for the first time. I know that I had something to do with that. Money is important but it is never worth sacrificing my passion for.

I have to be creative in combining opportunities into a career. I have been able to find a balance between spending a lot of time in Manhattan while still getting back to Ireland regularly. I would rather have the freedom to live in both worlds than to give my life to a corporation and only get two weeks off. Once I finish my PhD I will hopefully find a full-time job teaching Irish history and Irish language in the US, as I love being part of the Irish diaspora and the Irish community outside of Ireland. My unconventional career created around the Irish language is perfect for me. It is a balancing act but it keeps me grounded and it brings me joy. That is what success and happiness are all about.

Corinne Dillon

Corinne Dillon is on a journey to embrace, promote, and preserve the unique characteristics of cultures around the world. Corinne's life journey has exposed her to a melting pot of cultures, including Irish, American, and Chinese, and she has found a way to embrace all three. She turned her passion for sharing her knowledge of language and culture into her profession. She hopes to expose others to the excitement of embracing something new and different from the familiar. In 2009 she founded her own business, Discover Mandarin, providing Chinese language learners with a fun and efficient way to learn Mandarin through personalized, one-on-one classes online.

Corinne's Story: Irish Connection

My parents, Kerry Dillon (nee O'Hare) and John Dillon, come from a long line of Irish immigrants—as far back as my great-great-grandparents. My great-grandfather Michael Cotter came from Inchigeelagh, County Cork, and immigrated to the United States in 1902. His wife, Nora Sullivan, was also from Inchigeelagh, but she didn't come until 1909. They met in the US and married in New York in 1912. Their son, my great-uncle, William (Bill) Cotter was the assistant postmaster general of the United States and worked for the CIA during and after World War II. My great-great grandparents Michael and Sarah Dillon came to the US separately, arriving in 1870 and 1873, respectively. According to Dillon lore, they hailed from County Roscommon. My great-great grandfather on my mother's side, James Thorpe, was a County Kildare native who immigrated in the late nineteenth century and set up a butcher shop with three of his brothers in Brooklyn.

Knowing the kind of struggles and discrimination my ancestors faced in both Ireland and America always inspired me, even at a young age, to work hard and do my best as a tribute to their sacrifice.

I have always been fascinated with literature and cultures, especially Irish. While at Harvard, I majored in English literature, with a focus on Irish theater and literature, and minored in Mandarin. The combination definitely isn't orthodox, but it reflected my lifelong dual interests.

Chinese Connection

My connection to Ireland comes from my parents and my upbringing. My connection to China comes from my childhood experiences when my father was transferred to Hong Kong and we lived there for three years. I always knew that one day I wanted to go back to China and learn Mandarin.

My father raised me with the Irish philosophy of "You are not better than anyone else, but no one is better than you," meaning that you should treat others with respect, but have enough confidence in yourself to approach any challenge life might throw your way. His Irish heritage is a great source of pride for him, and he had the utmost respect for immigrants coming to America, saying that immigrants were the bravest people of all because they give up everything familiar to start a new life and create new opportunities for their children.

It may seem ironic then that I myself would become an immigrant of sorts—to China. Considering that I spent three years of my childhood in China and another two summers during college, it kind of makes sense. When I moved to Beijing in 2007, I could speak some Mandarin, but not very well. Even though I did not know it at the time, my Harvard Mandarin professor had strong confidence that I would move to China and succeed. Most people's Chinese names are transliterations of their native names. But my professor at Harvard gave me a different name. He called me Di Qing. It was the name of a real Song Dynasty general. My teacher said, "I think you are very *lihai*, which means 'great,' and you have potential to go to China and do great things." There is a saying that if Di Qing is in the vanguard, you'll win. I certainly don't feel deserving, but I am very proud of this name and his confidence in me.

So with my professor and parents' encouragement, I set out to find my calling in Beijing. When I arrived in Beijing, I was so self-conscious about my ability to communicate in Chinese that I would not even let my husband, Alex, also a nonnative speaker, listen to me speak Mandarin. I had him cover his ears when I spoke.

Speaking a foreign language is about confidence, and confidence comes from opportunities to practice in a one-on-one environment with qualified native speakers who correct your mistakes. I realized that my insecurity was getting me nowhere, so I decided to find a teacher to help me. During my quest I not only found one teacher but an amazing group of teachers. We had an immediate rapport and developed a fun, real-world curriculum using materials like movies and blogs. Before long, both my speaking ability and my confidence took off. I decided that if it could work for me, it could work for others. So I formed a business called "Discover Mandarin." These same fantastic teachers from whom I learned fluent Chinese are now my core Discover Mandarin teaching team.

My company is based in Beijing and has five full-time teachers who give live, one-on-one lessons over the Internet to predominantly English-speaking students located around the world. The Chinese economy just opened up in 1978, so it's newer, it's fresher, and people have drive and entrepreneurial ideas. Because of the global economy, more and more people have a desire and need to learn Mandarin. My company fills that need. I was very proud to have been profiled in *Businessweek* magazine last year and to have been featured on *The New Yorker* magazine's China blog.

Know How to Laugh at Yourself

My favorite quote about the Irish is by the playwright Sean O'Casey: "[The Irish] take a joke as a serious thing and a serious thing as a joke." When I was at Harvard, there were a lot of serious people around me all the time. Wonderful serious people. They were serious about who they were and what they were setting out to do to achieve their goals. Too many of the students couldn't laugh at themselves, though.

If you can't take a joke or laugh at yourself, you can never make a mistake. The problem with perfection is that it is failure that gets us to where we want to be; failure is part of the process. Whether it is living abroad, learning a language, or starting a business, when we become too serious to laugh at our own mistakes we get stuck.

Living a life by my own definition of success leaves room for error and laughter. I define success as having self-confidence and a feeling of contentment with what I am doing, on the path I have created. I recognize that where I end up may vary from my original dream, but as long as I'm living life the way I want to and am proud of what I am doing, I am content and fulfilled. That has a different meaning for every woman. For some it is raising a family, for others it is running a business or even moving to China to teach Mandarin.

What is important is pride in what you are doing and what you have accomplished.

My favorite Chinese idiom is: "Be prepared; have no worries." It's a good motto for business. If you prepare in advance, all will be well. Preparation takes the worry out of life. A similar Irish saying is: "Plan your work and work your plan." Both cultures recognize and live by how important it is to take the time to prepare for what you want to accomplish. When you prepare for life and set goals, you will thrive.

Chapter Four

Irish Gumption

*T*he Irish are known for their ability to work hard. No job is too menial or too difficult if it means taking care of family or working toward a desired goal. Along with that willingness to do whatever it takes to survive, the Irish apply imagination, sweat, and guts to turn a trouble into an opportunity.

As a people, the Irish have had much to grapple with: famine, invasion, the fight to preserve culture and heritage, waves of emigration, economic woes, and a rocky road to independence. Throughout it all, they held their heads—and their beer glasses—high and kept their hearts filled with poetry and song. They have emerged with an adventurous, courageous spirit that has become as synonymous with what it means to be Irish as red hair and freckles.

Upon being presented with a challenge, many Irish embrace it as an opportunity to begin a new or more successful life. This courageous spirit can be seen today in the stories of the four wise Irish women in this chapter, who became independent entrepreneurs and took control of their destinies.

In this chapter you will meet Lulu O'Sullivan, who took out a small business loan and used it to create the first and largest Internet sales website in Ireland. You'll meet Rachel Gaffney, who learned excellent customer service from her newsagent father, which helped her change the world's *perception of Ireland through her company Rachel Gaffney's Real Ireland. And Mary Gosling, who at nineteen took a small cabin on her family's farm and turned it into a favorite tourist destination. Finally, you'll meet Sally Miller, who was forced out of one career by a terrible accident yet was able to use what she learned from tragedy and turn it into a triumphant new career. These women created their own destinies by living by the words of Eleanor Roosevelt: "The future belongs to those who believe in the beauty of their dreams."*

Lulu O'Sullivan

Lulu O'Sullivan was twenty-one years old when she returned to Ireland after living abroad. Realizing that she needed a job, she applied her imagination and grasped a new idea. She created the business known as InterTeddy—an Internet-based mail order company selling novelty teddy bears. She was one of the first Irish businesses to grasp the significance of the Internet for online sales. Lulu's teddy bear business grew to become the biggest online shopping company in Ireland.

Lulu's Story: Kitty O'Shea O'Leary

My grandmother Kitty O'Shea (O'Leary) was one tough cookie. She wasn't a soft little granny at all. She loved to play the piano. She smoked cigars. She sang brilliantly. She was the last to go to bed if there was a party. She also had this fantastic business head on her shoulders.

I was lucky to have her living right next door to me in Dublin so I spent a lot of time with her. My grandfather was a successful veterinarian, but although he was considered wealthy in those days and women did not usually work outside the home, my grandmother Kitty started her own business. This was unheard of.

With seven children to care for, my grandmother opened a chain of Newsagents (convenience/gift shops) all over Dublin. At one point she ran four shops on her own. She was one of the first women in all

Ireland to drive a car. It was not because she wanted to have a car; she just needed it for her work.

Then suddenly my grandfather dropped dead of a heart attack at the age of forty-five, leaving Kitty alone to raise seven children. Out of necessity, her "hobby" became a way to continue supporting herself and her family. By the time I was ten my grandmother had a sweet shop called Notions on Marian Road in Dublin.

Every Saturday morning I went with my mum and granny to the shop. It was a thrill to stand behind the counter. I watched, mesmerized, as Granny treated the customers like gold. They would walk past three shops just to buy their newspapers from Granny. She had a little word for each one of them as she brought them down to the end of the counter to pay for their paper. She made them feel important.

Granny watched her pennies on the business side. At break time I was only allowed to eat a chocolate that was broken or damaged. The other piece could turn a profit. I got most of my customer service and business sense from watching my granny run her candy shop every Saturday morning. I never forgot her lessons. They helped me become the business woman I am today.

In the Dublin of the 1980s, the prospects for me were nonexistent. My friends were off in college and each summer they traveled to America or Australia and experienced life. I was working full-time and attending college classes at night. I felt that I could not let everyone enjoy all the fun without me, so I decided to take a year off and spend six months in New York and six months in Australia. I arrived in New York and stayed with friends. I worked as a waitress and did odd jobs and had the time of my life.

In Australia I was offered a job in a dress shop. I always loved fashion and this was a great fit for me. Within a few months I was promoted and at the age of twenty-one, I was offered the opportunity to run my own shop.

I knew I was at a crossroads. If I took this offer it meant staying in Australia for the rest of my life. I was not ready to give up my connection to Dublin and my family so I turned down the offer and headed back to Ireland.

It was 1986 and Ireland was going through yet another horrible recession. Job prospects, especially for fashion and dress shops, were nonexistent. I went on a few interviews and nothing came up. I felt like I had made a mistake by leaving Australia and opportunity behind, but I was not going to sit around licking my wounds so I got to work on how to start my own business. I signed up for a course with FAS, an organization in Ireland that provides entrepreneurship training, and I worked on my business ideas.

InterTeddy

My first choice would have been a fashion store, but I didn't have the money for that and no way of getting it. While in New York I'd seen the idea of delivering teddy bears which, doesn't require a store or much money. The FAS course provided guidance on writing a business plan, cash flow, funding, and marketing plans. I named my company "InterTeddy" and I borrowed IR£2,000, spending IR£1,000 on marketing and the rest on stock. I rented a tiny office for IR£16 a week and set up one phone line.

I gave a public relations agency IR£1,000 and asked them to get me whatever they could for that money. My idea was novel and as a twenty-one-year-old female entrepreneur I was a bit unique. In 1986 there still were not a lot of women-owned businesses in Ireland. I managed to get written up in several newspapers and I was lucky because I could not have bought the advertising space that the free PR campaign gave me. The InterTeddy name took off.

Over the years we expanded to selling hampers (food baskets) and we grew the business over 1,000 percent. My company was one of the first companies to go online in Ireland. Not only was I the only person in Ireland sending teddy bears, I was also introducing the public to a new way of buying. I had to build customer trust in the Internet buying cycle. They wanted to know that their product would arrive. I committed to each customer that I would deliver it personally if I had to. It was all about building trust and setting up a company based on integrity.

Even though many naysayers told me I was bonkers to sell online, I knew it was the wave of the future and was not going away. I expanded the business to do worldwide online sales and we were the first in Ireland to do that as well.

The company expanded from baskets, teddy bears, and champagne to selling all kinds of gifts worldwide. The company is now known as Gifts Direct. We are the largest online seller of gifts in Ireland. In 2010 we set up a second website called Siopa.com. *Siopa* is Irish for shop. It was born out of my passion for beautiful Irish products. I handpick the best Irish gifts from known established brands. I also search Ireland for new local artisans and showcase their work as well. Customers can read about the artists and their profile while shopping online. This website caters to people all over the world who want to shop in Ireland as if they were there.

Had I thought about all the reasons not to set up my business I never would have done it. Thinking about all the ups and downs is a way to never do anything. If it doesn't work out it doesn't really matter. I never think about whether it is going to work or not. It is really more about the end goal. The end goal is that you're doing something you're passionate about. Even if it fails at least you can say, "You know what? I gave it a really good try." And it might hurt for a little while afterwards if it doesn't work out, but you won't ever be sorry that you gave it a go. Chances are you'll get back up and do something else. Often the strongest people in business are people who have had the failures.

Fighting Spirit

I've lived in four different countries and I believe that the Irish are unique in our fighting spirit. We take our fair share of bashing and we get up and fight again and again. We look on the bright side and we get through it. Over the years my company has been on a roller coaster ride. Sometimes I am up and things are fantastic. Then something goes wrong and down we go again. It is a cycle. I look at the setbacks as a lesson I must learn. I can't blame someone else. I have to learn the lesson for myself. The trick is to learn the lesson as fast as I can and move on so it does not have to be a big lesson. Learning lessons quickly is better for business and better for life.

Even though we are the largest business of our kind in Ireland, we always want to be number one. We have been able to sustain that by working hard and constant improvement. We cannot be stagnant. Now with our new website, Siopa.com, we want to be the number one Irish website worldwide, selling the best of Irish goods to a global market.

Managing Priorities

I have four children and a husband who is also an entrepreneur. I recognized early on that there was no such thing as having it all. I had to make adjustments and find what worked for me.

Sacrificing my relationship with my family was never an option. For me it was about setting priorities. For example, it was not a priority for me to pick up the kids from school. Yet it is a priority to be home at 6:30 p.m. and have dinner and spend time with the kids. When work is not complete I do it after the kids are in bed. If someone got sick, I knew I would be there no matter what. There was no point going to the office and spending the day worrying. We have a house in the west of Ireland that we go to every other weekend and there is no TV. It is family time.

I also realized not only does my business need an excellent CFO; my home life requires excellent child care. I used the same process to hire a CFO as I did to hire a child minder. I interviewed many people for the job to make sure it was a good fit. I also think my kids benefited from having another positive, kind person in their lives who they could depend on and learn from. Overall my kids are fantastic and I am very proud of them. Raising kids and building a business at the same time is not easy but it is definitely manageable. It requires planning and passion just like anything else worthwhile in life. I also recognize that even if I had stayed home I would have had issues too. There are always issues. Nothing is perfect.

Ireland has not done much to accommodate working mothers over the years and there certainly is a need to improve childcare options. It is clear that working mothers are a fact of life. If women want to set up their own companies to prove that it can be done then I applaud them and am happy to stand out as an example that it can be done and it can be done well.

My goal is to continue growing my business. I hope to continue learning from my mistakes and coming through each with a stronger, better business. My idea grew from necessity but now it is a passion. I like to believe that my fighting spirit will carry me through any hard times ahead.

Rachel Gaffney

Each year on March 17, everyone in the world becomes just a wee bit Irish. Green beads, green beer, green rivers, corned beef and cabbage, and "Kiss me, I'm Irish" come out of the woodwork for Saint Patrick's Day.

For many people a Saint Patrick's Day "drink fest" is what it means to be Irish, but not for Rachel Gaffney. Born and raised in Cork, Rachel left Ireland after college, headed for London, and eventually settled down in Dallas, Texas. It was not until she left Ireland that she realized the Ireland she knew is completely misunderstood by much of the world. Rachel is proud of the real Ireland and has devoted her life to giving people a better understanding of her home country, far beyond the trappings of Saint Patrick's Day.

Rachel brings the "Real Ireland" to life through her consumer goods, cooking classes, travel, writing, sharing, and study of its history and entertainment. A true "connector," Rachel is constantly out meeting people and bringing them together. "I absolutely love connecting with people, whether it's through my *Rachel Gaffney's Real Ireland* cooking classes and TV segments, or through the products I sell. I am learning so much about my own homeland through other people."

Rachel promotes the best of what Ireland has to offer and is a shining example of the everyday experience of the true Irish culture. Rachel's story exemplifies Irish pride—in herself, her family, and her country. Rachel's mission is to have Irish products in every major department store throughout the world. It may take a little time, but watch out because Rachel is on a mission.

Rachel's Story: The Real Ireland

For the record, in my entire life I never heard anyone in Ireland utter the words *begosh and begorrah*. I never had a green beer until I moved to America in 1996. Not once did I wear green Mardi Gras beads or "Kiss me, I'm Irish" buttons. I never met a leprechaun. After leaving Ireland I recognized that the world's perception of Ireland through the bottom of a green-colored beer glass on Saint Patrick's Day was not and never would be the real Ireland. My mission in life is to educate the world on my Ireland, the real Ireland, so in 2003 *Rachel Gaffney's Real Ireland* was born.

The Irish recognize that there will be good times and there will be bad times and that is the cycle of life. Sometimes we learn from our past, sometimes we don't. Somehow, being Irish we seem to innately understand this.

The Irish are a passionate people. We love, fight, argue, write, and feel passionately. We give it our all. To some, this is difficult to understand. Perhaps it has something to do with our history of national struggle. We also have this abiding sense of humor that lives within us even through the darkest times. We only have our past to help us to understand this. We have long been a persecuted country. Yet our heroes are resilient and rise again.

Ireland has historically endured much as a nation yet every time we bounce back. Not only do we survive but we thrive. In the words of William Butler Yeats, "Being Irish, he had an abiding sense of tragedy which sustained him through temporary periods of joy."

On March 17, 2007, I was asked to be on the *Martha Stewart Living Show*, to make traditional Irish butter shortbread on national television. Meeting Martha Stewart in person was a wonderful experience. After the segment I went back to the hotel to get ready for an afternoon of Irish festivities and celebrations. I walked into the hotel room and the phone rang. My son had fallen on the ski slopes in Colorado and was in the hospital. I immediately packed my bags, rebooked a flight, and spent the next eight hours trying to make my way to him. All worked out well and he recovered from a broken wrist. As my head hit the pillow that night, it suddenly dawned on me that I had actually taught Martha Stewart how to make Irish shortbread.

I laughed to myself, "OK, woman! You had your moment of joy—now it is time to get back to reality." My abiding sense of tragedy sustained by my own personal temporary period of joy.

Whatever You Do, Do It Your Best

Instant gratification is not something that I learned as a child. I worked for what I had. I was by no means poor but that was not the point. My father, Anthony Gaffney, owned a chain of convenience shops—Newsagents as they were called then. I stocked shelves, cleaned floors, wiped down counters, and put out the newspapers. It was not glamorous work but I learned the most important ingredient to a successful business—customer service. My father lived and breathed good customer service.

One of my father's most lucrative shops in the 1980s was located between a hospital and the University College Cork campus in Mardyke Parade, Cork City. This was long before gift shops in hospitals and vending machines on college campuses. Also nearby was a shelter for battered women. One particularly busy day a woman from the Battered Women's Shelter stopped to buy her young son a 5p lollipop. She looked forlorn and tired. My father went out of his way to treat this young woman with the same level of respect as the businessman purchasing flowers and chocolates for his wife. I was acutely aware that my father treated every single person with respect. I was lucky enough to live it firsthand and adopt it as a rule to live by.

At sixteen I landed a job over Christmas slicing and wrapping meat in a butcher shop. O'Donovan's Butcher shop was an institution in Cork. It was famous for its spiced beef. I wore a white coat with a red and white striped hat with my hair pulled back. My friends came by and teased me relentlessly. After all, most teenage girls wanted to work behind a cosmetics counter. I remember my Dad saying, "If you are going to slice meat for a living, be the best meat slicer there is!" I have learned that when I take pride in my work my customers share in that pride and become customers for life.

In 1990, I moved to London and worked for the London Tara Hotel. One late night when my shift had just ended, an American businessman, Peter Leahy, walked into the hotel. He was tired having just flown in from Paris. He explained that his family was stranded due to some visa complications. In spite of the stressful circumstances he noticed that my name tag read "Rachel Gaffney, Cork, Ireland." In a strong American accent he said, "I'm Irish too! From Cork also!" I replied, "I don't know too many people in Cork with an accent like yours." He laughed at my obvious sarcasm.

My shift was over, and I did not know the predicament he was in. He had no cash, no access to a bank, and no credit card. I could not locate the duty manager that night. I did not hesitate. I knew that at best everything would work out and at worst I would be down money in my till. I forwarded him a little cash and added it to his bill. I simply decided to do what my father would have done and help the customer out. I believe in trusting my intuition. It's just another brain given us by God.

Sure enough, as my father would have expected, everything turned out for the best. This customer, the director for marketing services for Coca-Cola Great Britain, later moved back to the United States to become national vice president of sales for Hills Pet Nutrition, then vice president of national accounts for Coors Brewing Company.

How do I know what happened to the customer? Because Mr. Peter Leahy and I continued to stay in touch. Not only did he go on to have an amazing career, he helped me launch my company. He is acting partner and COO for Rachel Gaffney's Real Ireland. Imagine how different my life would be had I not stayed late and given a customer the benefit of the doubt.

Tough Times

Today's quest for instant gratification saddens me. What happened to having a strong work ethic and being satisfied by a job well done? Many people seem to have lost their heart and drive, but what I notice more and more is that people give up all too easily. It took five years to develop my shortbread recipe for commercial production. I knew how to make it on a small scale but wanted to take the same recipe without changing the quality or integrity of the product. I was told it could not be done, that I would have to change my ingredients, using inferior butters and lards. This was not an option for me. Those five years were not a waste. I was simply eliminating all the obstacles until I found the way to make it commercially. I still remember the day the shortbreads came off the line, their golden color winking at me as they meandered by. I had tears in my eyes. It's not a feeling that can be attained by any money but by the satisfaction of simply accomplishing a task.

One of my most memorable business deals occurred when my shortbreads were accepted by Central Market, a high-end grocery chain throughout the state of Texas. They placed an order for five hundred cases. At the time I was subleasing a bakery, so I was baking during the early hours. I baked all night several nights running. I met my deadline and was ready to load the truck when we discovered that some of our inventory had been stolen the previous night.

It was 5:00 a.m. and the truck had to be on the road at 10:00 a.m. to meet our deadline. These orders needed to be delivered across the state to Houston, Austin, San Antonio and many more towns. Peter Leahy and I quickly decided that the stores farthest away needed to receive their delivery first and that there was no other option but for me to get back in the bakery after twelve hours of baking and start again. You only get one chance to make a first impression, and calling my client to tell them they would not be receiving their order was not an option for me. That is what is required to be successful. You do what it takes. There will always be challenges and road blocks. It takes heart and drive to survive.

Choose Laughter

Sometimes things happen in life that you can choose to cry about or laugh about. For the most part, I choose to laugh. I was scheduled to do a demonstration in the Dallas Central Market store. It was a beautiful spring morning and I was excited about the new adventures to come for *Rachel Gaffney's Real Ireland*. I entered the store through the receiving doors in the back and the loading dock was a hive of activity with trucks delivering beers, dried goods, and meats. I greeted the girl in receiving and signed in as required. I picked up the box of materials I needed and began to work through to the store. Unbeknown to me, the cord to my linen pants had looped itself around one of the carts. I took a step and the cord pulled itself undone. There I was standing with my linen trousers around my ankles and me holding a box of shortbreads. I placed the box down, redressed, picked the box back up and walked through the sea of delivery men. I'm pretty sure my scarlet face was a fair indicator as to how I felt.

Two weeks later I returned to the store, but this time I was with Peter Leahy. I had checked in as he parked the car so I told the girl to play a joke on him. You see, he did not have identification on him so I asked her to play along and say he could not come in without it. When he arrived, she asked his name, then asked for his identification. "I'm with the lady who likes to drop her trousers in the receiving area," came his reply. By then the joke was on me. I laughed and I still laugh about it to this day.

Today, my company has evolved, as it should. The core values and mission remain the same—to bring the real Ireland to life. Recently I was doing some research with my sons and discovered that the Gaffneys are descendants of "Niall of the Nine Hostages." Niall was King of Ireland from 379 to 406. He traveled to England and Wales and captured nine people. Among them was a boy named Patricus and his sister. Today, we know Patricus as Saint Patrick.

So my family's claim to fame is that we kidnapped Saint Patrick. I'm not sure whether to be embarrassed or proud.

Even Saint Patrick hit some rough spots. He stayed alone, naked, freezing, and hungry in fields minding sheep for seven years. As every good Irish man, woman, boy or girl knows, Saint Patrick overcame his lot in life and changed the course of Irish history forever. He turned adversity into triumph and peace. He taught the people of Ireland faithfulness and created undying loyalty to Ireland for the entire culture. He most definitely made the best of the hand he was dealt and changed the world for the better in the process. Legend says that as a child Saint Brigid got to see Saint Patrick speak and was overcome with ecstasy. This started her life of devotion to spreading Christianity through Ireland. Not an easy feat for a young woman to start a monastery and spread the foundation of Christianity throughout Ireland, but that is what she did.

Overcoming adversity, pursuing passion with heart and drive, making a difference in the world—that is what dreams are made of. That is what the Real Ireland is all about.

Mary Gosling

Mary Gosling was raised on a farm in a rural area of southern Ireland near the coast. It was a popular summer tourist destination. At the young age of nineteen, Mary realized that there were no facilities in the area to serve these tourists. So she repurposed a small cottage on the farm into a tearoom and refreshment center. It was a hit, and soon her tea shop became a regular stopping point for visitors to the south.

After marrying, she expanded her tearoom to include some bedrooms and created a bed-and-breakfast. Then she realized that her visitors needed suggestions on where to go and what to see, so she and her husband created a board game that helped the customers explore the area. The board game, "Discovering Ireland," was another hit and became popular throughout Ireland.

Mary's Story: A Tea Shop

I grew up on a farm in Long Strand Castlefreke, a tiny town in West Cork, where there was never much going on, although the coastal scenery attracted tourists each summer. Our farm overlooked the coastline, and it was beautiful but very remote and quiet. It left a lot of time for thinking. My mother had five children to raise—our father died when we were very young. My mother had her hands full so she raised us by the philosophy that as long as we were out of harm's way, we were out of harm.

Our farm had a tiny cottage on the land, with little value. When I was nineteen I started thinking—the tourists came every summer and there were more and more every year. But there were no facilities catering to tourists; nowhere for anyone to get refreshments or have a cup a tea. I said to my mom, "What if I did some nice refreshments for the tourists and see if I can make a go of a tea shop?"

I always loved to cook and bake. I started off making tea and coffee and ice cream. Things started to go well. People told others about my little shop. I started offering cakes and pastries that I baked myself. The next thing I knew my little tearoom became very busy. I had a following. Customers would come back each year. I expanded my menu each year, just a little bit. I made homemade scones early in the morning and apple pies. I added homemade soups. My little tearoom, called the Tea Shop, was the first one in the whole area.

Winters were too cold and dreary for tourists so I spent winters in London and worked my little shop from Easter to September. I loved to travel and I thought this was the best of both worlds. I expected I would do that the rest of my life.

While working as a waitress in London I met my husband, Graham. He was one of my customers and we started dating. We got married the following year and spent the first two years going back and forth to London.

When I had my daughter Nicola, all of that changed. I needed to be anchored. So we stayed in Ireland. I had no intention of living permanently in London. The Irish coastline is just too beautiful. The lifestyle is peaceful. So Graham decided to come with me and make Ireland his home. We expanded the tearoom a little and we built some bedrooms upstairs. We opened a bed-and-breakfast with two spare rooms. We had no problem filling the rooms. Longtime customers were happy to stay at our place.

Our location was amazing and there were so many places to see and things to do. It was great for a day of exploration. Our customers often came to us each morning with their maps in hand and asked us where they should go. Graham and I made suggestions while they took notes. Back then the sign posts were nonexistent. They would come back every evening with a story of how they took the road to Bantry and ended up in Bandon or how sheep in the road created an unexpected detour. They thought it was a great adventure.

Discovering Ireland

One night Graham came up with the idea of making a board game out of the map of Ireland to give to customers on their explorations. He colored little boxes on a map of Ireland and got little buttons to put in the boxes. Depending on how long the customers wanted to explore we altered the destinations and the places they could go. The guests loved it. The kids loved it. They played it with their children. We played it with our children.

One day a guest told me about a course he was running teaching people how to start their own business. I showed him the prototype for our game. He said it was a brilliant idea and told me to visit Enterprise Ireland, a government agency that helps small businesses get started. I went and they agreed it was brilliant. It took about three years for the game to launch but once it did it became a best seller. That was twenty-five years ago. It is still one of the most popular board games in Ireland today. We have followed up with Discovering London and Discovering Europe and we have expanded into other games as well.

Running the board game business became a full-time job and I had to close down the tearoom. About five years ago I noticed some signs that the so-called "Celtic Tiger" was sputtering out and that

Ireland's economic resurgence might be coming to an end. I knew that it was time to find a new item for the gift market. The economy was tough and people encouraged me to go back to the tearoom; reopen it and start over. The problem is that I never want to go backward. I believe we should always be moving forward. I wanted a new game, something that had never been done before. I came up with the Make It Bake It Cupcake Tin, featuring the artwork of Courtney Davis.

The tins come with cupcake ingredients. Kids must first complete the puzzle to have the baking directions. It is the first of its kind and we will have new ones every year at Christmas. Today our business sells games all over the world from our home in Clonakilty, Cork, Ireland.

Small business is what leads the economy. It is unfortunate what the bankers and their greed did to our country—the people are the ones paying the price. But I believe that a recession brings out the best in people. The best ideas for business come out of it. People start their own businesses out of need and create the vision for the future. Families start spending time together and stay home. They play board games and start talking again. We remember what is most important. We slow down enough to find empty space to think of ideas and improve the future. We remember the basics. Coming up with creative ideas for expanding our business has always been a joy. I am happy to be in a business that brings families together. I know that we are ready to pull together and ride out this recession.

I do not believe in blame and negative thinking. Negativity paralyzes people. Watching the news and the doom and gloom is just a waste of time. I surround myself with positive people and I believe that I can always move forward. As long as I am moving forward I am going in the right direction.

Sally Miller

Sally Miller is an Irish transplant who was happily engaged in a career she loved as a trauma nurse when a terrible automobile accident required that she change direction. Drawing on her skills and her love of helping people, she embarked on a new career focusing on relaxation and skin therapy. Now she is the successful creator of the Sally Miller Collection, a line of skin care products sold all around Ireland and the world.

Sally's Story: Trauma Nurse

Growing up in England I had a simple and for the most part ordinary life. From the time I was three years old I knew I wanted to be a nurse, so that is exactly what I set out to accomplish. By my early twenties, I was working as a nurse in the casualty (trauma) center and I loved it. Every day meant a steady stream of activity and flurry—a challenge both physically and mentally. I thrived on the adrenaline rush. My whole world was tied up in the long hours I devoted to my work.

One day everything changed. I was involved in a car accident that left me seriously injured. I suffered trauma to my neck and back, which left me with severe neck pain and damage. I had to undergo surgery to have three discs in my neck taken out and a bone graft from my hip put in their place.

The accident left me in a predicament. I had to rethink my whole career—in fact, my whole direction in life. I was faced with the reality that, although I was only in my early twenties, I was forced to retire from the career I had planned and worked toward all my life. I was devastated. I had loved my work and the excitement. Suddenly I was faced with a new set of rules and limitations. I was no longer able to be a trauma nurse. I had to choose a new way to move forward. So that is what I did.

Move to Ireland

When I moved from England to West Cork, Ireland, eleven years ago, I took stock of my skills and talents so I could repurpose my life's work. My nurse's training gave me medical knowledge and I started to train in massage, aromatherapy, and reflexology, so I set up treatment rooms in the Celtic Ross Hotel. I was able to offer a service to the customers of the hotel using my skills.

I enjoyed my new work helping people relax on their vacations. I got satisfaction from my ability to make their stay at the hotel more memorable and enjoyable. My days were filled with a busy schedule of massages.

As my reputation grew and I became more settled in the community, I was contacted to assist with cancer patients in need of massage therapy. Suddenly I found myself with a very busy schedule indeed, working in two different places with clients with very different needs. Whilst working with different clients they asked me to make products to help them relax or creams for their skin using my aromatherapy knowledge. Little by little I started concocting different creams and soaps at home and giving them to my clients and patients to try.

The Sally Miller Collection

One of the best products on the planet for skin care therapy is Shea butter. I found that it was great for relieving some of the side effects my patients experienced. It is expensive, however, and must be imported to Ireland. I began exploring how I could import it responsibly from Ghana, Africa, one of its main sources. During my research, I found out about an international program under the auspices of the United States Aid for International Development (USAID) that helps businesses around the globe pay fair wages in Africa so that Ghanaian women can set up their own businesses and improve their quality of life. I launched my own line of handmade, all-natural cosmetic products under my name, The Sally Miller Collection. By growing my business in Ireland I am able to help women in Ghana sustain themselves and improve their lives. It is a win-win for everyone.

Our products are popular in Ireland, and since that is where we are located it is our biggest market. More important, I feel that my products are making a difference in the lives of my patients and clients. I have grown my business to include a whole line of all-natural cosmetic products. Most of my cosmetics and bath products are hand produced in my workshop. My dream is to grow and expand so that I can market all over the world, particularly in America. I love my products and I love my business.

Being an entrepreneur and setting up my own business was the best decision I ever made. For a long time I was a bit lost, searching for the buzz and the adrenaline rush of the trauma room. It was difficult for me to realize that I could be successful without having to constantly experience the excitement and stress of my previous career. My business is successful, yet it runs at a very different pace. In some respects, I have repurposed my life from one extreme to the other: from the ultimate adrenaline rush to the seeking of peace and tranquility.

I take my time searching for the right ingredients and items to bring into my business. The pace is different and the satisfaction of doing it on my own is amazing. I feel as if I create a work of art every time I introduce a new product to my collection. Every day is a challenge and makes me feel good about what I am doing.

My home in Ireland overlooks the Galley Head Lighthouse in West Cork. It is beautiful and tranquil. Although I am English, Ireland is now my home. The Irish people are cosmopolitan and kind. Ireland is one of those places where everyone is welcome and new people are embraced. I believe that I have found my life's work and am able to combine the best of my skills. I hope that my collection of products share a little of the peacefulness of the Irish country life with all my clients.

Chapter Five

Irish Luck

O *ne of the most common Irish expressions acknowledges the Irish ability* *to overcome catastrophe or calamity. Nearly everyone has heard of the* *"luck of the Irish," and perhaps has envied the person who seems to have* *the lucky shamrock shadowing his or her life. Of course, most people realize* *that luck is often made. The Irish are particularly good at making luck and* *embracing opportunities. Many Irish American fortunes were made when* *a clever and determined Irish man or woman seized an opportunity and* *turned it to gold at the end of the rainbow.*

Embracing an opportunity and having the courage to act and the *confidence to embrace risk are traits that have led thousands of Irish men* *and women toward the attainment of their dreams. Sometimes the Irish* *make luck out of necessity, sometimes it is the result of a desire, but always* *the Irish are strong enough to take a chance and open a door.*

They are people like Naomi McMahon, who thought "Why not?" when *she sent a long-shot e-mail to Harley Davidson—and found herself working* *for the motorcycle giant in America. Or Patricia DeNucci, who feels herself* *lucky because she had ancestors who took the time and trouble to write* *down their stories of turning hardship into triumph, thereby inspiring their* *descendants. Or Audrey O'Gorman, who saw bad luck firsthand in the lives* *of her mother and grandmother, who had little choice in how they lived but changed her own luck by learning from them—and winning a Visa Lottery. Or Renee Gatz, whose good luck failed along with others on 9/11 in New York City, ultimately resulting in the loss of her marketing career— but who regained the luck of the Irish when she was wrote a book about the Irish sayings she grew up with. Or Joanna Wilson Vargas, whose career skyrocketed when she was featured in a popular local magazine and then in* Vogue *magazine itself—right after she decided that family came first.*

Learn how these lucky women took their luck—good or bad—and made it work for them.

Naomi McMahon

Naomi McMahon exemplifies the modern day Irish woman. Educated, hard-working, intelligent, stylish, confident, and kind, Naomi personifies the best of what Ireland has to offer. Combining her love of Ireland and her love of New York, Naomi is creating a platform for the world to see and hear about the "New" Ireland.

Naomi is someone who creates a vision for herself and then maps out a plan to achieve it. Naomi plans to take her advertising, marketing, and branding experience and create a new dream for Ireland. She explains, "Having lived away from home for a number of years now, I have gained an even greater appreciation of the unique richness of Irish culture and creativity, and the importance of a strong family connection. Through my Irish community I embrace the richness of Ireland and am constantly seeking new ways to share the wonders of our country with the rest of the world."

Naomi's Story: A Dreamer

When I was a child my teachers told my parents that they had no idea how I got such good grades. I would sit at my desk and spend most of the time looking out the window just daydreaming. Yet I was still able to grasp the information being presented and use my skills to apply my knowledge to my schoolwork.

I have always been a dreamer. I carry a moleskin journal with me everywhere I go to make note of various ideas, quotes, sayings, or things that I pick up during the day. Sometimes I have no idea why I write something down. Things often don't make sense initially but sure enough I will look at it a few days later and lo and behold there is a connection. This is how I exchange and dialogue with my subconscious. I think it's important to remain aware of the world around you, yet also be conscious of what's within you.

Harley-Davidson

In the spring of 2003 I took a marketing class at Trinity College in Dublin, studying how brands become more than just a symbol; they become part of a community and a culture. When a marketing team hits pay dirt, people become so passionate about a brand that they eat, sleep, drink the brand and even devote a big portion of their life to it. My professor gave us one example of a brand that has been able to accomplish this—Harley-Davidson.

At the end of the day, Harley-Davidson sells two-wheeled, chromed-out motorcycles. Still, it has become so much more. For many people, Harley-Davidson is a way of life. People tattoo the logo on their bodies and dedicate their weekends and even their lives to be a part of "the experience." Doctors, lawyers, husbands, wives, bikers, and engineers, Harley-Davidson crosses cultural barriers and socio-economic classes and—despite some negative stigma—brings America together.

I sat in marketing class mesmerized. How could this little business that started in a shed in 1903 in Wisconsin when two brothers crafted their first motorcycles have grown to become such an American icon? How could Harley-Davidson survive two world wars and sit on the brink of bankruptcy twice and yet still manage to solidify its brand image and become a symbol for freedom and individualism? I learned that it was because they stayed true to their core beliefs. With that realization, I knew there was no other company that I could learn more from about marketing.

In the summer of 2003 Harley-Davidson was getting ready to celebrate their one hundredth anniversary. Hundreds of thousands of people were going to converge on Milwaukee, Wisconsin, for a three-day celebration. I wanted to be a part of it, so I wrote an e-mail to the head of marketing explaining what I had learned in class and how I felt compelled to be a part of the celebration. I asked for an internship to work on the marketing team, and after a few days, I got a response: "Yes, absolutely!"

I found myself on the way to America to embark on the opportunity of a lifetime. I was the only international intern on the team, and although I was not fully prepared for the magnitude of the events to come, I was willing to work hard, take on anything that was thrown at me, and figure it out. It was the best on-the-job training I have ever had, a total immersion into the American culture, and I set out to enjoy every minute of it.

I am thankful that I have had managers and mentors in my career who have collaborated with me and also given me the green light to figure things out. I admire and gravitate toward people who go out against all odds and try things simply because they believe they can make a positive change. That is how I learned to build a thriving career. Those that live in the middle of their vision are far more successful than those who sit outside looking in, or allow someone else to own it. A vision without a plan is just a dream; you have to have a plan and be prepared to work at it and modify it as needed.

Back to America

After my internship I knew with certainty that I wanted to return to America, so when in 2005 I was offered a marketing position with Enterprise Ireland New York, I immediately seized the opportunity. Working with a talented international team and some of Ireland's finest entrepreneurs, technology leaders, and visionary designers, at the forefront of Irish industry, was a humbling yet fulfilling experience. It provided me with a great foundation for success, which I would later build upon when the next opportunity presented itself. In 2008,

I joined the VIA Agency to reestablish their New York office. I entered the advertising industry at the height of the digital revolution, and through dedication, passion, and solid teamwork, within a few short years the agency was named the top small agency in the US. I am so proud to have played an integral role in this success.

Towards the end of 2010, I began to wonder, "What is next?" I scheduled some time with my mentor and boss to discuss my future. I wanted to ensure that I was in the right place to take the company forward. At the same time, I had also been pondering the worsening economic situation in Ireland and wondering how I could be of greater service to my country. After a long discussion we agreed that it was time for me to leave VIA and focus fully on my next career move.

It was a great feeling to end one journey and begin another on such a high note. I am fortunate to have forged strong relationships and connections throughout my career, which continuously enrich my life experiences and help in shaping my future decisions.

Early on when I thought about talking to my boss I felt a lot of fear about having the conversation—fear of losing my security and fear of how he would react. I soon recognized that all of the fear was within me. There were no external forces pressuring me to do anything. When it dawned on me that I was fully and completely in control of my decisions and the outcomes, I was able to embrace the power to change it all. I have the power to decide where I want to live geographically, the people I choose to surround myself with, and the kind of work I want to do.

Fear is omnipresent in life, you can let it overpower you or you can harness it to empower yourself. I chose to use it as fuel. To have the courage to leap, and ultimately, regardless of the economy and various business issues, believe that the net would appear.

Comfortable Being Uncomfortable

I have learned over the years that I am comfortable being uncomfortable. Comfort brings with it a sense of security and belonging. It can also promote stagnancy and complacency. When I create room in my life for discomfort and change, I create the room to grow. My interests change. The people I interact with change. I am exposed to fresh ideas and challenges, new adventures, and inspiring new people to work with. Companies often hang on so long to what has worked well in the past that they lose sight of what is coming next. When I moved out of the way to create an opportunity for new insights, I actually did my company a favor too.

Ireland is a massive collective of stories and shared experiences. Nearly everyone on the planet has a perception or experience related to Ireland which is unique for a small country. Because our people have dispersed to every area around the world, the world has experienced Ireland. Often the perception of Ireland that people have grown to know over the years is very different than what is truly going on in the country. I see myself as a "connector of the dots."

Graduating from college and moving to New York, I constantly found myself surrounded by people who think globally— "big picture" thinkers. I'm lucky to have such important role models and mentors in my life. Thinking globally is now part of my DNA. When I consider the future of Ireland, I believe that the Irish have gotten caught up in the smaller details while the world continues to create a perfect canvas for creating the "big picture." All our current challenges cannot be solved within Ireland. We must look to a global solution for our future.

As a relatively young business woman, my advice to women is to know, trust, and believe in yourself. Self-knowledge comes from giving yourself the time and space to make informed decisions. Women tend to rush from one moment to the next, one job to the next, or stay put because "it's safe." I give myself the opportunity to dream. I give myself the gift of time to be truly aware of what I want in life and to craft a plan to get there, without compromising my values and integrity.

The second piece of the puzzle is exploring and developing the skills to communicate on a professional and intrinsic level. Building relationships—both personal and professional—is critical to success.

Every person I meet has a story, and every interaction, be it in the boardroom or over a cup of tea, is a unique window of opportunity to learn and connect. You'd be surprised how much can be accomplished over a cup of tea. Each meeting gives me an opportunity to present my true self, with the confidence and skill set to communicate my vision and goals and articulate responses in a professional, concise manner. Networking and listening are keys in creating a life filled with adventure and passion.

Finally, you have to be willing to work hard, love what you do, and remain committed. Have faith in yourself, follow your heart and intuition, believe in endless possibilities, and trust that although the next steps may not always be completely clear at first, the dots will connect in the future.

Patricia Parks DeNucci

Patti DeNucci spends her life connecting people. As an entrepreneur she teaches the art and science of intentional networking and attracting strategic referrals. She attributes her ability to connect to others in business to her English Irish heritage and skills she learned from her father and ancestors. "Entrepreneurship was always in my family," says Patti. "My great-great-grandfather sailed around the world as a captain for the British Merchant Marine, toting his entire family with him on many of the journeys. He was an example of taking charge and making choices to balance work and family life. I often rely on the strength and skills passed down from my Irish ancestors to move me forward in my business. I learned how to communicate and bring people together, and that is an Irish trait."

Patti teaches others how to network through consulting, speaking, and training. Her book, *The Intentional Networker,* offers stories and techniques that teach business organizations how to purposefully network.

Patricia's Story: Away at Sea

I am one of the lucky ones. My ancestors left a lot of clues and folklore so I know who I am and where I come from. My great-aunt Sally Archer Burton, daughter of Sea Captain Fred Wherland and his wife, Sara Deane, authored a family book called *Your Mother Remembers* that provides a unique look back in time. It shows just how adventurous and courageous the Irish branch of my family had to be to make it to America and start a new life in the Midwest.

Sally's father, Fred Wherland, was only thirteen when he lost his mother. Broken-hearted and alone, he left Cork, Ireland, and ran off to sea. The ship's owner, Mr. S.R. Graves, First Lord of the Admiralty and an acquaintance of the Wherland family, saw Fred and asked him what he was doing on a ship at such a young age. Fred told Mr. Graves his circumstances and Mr. Graves replied, "You belong to a wonderful Irish family. I'll have to alter your position for your next voyage." And with that young Fred was made a cadet and started a long, successful career at sea.

By the time Fred was twenty-one he became captain of his own ship and went on to sail around the world. Captain Fred Wherland's life captures the adventurous, entrepreneurial spirit that was passed down to each generation of my family. Not only was he a free spirit, sailing around the world, surviving famine, fires, storms, earthquakes, and disease, he also took his wife and family with him on many of his journeys. It is an early example of combining work and family life.

At twenty-five, Captain Wherland met and married sixteen-year-old Sara Deane. Together they embarked on the *Columbine*, a sailing vessel headed for Peru, South America. They were at sea for fourteen months and produced a son named Fred, who tragically lived only seven months. Sara was so lonesome and sad over the loss of her child that she decided to go with her husband on the next trip to India. While on that trip she contracted cholera and was almost lost. She was taken to a hospital where they tried everything possible to save her. According to the accounts by Sara's daughter Sally, "The only thing that saved Sara was a dose of brandy and soda water. This miracle goes to show that liquor is actually good at times."

My great-grandfather, John Neptune Wherland, was born on the ship while crossing over the equator. He was rightfully named "Neptune," meaning "god of the Sea." The family sailed for many years together with all the children in tow. When the Captain finally decided to settle down he relocated the entire family to a farm in the Midwest. This created a new life full of hardships and adventures not seen in our comfortable society of today.

Sally Archer Burton

My Great-Aunt Sally went on to marry and start her own family. Sally's husband had one serious affliction, however, that Sally could do nothing about. Money ran through his fingers like sand. Sally stood by as the dutiful wife and quietly watched as her husband lost their farm. This created difficult living conditions for Sally and her children. As Sally got older, unlike many women of her time, she took matters into her own hands. In Sally's own words, "When my last baby was two years old, I ventured into a business career, strange as it seemed, for I had never faced the public before. I had to learn the life as I went along. My experience has taught me that politeness and kindness did more for me in life than anything else. It costs nothing and does so much."

Sally refers to many false starts and "starvation points" where her hard work did not reap any benefit. Finally in 1910 her luck seemed to change when she and her oldest son, Vivian, started a new restaurant. Vivian said to Sally, "Now Mother, get behind the wheel and make good for your alter days" (old age). Within the first year of Sally's restaurant she turned a profit and went on to build her very own home, paid for outright within a year. According to Sally, "God helps those who help themselves. I certainly tried this out ever since I have been in business. It is awfully hard work at times, like pulling hard against a stream."

For a woman in 1910 to start her own business and get her family out of debt was unheard of. It inspires me every day knowing that the entrepreneurial spirit runs deep in my roots.

In My Blood

I always knew I would be an entrepreneur. I could feel it in my blood. Captain Wherland, Sally Archer Burton, my paternal grandfather, H.A. Parks, and my own father, Kenneth Parks, were all entrepreneurs. My father ran his own car dealership. I guess that is why I was never afraid of the "cycles" of entrepreneurship. I was raised in a home where sometimes money was tight, sometimes things were good; I understood that when you are in business for yourself you are in control of everything. If business is tight and the economy shrinks that means you may not get paid but you hunker down and get through it. That is just the reality.

Often I think about my Irish ancestors and how difficult they had it, both in their homeland and in coming to America. Sally's book highlights how the weather, the seasons, and a husband's habits and decisions influenced the course of a woman's life. Women of today have it easy in comparison to what Sally faced. We need to remember that. I have pictures of my ancestors in my house and I look at them often for inspiration. If they can sail around the world with their kids, settle down in a new country, and literally create a new life, surviving famine, disease, bitter winters, hunger, and cold, I can certainly do anything I set my mind to.

I was always a writer. When I graduated from college I got a job working in a PR and advertising agency. When my husband and I were ready to start our family, I decided it was time to go freelance and start my own company. It was important to me to have flexibility and I did not want to have to ask anyone's permission to be a mother and take care of my child. In my line of work it was relatively easy to transition from employee to freelance work. Our agency had established relationships with freelancers so essentially I just became one and continued to do some work with the firm as well as many other companies.

Along with writing I thrive on connecting people to opportunities. I have a knack for meeting people and making a strong personal bond. I am then able to facilitate helping those people connect to others in my network. Recognizing this as a strength, I decided to build a business around it.

My book, *The Intentional Networker,* educates people on how to mindfully do this for themselves. We can only turn our dreams into reality through making connections to others, and that is what I do best. The Irish are known for their innate ability to connect to others. Many people take this trait for granted. I learned it from my family. Back in Captain Wherland's time that was how you did things. He got his start in the British Merchant Marine through a family connection. These connections are the key to making opportunities.

Follow the Stepping Stones as they Appear

I am most proud of being a mom. I was fortunate to have great role models and grow up in a loving, supportive home. My parents expected excellence but they also encouraged me to pursue whatever spoke to my soul. I hope I have passed that down to my son as well. Unconditional love and support is the greatest gift you can give your child. The Irish are all about family and making it through the good and the bad together as a unit.

My son just went off for college and I consider this time in a woman's life similar to adolescence. I'm going through something completely foreign, emotional, and life-changing. Women devote their lives to their children and when they go off to live their own adult lives we find ourselves feeling alone, lost, and even distraught. Couple that with menopause and you can have an interesting challenge on your hands.

But if women approach this time in life with a philosophy that this is a time for self-reflection and self-development and a necessary part of life, they can come through it grateful for this part of their journey. I remember reading what Stevie Nicks from Fleetwood Mac said about big birthdays. She noted that every decade birthday is time to reflect and determine what this decade is going to be about for you.

Celebrating each decade and setting a theme and a course of action changes your life experience. When kids leave home it is a new beginning not just for the child but for the mother as well. It is time for you again. My fifth decade is when I made the decision to write my book and expand my business to include speaking, consulting, and workshops. This is an exciting time where I am creating a path and following the stepping stones as they appear.

I am determined to make each decade count.

Audrey O'Gorman

The Irish people share a rich folklore and a mythic tradition that includes the likes of fairies and leprechauns. Unfortunately for many of the women of Ireland just a generation or two ago, wishing on rainbows for pots of gold yielded little to ease the tough reality of their plight. Audrey O'Gorman observes this in recounting the story of the limited choices available to her grandmother when raising a large family in Dublin in the 1930s and 1940s.

Audrey has been an American citizen for a decade now and has embraced the idea of pushing beyond preconceived cultural limits. She encourages women of every nationality to claim the right to make their own decisions and define the quality of their lives—as mothers or as women who choose not to be mothers. One of Audrey's life goals is to contribute to the empowerment of women to do just that. She is studying counseling to that end, and with a little Irish luck and a lot of hard work—but no wishing on rainbows—Audrey has set out to live her own unique and satisfying life.

Audrey's Story: Complicated Relationships

Like most relationships, my relationship with Ireland is a complicated one. Ireland in many ways has a wounded soul. The country's history and traditions make it an enormously rich culture but can also hold back its population in significant ways. The Irish have not yet learned how to be prosperous, or we have a limited definition of what true prosperity, true empowerment, really looks like. The hangover and conditioning of the past contributed to the terrible mismanagement of the economic boom at the end of the last century. This led to the tragic demise of the "Celtic Tiger" and the emergence of a brand-new wave of necessary emigration that will affect our country for years to come. The history of the power of the Catholic Church and the centuries-long conflict and oppression from England traditionally kept sustainable positive change at bay, but when some real financial power did come our way, we were caught like deer in the headlights, with no clue what to do with it. And so the Celtic Tiger became (as I remember reading in one article in the *New York Times* a few years ago) the "Celtic Garfield."

The sad truth is that, instead of suffering the familiar oppression from our neighbors to the east and the humiliation of having to seek a living in the heart of the country which had so long reviled us, as was the case historically, Ireland began to inflict a different kind of oppression on itself. Which one of those scenarios is more of a recipe for cultural distress? Perhaps an experienced mental health professional would be the one to ask.

I was born in England in the 1960s during one of the many times that Ireland had too many people and no means to support them. Both my parents are Irish—Mom from Dublin and Dad from Waterford—and like others they moved to London after high school to find work. My parents met, married, and started their family there and I lived in London until I was eight years old. I went to English schools, played with English children, and had a proper London accent. I was an excellent student, made good grades, and took pride in my academic abilities.

We moved back to Dublin, Ireland, after my father's father died. My dad missed his homeland and was struggling to maintain employment in London (although my mom was advancing in her work), so off we went. That was my first real experience of traumatic disempowerment. Not that an eight-year-old should get to make final decisions about a family's well-being, but why did no one ask me what I thought about it?

When I arrived in Ireland, a precocious eight-year-old ready for third grade, I was dealt a heavy blow. The local Catholic school required that I study Irish and the nuns in charge were appalled that I hadn't yet made my first Holy Communion. So in their wisdom, they kept me back a year and made me repeat all the lessons in English, math, and so on that I had already covered.

I was bored, frustrated, and angry with every adult in my life, parents and teachers included. The decision had nothing to do with my ability to do the schoolwork, but it had everything to do with religious tradition (which meant nothing to me at the time) and secular control. I had no control or choice and it established a powerful theme that has run through my life thus far: the vulnerability of individuals in the grips of dysfunctional systems. Is it any wonder I eventually found work involving the facilitation of individual and personal empowerment?

Observations and Questions

So began my questioning of the Catholic Church in Ireland and its influence and control over the Irish community. As I got older, I wondered why the priests lived in houses with housekeepers and drove fancy cars while the nuns lived in communal residences without any transportation other than the local bus system, eating their boxed lunches at school just like we did. I wondered about the practices and traditions and recognized that they did not suit me and my belief in my own potential as an intelligent female. I didn't need to have a big house and nice car like the local priest did, but I did want it to be an option for me should I choose to pursue it. It seemed like simple logic to me, even at a young age.

My mother's family in Dublin had been quite poor and was very large. She told me about growing up and never having enough food to feed all the eleven mouths in the two-bedroom home in the suburbs of the south side of Dublin. Because there were not enough eggs at breakfast to go around, the top of her father's egg was cut off to give the children a taste, and it was a big deal to be the one chosen to receive it. Often the kids were sent out of the house while their parents ate their dinner, and then they returned to have a much less appealing meal of their own. One day my mom and her brother were peering through the kitchen window and saw their father eating a dinner of meat, potatoes, and vegetables. My teenage uncle put his fist through the window because he could not contain his frustration. There was never enough for all of them. Often the neighbors would feed my mother dinner if she was looking particularly scrawny that day.

My grandmother was powerless to change anything, yet she and my grandfather continued to reproduce. It was not until years later that I had the insight to realize why she would get pregnant every time her husband, my grandfather, came to visit her from his wartime factory job in England. He had another life in England for several years (including a son by an English woman.) In fact, my mother did not meet her father until she was two years old. He only came back to Dublin for short visits, but the most important thing was that the monthly check he sent home for the upkeep of the family keep arriving. That was my grandmother's only resource to keep the roof over their heads. So almost every time he came home for a visit, she got pregnant. Perhaps it felt like it was increasing his ties to her. Even though he had an entire other life in England, my grandmother was completely and utterly vulnerable. Each child may have been, perversely, a form of insurance to ensure the breadwinner's connection with his family. Like many other women of her time, she had no other way to survive. The moral imperative about birth control preached by the Catholic Church served to convince her that reproduction was one of her sole duties as wife and mother.

Another odd phenomenon of this time and place is how the children were raised and thought of. Boys were considered potential wage earners for the future. They were put on a pedestal, nurtured for the potential security they might later be able to provide. The girls were left to fend for themselves, but that included an expectation of early and useful marriage. Forget self-esteem, dreams, and education. It was all about survival, and the boys were considered to hold the future of the family.

Perhaps watching my mother struggle with the repercussions of this culture and lifestyle is why I never had children myself and have spent my life pursuing education. The combination of the rules and expectations of the Catholic Church to create children, coupled with the widespread poverty and emigration, was the perfect storm.

There were not many options for my mother and like many children, I tuned in to her feeling of being trapped by her circumstances. I set out to ensure that I had more options and I have been lucky enough to live in a time when more choices have been available to an Irish woman of limited means.

Seeking Change

After finishing college, I realized that once again Ireland had few opportunities to offer its young people, and I was ready for a change. I applied to the Donnelly Visa Lottery for an opportunity to immigrate to the United States and ended up, like so many others, with the coveted green card. I had to arrange for a job in the United States and an employer to sponsor me. Through a college professor I knew, I found a public relations company in Cleveland, Ohio, run by a Dublin woman who offered me a job and sponsorship.

Having never been to America I had no idea what to expect. I certainly did not expect the huge amount of snow that blankets Ohio for months in the winter. I had no transportation. I had little money. This was the "shock experience" that required me to face up to the reality of being an Irish emigrant. I stayed about six months and headed back to Ireland, too homesick and lonely to last any longer.

After several other stops, including a five-year stint in London working in the TV industry, I applied for a short-term contract position in New York at the United Nations. Short-term turned into eleven years. As I got older and did the same thing every day, I began to notice that over time people who accepted the status quo and stayed static within another malfunctioning bureaucracy became shells of their former selves. I recognized that this was likely to happen to me and I was, as I had been when I went to school in Dublin, being required to neglect my own abilities and to deny some of the best parts of myself.

I had at least one more adventure left in me and I needed to act on it while I still had the energy and the courage. My best friend at the UN, Michael from Oklahoma, and I decided to quit our jobs at the UN and move to Austin, Texas. I did not have a plan, a job, or a specific agenda, yet in the fall of 2007 I gave notice to my boss after eleven years in the same office. The next thing I knew I had sublet my apartment and shipped my belongings to Austin. It didn't really hit me until I was driving across America to spend Thanksgiving in Oklahoma with Michael's family that this was, even after all my years in the States, my first real experience of the American heartland and perhaps somewhere where a more satisfying version of the American dream might still be available to me.

After about a year of exploration and some freelance writing work to help keep me afloat, I enrolled at the Seminary of the Southwest in the masters of arts in counseling program. I knew immediately that this was my niche—helping people to manage change, to understand and be kind to themselves, to deal with adversity and enhance the quality of their lives. To my surprise, in Austin I also found a community where I feel I belong, as well as an expression of faith in God that matched my own core values—one that treats women more as equals, is not as rife with blatant hypocrisy as the Catholic Church of my upbringing, and one that is capable of enhancing a spirituality more in keeping with modern times. I funded my studies with my United Nations pension (very much a case of putting all my eggs in one basket), and although I am currently as poor as the proverbial church mouse as I near the end of my program and the beginning of a new professional life in the field of mental, emotional, and spiritual health, I am happier than I have ever been.

Irish women are tough but despite our challenges as a culture, we have for the most part maintained the ability to access our compassion for others. We recognize that everything we have, we have worked to get. For most of us, nothing came without substantial effort. Because of this, we never forget how important it is to support and connect with others. Americans have mastered the arena of competition, but sometimes at the expense of their humanity. I would like to be part of redressing that balance in some small way through my future work.

I believe that women of all ages and nationalities must give themselves permission to enter into the competitive fray, not to get bogged down in cultural tradition and preconditioned limited expectations. We sabotage ourselves with an endless list of reasons we can't achieve, internalizing the idea that only masculine traits can lead to success and depriving ourselves of the opportunity to explore alternative possibilities. As women, we must give ourselves permission to do what speaks to us in the quiet of our hearts. This is what will change the world.

I have found my path, a source of challenge and satisfaction and learning and community. This new world opening to me has the potential to bring much contentment, and I can only wish that kind of contentment for every woman who was once convinced that the limited womanhood of her mother's generation was all she could aspire to.

Renee Gatz

Uncertainty in our professional lives has become a way of life for many Americans. Renee Gatz is no exception. After working for ten years to earn a degree to prepare for a career in marketing, she faced layoffs, downsizings, and mergers that resulted in unexpected career changes.

Through it all, Renee drew upon the women who came before her: her Irish mother and grandmother. Remembering them got her through her trying times. Their wit, strength, and wisdom continued to resonate with her.

Recently, Renee captured her grandmother's best-known phrases in her book, *Wise Words and Witty Expressions*, where she celebrates her strong Irish American upbringing and shares some of the expressions and sayings that she loved as she was growing up.

Renee's Story: Connection

I always felt a strong connection to my grandmother, who came to America in 1907 from Hollymount, County Mayo, Ireland. Bridget Ena Madden McCaffrey, also known as Della, arrived at Ellis Island after two weeks in steerage aboard the ship *The Baltic*.

Della grew up on a farm and was perfectly content to stay in Ireland, but Della's sister, Mary Ellen, had visions of leaving the farm for a faraway place. Mary Ellen wrote to a friend and arranged for passage to America to join her in New York. Della's family made all the arrangements for Mary Ellen to travel abroad and meet her friend in New York. She planned to find work as a maid and cook for a wealthy family in the Big City.

Then the night before the journey was to begin, Mary Ellen got cold feet and refused to leave. The family, having already made the arrangements and spent a small fortune on the ticket, decided that the only practical thing to do was for Della to go to America in her sister's place. From one day to the next, Della had left her comfortable life on a farm in Mayo and was confined in the crowded quarters of steerage on a boat bound for America.

Though only eighteen when she arrived in New York City, Della immediately began working as a maid. The job gave her the means to help three of her brothers immigrate to America. One could not handle the homesickness and no sooner than he arrived he returned to Ireland. Her other brother arrived in America and before too long became ill. Della stepped up to take care of him. She managed to scrape together enough money to rent a small room. Soon he succumbed to his illness and passed away. Della felt responsible for ensuring that he had a decent burial. She contacted a local funeral home and talked the funeral director into letting her make payments. She struggled for some time to pay off the debt but it was a matter of honor.

After a few years she met Phillip McCaffrey, a native of Philadelphia with Irish ancestors, fell in love, and married him. Phillip and Della went on to have eight children, four boys and four girls. Della's youngest son, Francis, died shortly after his birth. She had one more baby, my mother, Patricia, who arrived as a surprise when Della was forty-four. Having seven kids to raise during the Depression took its toll on the family. In spite of the financial challenges Della did her best to keep a happy home.

Phillip supported the family as best he could working hard labor jobs, including the building of the Delaware River Bridge, now known as the Ben Franklin Bridge in Philadelphia. His last position was as a boilermaker.

Philip died when Patricia was ten years old. Della's older sons were grown by this time so they stepped up and helped support the rest of the family. My mother was one of the last at home so her brothers took a vested interest in her upbringing. She often commented that it felt like she was an only child with extra sets of parents. They made sure she did not want for anything.

Della loved her adopted country and took great pride in the fact that her three boys served in the United States Army. Her pride in America never wavered even after the tragic loss of one of her sons, Jimmy. He always seemed to have a premonition that he would not enjoy a long life. He mentioned to Della on more than one occasion, "I will not live to comb many grey hairs." Shortly after returning home from serving in World War II, he died from a pulmonary embolism that developed after neck surgery. Della never let the tragedy of this loss dim her love of this country. She was always grateful for her many blessings.

Della was close to all her children, including my mom, Patricia. I was only three years old when Della passed away. Mom took her death terribly hard. Della's passing left a big hole. She was the backbone of the family, with a strong faith in God and a never-ending sense of humor.

My mother felt it was her obligation and honor to share Della's story with her own three girls and keep her mother's memory alive in us. I grew up hearing wonderful stories about my inspirational grandmother. Those stories made me feel as if I had known her and fostered a strong affinity with Della, Ireland, and the Irish way of life. So strong, in fact, that these tales inspired me to write my book, *Wise Words and Witty Expressions*.

Della's Words of Wisdom

Life is funny. As a child, I remember my mom sprinkling her conversation with sayings. If I daydreamed aloud about something I wanted, her wry response would be, "If only wishing made it so." I'd roll my eyes at her and think, *There she goes again. Will she ever stop?* As I got older, I was horrified to find the same sayings coming out of my mouth. I realized, "Oh my God, I sound like my mother."

Later, I realized those sayings had value—and they kept coming back to me, whether I wanted to block them or not. They were just part of who I was, like my blue eyes, and I finally learned to embrace them. My grandmother's beliefs and values were transferred to me through my mom by her use of my grandmother's wise words.

One of my favorites is, "Watch the pennies, and the dollars will take care of themselves." My mother was a Depression baby born in 1932 and said this constantly. Like most children growing up in that era, my mother was conservative about money—everything reusable was saved; every purchase scrutinized. She may have enjoyed nice things, but she wasn't going to throw away money, either. She taught me to recognize that the number of little expenses can add up and prevent the accumulation of wealth.

"They have more money than sense" was another family favorite. We were taught to be careful with money, and respect it for the security and freedom that came with it. Because the value of hard work was one of the core traits in my family, I was not afraid to commit to doing whatever it took to meet my goals.

"Doing anything you set my mind to" was another of Mom's favorites. After graduating from high school, I did not have a particular career in mind so I trained to become a secretary. I attended the Katherine Gibbs School, a well-known secretarial school. After completing my training and starting work, I realized that I felt frustrated by the limitations that my career presented. Often, I felt like I could do more and I soon realized that I was just as smart as many of the professionals that I was working for. I realized that my opportunities were limited without a further degree so I decided to earn one.

Thanks to my parents, I never for a moment doubted that I would succeed. I just had no idea how very demanding it was going to be to juggle a full-time job with college courses at night. Looking back on it I don't know how I survived. Going through it, I just did what I needed to do.

Here's another saying: "If wishing alone would make it so." I knew that I would just have to do the work. "This is too hard. I'll put it down and I won't do it" simply was not an option. It was not in my vocabulary. And Heaven help me if my family had heard of me doing so. My family was supportive but didn't believe in not living up to one's potential.

"We earned our own, and I would not want to deprive you of the privilege of earning your own." Talk about backbone. I knew that my parents—and my grandmother before them—had endured much more difficult times than I had, often for less of a payoff.

You'll Survive to Tell the Tale

It took me ten years to graduate with a BS degree in business management from Saint Peter's College but I finally did it. When I finished my degree I was at a crossroads again. I had a well-paid job as an administrative assistant, but if I wanted to put my education to good use, I knew I had to start over again. I had to let go of security, money, and comfort, and move into the unknown. To start over in a career in marketing that actually utilized my degree meant facing a pay cut, bigger challenges, and starting all over again at the bottom. I always thought that the college degree would open the doors to stability. I have learned that there is no such thing as stability. Change is the only thing that is constant in life.

I quit my secure administrative assistant job and embarked on a career in marketing within the financial services industry. My first position was not what I hoped for. Instead of a marketing role with a great salary, my first position was writing proposals. I hated it. Being true to Della's words I decided to offer up my unhappiness to the "poor souls in Purgatory." I sucked it up. In the process I gained writing skills, corporate experience, and key relationships.

To my surprise my degree did not give me the stability I expected. Before too long a company merger left me downsized for the first time in my life. Suddenly I was out of work. To make matters worse, I had just lost my beloved father to a long battle with cancer. I had just bought a new home. My life seemed out of control and I felt lost.

My next job—marketing of financial product—was more suited to my goals and skill set. This time I thought I was set when once again there was another mass layoff. The timing could not have been worse. I was laid off shortly after 9/11 and no one was hiring. Wall Street and the entire financial world were reeling from the tragedy and no one knew when the trend would change. As always, I relied on my upbringing, hearing the words of my grandmother: "If you're at the end of your rope, tie a knot and hold on." I scrambled as best I could and managed to find something; I landed a contract position writing proposals once again. I was back doing the thing I hated but I was lucky to get any work and grateful to have it.

The next few years saw me move jobs three times in seven years. I have developed a priceless gift through all this: the ability to network and market myself. I have come to expect that change can happen with little or no warning. I always keep my resume updated and I continue to keep my mind open to new opportunities.

Most important, I have learned that who I am is not what I do. I observed people who had been laid off after decades with an organization and saw them go through great distress. The first time I was laid off, I took it personally. Now I realize that it is not personal; it is a business decision that happens to impact me in a personal way. Ultimately, I am a survivor and happiness is a choice.

Words of Wisdom

Among my favorite sayings of my grandmother is: "The Irish have a way of telling you to go to hell so you can look forward to the trip." I felt the need to bring her indomitable spirit to life. Two years ago I felt a yearning to work on a project to satisfy my creative side and sensed a quiet, encouraging voice in my head. As I have gotten older and found myself quoting my grandmother and mother, friends and coworkers have encouraged me to write their sayings down so they can be shared. I decided I had to share my grandmother's legacy as well as her sense of humor and fiery nature so I started writing down all her sayings. They became my first book.

Wise Words and Witty Expressions is a labor of love and was a joy to write. It is a collection of Irish expressions full of wisdom and humor and a wealth of good common sense to get us through our lives. My writing has provided a haven from the instability of my professional career. Because of my little book I have met the most amazing people. Through speaking and promoting my book I have connected with people who have felt touched by my grandmother's words. They have shared their own stories with me and left a mark on my heart. A ninety-nine-year-old woman who told me she would be one hundred in two months came out in the dead of winter just to attend my book signing and to let me know that it touched her heart and reminded her of happier times. Through this simple project, I have been able to bring credit to my grandmother which resulted in her being honored in her hometown newspaper back in Ireland. This project has allowed me to publicly honor my parents and express appreciation for the positive influence they had on my life.

When challenges come my way I remember my mother saying, "You can do this! You will be just fine! After all, you come from good stock!" If my grandmother can get on a ship alone at eighteen, start a new life in a new land, and live with dignity, integrity and honor, then as her granddaughter I know that I must live a life that honors her.

Joanna Wilson Vargas

Inner beauty is a personal quality. It is an attitude or a look, a feeling or a gesture. The most beautiful model in the world is not truly beautiful if she has a bad attitude. While much of the world today is obsessed with physical beauty, Joanna Vargas has made a career out of helping women look their best, starting from the inside out.

Joanna attributes her rise to success as one of the "Top Ten Women Business Entrepreneurs in the United States" to a strong work ethic, kindness, and customer service—and encouraging clients to recognize their own inner beauty. A little bit of Irish luck didn't hurt either.

Joanna feels lucky that her cultural heritage is a blend of two distinct yet complimentary cultures. She melded her experiences as the child of an Irish father and Mexican mother, both immigrants, to find the true meaning of beauty that is present in all cultures.

Joanna's Story: Mexican and Irish

Growing up as a second generation American, my culture and the opportunities that America provides were a constant topic of conversation. My father, Pell Wilson, was a first generation Irish American and my mother, Wanda Luna Wilson, was a first generation Mexican American. My parents had a deep appreciation for the unique opportunities available to those fortunate enough to come to the United States. They found a way to embrace America's opportunities and mesh them together with the traditions and cultural values of Ireland and Mexico.

Although my appearance seems 100 percent Irish, with my auburn hair and pale skin, I am a combination of two countries. I speak fluent Spanish and embrace the best of both cultures. My parents were such a good example of how cultures can mesh together that I was able to recreate it in my marriage to my Nicaraguan-born husband, Cesar.

Real Beauty

I always knew I wanted to do something in the beauty industry. At twelve, my prized possession was my complete Tinkerbell makeup and skin care collection; it provided me with my first opportunity to experiment with beauty products. From the time I was a little girl I experimented with my hair color, much to the aggravation of the nuns at my Catholic school. In spite of their disapproval the nuns often told me that one day I'd be a contributor to the beauty industry. It was at this all-girls Catholic high school where I learned to use my own voice to create opportunities. Even at this young age, I knew that if I did not ask for what I wanted the answer would always be no.

In college I created my own opportunity simply by having the courage to ask. I was interested in two distinct paths: photography and women's studies. I wanted to study both so I approached the dean's office and structured my own degree plan. My thesis project involved taking pictures of fifty women wearing their favorite outfits. The only caveat was they could not wear makeup. My vision was to show that with confidence women do not need makeup to be beautiful.

Like most young ambitious women, I was dedicated to my career and ready to climb the ladder. I knew I wanted to be a facialist. I spent many years honing my craft. I worked in an esthetician's office so that I could absorb and learn the science behind skin care. I then worked my way up in celebrity spas and salons until I finally made it to the proverbial top. Every day I mingled with the richest, most famous people in the city, and I trained under some of the best dermatologists, estheticians, and facialists in the world. I expected to continue to work and believed that I could master the balance of being a working mom with family demands while maintaining a high-profile successful career. I thought I could have it all. I thought I was happy.

Hold Dearest Matters of the Heart

My son Odin was named for a Norse god. It did not occur to me when we named him that he would have to use every ounce of the strength in his name just to survive to see his first birthday. Odin was a happy, vibrant baby boy. I went right back to work shortly after he was born. As is traditional in Nicaraguan culture, my mother-in-law took care of the baby. In the spring of 2006, when Odin was about ten months old, he came down with a stomach virus. He stopped eating. He could not keep any food down. We went to the pediatrician, who diagnosed Odin with a virus, and me with "new mom worry syndrome." Four days passed and Odin was still throwing up. We went back to the doctor, who said he must have reinfected himself and to give it another few days. Three more days passed and again the doctor said, "It is just a virus. It will pass in a few days."

Odin lost six pounds. When I got home after the third doctor visit, a nurse called me from the doctor's office and told me, "Something is wrong with your baby! Get another opinion before it is too late."

Out of desperation and at the advice of my sister-in-law I took Odin to a well-known alternative medicine doctor in New York. He took one look at Odin and said, "Your baby will grow up to be very strong. Very strong stomach!" I felt relief for the first time in weeks. I held on to the healer's words praying that they would come true. Odin had an intestinal blockage that his pediatrician had missed. The Chinese healer's treatment of acupuncture and a special tea worked and Odin finally passed the painful blockage. A big ball of tar came out of him. After two blood transfusions at the hospital Odin was finally better. By the grace of God we got through it and he is a happy, healthy, active boy today. True to the wise healer's prediction, Odin has never suffered another stomach problem.

This ordeal lasted ten days and it changed my life for good. Through all the worry and stress, sitting in the hospital watching my baby struggle to survive, I started thinking about my career choices and how I got to this place in my life. Before Odin got sick, an outsider looking in would think I was the happiest, luckiest person in the world. I had a great husband, a high-profile job working in high society. I had a wonderful baby boy and all the trappings of a successful life. Yet just beneath the surface, just a little deeper, there were many parts of my job that I did not like. I was working too many hours to spend quality time with Odin. I was stressed out most of the time. I wanted to try new treatments and concoct my own inventions in the world of skin care but I did not have permission to do so. I was actually living in limbo and not following my passion. I was not doing what my Irish father, Pell Wilson, had always encouraged me to do: "Hold dear matters of the heart."

As Long as the Grass is Still Growing, You are On the Right Path

It was time to make changes so I could live my purpose. My purpose was to be the best mother I could be to Odin while taking full charge of my career. I was passionate about helping women feel beautiful from the inside out. Yet I wanted to do it on my own terms, with control of my schedule and what I offered my clients.

In August of 2006 I went to the salon and gave notice. My husband and I emptied our bank accounts. We borrowed money from a family friend and from an investor providing short-term business loans. I rented a tiny space on the seventh floor of a building in Bryant Park in New York City. We invested every penny in equipment from Europe and started experimenting with products and treatments. The day I opened my beautiful little shop, I had only one client. I had no idea how I would make this work. I was scared yet happier than I had been in a long time.

My turning point occurred when six months later my business was featured in the *Daily Candy*, an online newsletter in New York. I was featured simply by luck. One of their writers visited my salon and the next thing you know they asked to interview me. I got to work that morning and the phone was ringing off the hook. We had fifty phone calls a day for weeks. That article changed everything and my business started to flourish.

One of my most thrilling moments was in August 2009 when *Vogue* published an article titled "I Am Obsessed with Joanna Vargas!" I was coming out of the gym that morning with my best friend, Karin. We picked up a copy and walked down the streets of New York reading the article out loud. I never imagined things could be so amazing and that I would meet with such success. I never forget to relish the great moments and to be grateful for each and every experience.

Everything happened for me once I grabbed the reins and took control of my future. My business strategy has all been grassroots and word of mouth. I keep my clients happy. I look for the best technology on the market and I make it my own.

In the beginning starting my business was even more work than the job I had left. The difference was that I set my own schedule and I carved out what was important to me. I was able to put my son to bed at night and spend time with him during the day. It is the little things that make the difference for me. I volunteered as a room mother at my son's kindergarten. One of the happiest days of my life was going apple-picking with Odin's class. I take my son to school every day and we often stop at Starbucks for breakfast. I never miss the school events and I attend all his games. Since I quit my job and Odin recovered I keep a journal of all the things Odin says that I want to remember and our favorite experiences together. I realize that if had I never taken the leap of faith to start my own business, that journal would be empty. I would have missed it all. My son, my business, and I are all growing up together.

I believe there are three ingredients to growing a successful business. First you must love what you do and have a passion for it. My Irish dad would always say, "As long as the grass is still growing you are on the right path." My business continues to grow, thrive, and diversify into other areas that create new opportunities for me to learn. I am never bored and every day brings a new challenge or learning experience.

The second ingredient to a successful business is customer service. I treat clients as I would want to be treated myself. Many of the women who come to me put themselves down. They are their own worst critics. I remind them to have compassion and kindness for themselves. I will also point out to them when their lifestyle does not match their authentic inner self. If their goal is to have flawless skin but they are out late drinking and smoking, there is no such thing as a magic pill. I need to be honest with my clients as well as kind. I hold up a mirror for them to see themselves and perhaps empower change.

Finally the third ingredient to a successful business is creating an environment where I do what I love to do without sacrificing what is most important to me—my family. I learned the hard way what it is like to be expected to be at work when my child needs me. It was worth going through the uncertainty of being a new entrepreneur to be able to put my family first.

I love my family and I love my work. By going out on my own I was able to take control of both facets of my life. My success comes from a combination of hard work, integrity, and customer service—and yes, a little Irish luck. Because I love what I do I am blessed to be able to spend every day doing it. I am also able to share my passion with other women and I hope to help my clients find the inner beauty that lives inside every one of them.

Chapter Six

Irish Perseverance

*N*o matter how much you plan or try to control events, unpredictable situations and problems happen. What makes the difference between successfully surviving, overcoming, or even benefiting from a tragedy or problem is the attitude you embrace when dealing with these bumps. Sometimes the challenge is so great that you have to draw on the deepest part of your soul to move through it and do what you have to do.

Throughout Ireland's history, her women have put personal feelings, fears, and limitations aside and embraced what needed to be done. They worked when work was needed, nursed family and friends through illnesses, and kept the home front warm no matter how far their children roamed.

Here are the stories of four Irish women who persevered through challenges and even tragedies. They did not give up because they never lost hope. You will meet Eileen Lynch, whose son Jack tells the story of a young widow with four children to support who not only never gave up, but lived a life of joy. And Diane Stopford, who fell in love with all things food as a child and despite many naysayers made her love of food into a successful career. Here's Anne Martin, who reinvented herself many times, from attorney to a member of the US Navy to cosmetics consultant to wife and mother, determined to be the best she could be at each. Finally, meet Susan McBride Rothman—it isn't easy for anyone to become a VP of the

NFL, especially a woman, but that is exactly what she achieved because it never occurred to her to give up.

Eileen Lynch

"Getting by" was a common theme for women in the US during the 1940s and 1950s. The Irish trait of perseverance is what kept many women from merely surviving and allowed them to thrive despite difficult times. Eileen Lynch faced many challenges yet she met each one with dignity and grace and left her family a legacy of strength.

The main focus of her life was family and by her hard work and generous spirit she was an admirable example of selfless love. Eileen found herself a young widow and made a conscious decision to raise her children on her own. Her long career at Hyatt Roller Bearings brought her a great sense of fulfillment; she was head of benefits when the factory closed. That position well suited her nature to help others.

Eileen had a fantastic sense of humor and a strong faith. She was a woman to be proud of. Eileen's son Jack is so proud of his mother that he wanted to honor her passing on February 1, 2011, by telling her story in this book. Eileen Lynch will be truly missed, but as Irving Berlin wrote, "The song may be over, but the melody lingers on."

Eileen's Story, as Told by Her Son Jack Lynch: Bridget (Bridie) Walsh O'Neill

Eileen Lynch's mother, my grandmother, Bridget Walsh O'Neill, was born in 1892 in Cotterstown, Ireland, outside of Kilkenny. She was one of thirteen children. She grew up on a small farm where her father was a cobbler (shoemaker) and a farmer. The farm remains in our family today.

For most women in Ireland during that time, there were few opportunities and the United States seemed like the only solution to make a future. In 1909, at the age of seventeen, Bridget (we grandchildren called her Nanny) immigrated to the United States. Her sister Molly was already living in the Bronx and Nanny arranged to stay with relatives who lived in Brooklyn while she worked as a maid in Teaneck, New Jersey. It was not long before her two sisters Katherine and Margaret followed Nanny to the USA as well. Shortly after their arrival the two sisters, Nanny and her sister Margaret, met brothers John and Thomas O'Neill, from the same county in Ireland. Yet it took moving to New York for the families to connect. Connect is what they did—the sisters married the brothers. Nanny moved to Hoboken, New Jersey, with John and had six children. Margaret had seven children with Thomas and raised her family in Brooklyn.

Nanny became a young widow when her husband passed away in his early forties. Margaret, too, died young, leaving her seven children without a mother. Nanny took a job as a cleaner in the Jersey City public schools to keep the roof over her head and raise her six children. On weekends she went to Brooklyn to see after Margaret's children.

She didn't forget her family back home either. Nanny often sent packages to Ireland. Back then people did not travel the way they do now and money was always short. When I was a kid, Nanny would often help herself to my best and finest clothes and send them back to the family in Ireland. I remember helping her wrap my new white shirt and dress pants in a box. We wrapped it in brown paper and tied a cord very elaborately to make sure it was secure.

My mother, Eileen, a widow herself with four children, finally discovered that our best clothes were headed back to the old country. When Mom confronted Nanny about it, Nanny simply said, "Your kids don't wear them much but the kids back home will." She was right. When I went to visit Ireland for the first time as a senior in high school, my cousins commented on being the best dressed kids in the village thanks to the packages from Nanny. We never had church clothes for Sunday but I guess it all worked out in the end.

Mom often told me, "Your grandmother was always poor but she never noticed!" Her unselfish and generous nature allowed her to give whatever she had to someone else who needed it more than she did.

Eileen Lynch: Selfless Love

My mother, Eileen Lynch, set an example of selfless love and service. Every person faces tragedies in their life; what separates people is how they handle them. Mom faced her difficulties with strength, grace, and acceptance. When I asked Mom how she got through her challenges, her reply was simply, "What other choice did I have?" She knew no other course of action but to face her problems head-on and shoulder the responsibilities.

As a young widow with four children to support, Mom worked in the Hyatt Roller Bearings Plant, a division of General Motors. She started in 1962 working as a ball bearing inspector. She worked the night shift, 11:00 p.m. to 7:00 a.m., so she could get us all off to school each morning and catch a few hours sleep while we were safe at school. A few years later she was promoted to the personnel department and worked her way up the corporate ladder.

When I was a teenager and my friends and I looked for summer jobs my mom was able to help us. She gave us high-paying jobs in the summer with one proviso: she made us promise we would not stay at the plant after graduation. We must go to college. Mom never wanted us to think about high wages as a goal. She said we would lose sight of our dreams. My friends and I took Mom seriously and headed to college, working at the factory during our summer breaks.

By the time the factory closed twenty-five years later, Mom held the fitting title of head of benefits. Mom helped the employees by ensuring they received the full benefits they were entitled to.

After the plant shut down, Mom and her boss continued working in a new office for another four or five years during transition. In the end, she was the last person to turn off the lights on a company that employed almost three thousand people. She was rightfully proud of her contributions there. She found great fulfillment in work and the friendships she forged and was always grateful to GM for the life they gave her and her family.

Education and a Promise

In my whole life I had only one insurmountable disagreement with my mother. I was twenty years old when I came home from Boston University to break the news to Mom that I was dropping out. I knew that conversation could never go well so I took Mom out to dinner, figuring she would have to contain herself in public. When I finally got up the nerve to make my announcement Mom maintained her composure and said, "The day your father died, when you were just seven years old, I made a promise to myself to see to it that all four of you would receive a college education. The only thing I have ever asked you for is for you to get your college degree. After that I don't care what you do. You can sell guitar picks in Kalamazoo, Michigan, for all I care but you must get your degree!"

But I did not. I dropped out. This hurt my mother more than I ever imagined. I moved to San Francisco to work as a bartender. At twenty-eight, I realized that I forgot to get a career. I filled in some days for a jewelry designer, met some gem dealers, and decided that type of work appealed to me even though I was not that business-oriented. I would get to travel and work with creative people and beautiful things.

I moved back to New Jersey and lived with Mom while I attended the Gemological Institute of America in New York City and got my certificate as a graduate gemologist. As always, my mother was there to support me with a place to live and paid for my education. Finally, at age thirty, I started work in a new industry that proved successful for me. It also fulfilled my mother's promise to herself to educate me so that I would be able to succeed.

After graduation from the GIA in New York, I moved back to San Francisco and worked for a pearl importing company. Ten years later I started my own company, Sea Hunt Pearls.

The first thing most people mention about my mom is what a terrific sense of humor she had. She always had a quick retort or a story to tell and was the first to share a laugh and enjoy the party. It was very difficult to put anything over on my mother. After years of working with the rogues and miscreants of factory life, she had heard every tall tale in the book—and she enjoyed hearing them. She had her priorities right, but she didn't sweat the small stuff. Once, during my ungrateful teenage years, over dinner I made a derogatory remark to my mother concerning her domestic skills. She looked me right in the eye, gave her hair a fluff and said, "I am a career girl. If you don't like this, do it yourself."

The last conversation I had with Mom was when she was ninety and on her deathbed. She was home surrounded by her grandkids, cousins, and children. I remarked, "Wow, look at the number of visitors you have! You must be very popular." Without missing a beat Mom replied, "Jack, so what's not to like?"

That description sums up my mom. "What's not to like!" An apt description of a meaningful life filled with love, tenacity, and grace—a tribute to the Irish spirit of life. A life well lived and a soul well spent.

Diane Stopford

Throughout history, the Irish have had to be persistent out of necessity. Geography was not a factor in Ireland's favor. As a tiny island on the outskirts of Europe, Ireland spent its early years under frequent attacks and invasions. Each unwelcome visitor—the Celts, the Normans, the Vikings, and the English—brought change and impacted the evolution of the Irish people. While many of the changes were positive, such as in language, culture, and religion, the Irish people had to be persistent and fight to keep their land, their roots, their language, and their heritage.

As a result, the Irish are amazingly adaptive. The Famine of the 1840s is a historic example of how the Irish, despite extreme hardship, survived and reinvented themselves across the world while still embracing their strong sense of patriotism, culture, and above all, sense of humor.

The Celtic Tiger is the name for the phenomenon that propelled Ireland from what was essentially a third-world country in the 1980s to a booming contributor to the world economy. Once again, the Irish were challenged to reinvent, recreate, and revitalize the future.

Diane Stopford has never been afraid of hard work and has stood by her convictions with the persistence of her Irish ancestors. Her persistence opened the door to an amazing career as a chef and the opportunity to start a new life in America.

Diane's Story: Grandmother Dorothy

I was born and raised in Dublin, Ireland, the youngest of four girls born to Peter and Joy Stopford. From my earliest memories, I always had a love—a passion really—for food. At breakfast our family talked about what we were going to eat at lunch, and at lunch discussed what we were going to eat at dinner. Food was always the focus of our lives. Dad inherited a love of cooking from his own mother, Dorothy Stopford, which was passed down to me. To this day I have my grandmother Dorothy's cookbooks with me. Gran's handwriting in the margins of the cookbook takes me back every time I open them. It is my connection to the past and to family.

Dorothy always wanted to be a doctor. As the daughter of a clergyman in the Church of Ireland back in the 1940s, however, she was not allowed to pursue that dream. She set her sights on a degree in education and was one of a handful of women in her era who graduated from Trinity College in Dublin.

Dorothy rode her bike everywhere she needed to go. In her eighties the bike got too difficult for her to ride so my aunt bought her a moped that she named Snowdrop. Her final years were spent riding around town on Snowdrop, enjoying every minute of her life. Dorothy also created her own form of cooking career by cooking for the local nursing home. Dorothy cooked individual favorite meals for the residents. Once Dorothy sat down with me over a cup of tea and explained the dishes she prepared and how she made them. She commented on how she had to take care of the "old people," even though she was probably around the same age.

A Passion for Food

On Sundays, while my dad had the roast in the oven, the rest of us would bake a cake, brownies, or maybe an apple tart. Cooking and baking came very naturally to me as it was such an important part of our family life. So it was no surprise when I pursued a career as a chef. But the journey I took to get there was.

As a preteen in middle school, while other kids were interested in sports and movies, I was interested in cooking. I spent many a weekend at cooking competitions. My dad would take me and spend the day waiting to hear how I did. Instead of watching cartoons or teen shows on TV, I watched cooking shows.

I was about fifteen when I entered an intense cooking competition. One morning I caught Mum phoning my oldest sister begging her to come over to be taste tester. I overheard my mother desperately saying, "Please come and taste your sister's dish. I just can't face any more of it!"

My mum, not a great cook but my biggest fan, spent hours at the supermarket trying to find all the ingredients that I needed for the cooking competition. Monkfish was the worst. It can be very difficult to get during bad weather, and bad weather is often the case in Ireland. It is also not cheap. The fishmonger at our local supermarket, Superquinn, found out I was practicing for a cooking competition and started donating monkfish to my cause. I got to the finals but didn't win. It was ultimately the experience of taking part that counted and was a good lesson for running a professional kitchen. (I did win Tesco Irish Young Cook of the Year in 1997.)

If You Believe in Your Convictions, Then Don't Sit Behind Them

I started working in L'Ecrivain as work experience in secondary school (high school) when I was fifteen. The chef Derry Clarke let me come in for a week here and there during my Easter or summer holidays. He helped me practice the dishes that I later made for the cooking competitions. I continued to work with Derry throughout high school and he became my mentor.

When it came time to go to college I knew that a career in food was the only choice for me. I applied to a new program at the Dublin Institute of Technology and pursued my bachelor's degree in culinary arts. It was a brand-new program and at the time I applied, no degree like it had ever existed before. No sooner than I knew I had qualified for the course, my neighbor handed me a newspaper article in the *Irish Independent* saying that my course was canceled because the government wouldn't approve it.

I was immediately and totally heartbroken. The college canceled it. Just like that. How could this happen to me? I decided to fight it. I contacted the local newspaper and my local city council, and I told them and anyone who would listen about the unfairness of this decision.

A couple of months passed and then one day my city council representative (he was actually a minister or member of Parliament, not just a city councilman) showed up at our door and spoke to my parents. He said, "I want to meet with Diane." He was up for reelection and was out knocking on doors as candidates do to earn votes. When he met me at the door I was very angry. I exclaimed, "This situation is completely unfair and has ruined all my plans!" I went into a tirade about how important this program was for the university and for students like me who had planned their lives around it.

A few days later I received a call asking me to meet the minister in the Parliament in Dublin. I came to my meeting nervous but prepared, with all my newspaper articles and clippings highlighting the competitions I had participated in and awards I had received over the years. I explained to the minister that they were making a monumental mistake. The minister told me that he was going to bring this to the attention of the minister of education. A few weeks later I got a letter from the college indicating that I was accepted for advanced entry into the course. It was reinstated.

I hope I played a small role in saving this unique degree program—the only one of its kind in the world—from elimination.

I made a difference by speaking my mind and standing up for myself when I was only eighteen. I was in the first graduating class of the program.

I had the tenacity to speak up because of how my parents raised me. They taught me that if you believe in your convictions, then you don't sit behind them. The fact that I was only eighteen when I went through this experience was an excellent learning tool that I have applied to the rest of my life. In fact, I have found that speaking up for me has been a requirement in the male-dominated field of cooking over the years. It is how I have been able achieve success and still be true to my convictions.

Facing Challenges

One of the biggest challenges I faced in creating a career and a life in America was the complicated American immigration system. Many of my career choices stem directly from the ability to stay and work legally in America. I have applied for my green card under a category for extraordinary ability in my field. Typically this is a category for engineers, inventors, and doctors. Chefs are not the norm. I went through the process head-on and after a long wait I finally received a positive outcome. After many years of pursuit I received my green card.

My mother always told me, "Nothing comes handed to you on a plate." If I don't try I will never know. Whether it is a job, an education, or a green card, you have to work to get it. If it is worth it you will make it happen.

Four Irish Gifts

When I was a child, my father would often tell me in Gaelic, "*Aithníonn ciaróg ciaróg eile,*" meaning "One beetle recognizes another beetle" or "A heart knows its own heart." Wherever I travel in the world, I will always be able to recognize someone from Ireland. There is a strong connection regardless of where I am at the time.

Growing up Irish gave me four amazing gifts that I rely on every day. First and foremost is my supportive family. My dad was a Marine engineer and traveled the world. My mother often went with him before they had a family. They were not surprised when their daughters wanted to do the same. I may be thousands of miles away but I always know that I have my family supporting me. My sister and I talk regularly and I go to her for advice and comfort. My parents and I speak and e-mail regularly. We make the best of technology to shorten the distance gap.

My second Irish gift is the ability to network. We do this really well. Even though we don't refer to it as networking it is something that we learn naturally. The Irish think of it as chatting with new people. We don't go out the door with the expectation of building a network. The skill simply comes through our upbringing. As a child in a small house with four kids and two adults, on occasion when I had a difficult project to work on, my dad and I would head down to the Ballinteer House known as "The Beavers" for some peace and quiet—him for a pint and me to do my homework. Irish pubs are so special that you will find an Irish pub knockoff in every country. I actually got my first job at The Beavers when I was sixteen.

The third gift of an Irish upbringing is a sense of humor. It probably stems from generations and generations needing to overcome adversity to survive. The Irish have a knack for not taking themselves too seriously. I was about eleven when I learned that avocados were full of fat. I came up with the idea of making a chocolate cake using avocados instead of butter. In theory it made sense to me—if they were so full of fat, why wouldn't it work? I pureed the avocado in the food processor and added the green sludge to the mix and added the chocolate. It looked like lovely smooth batter. I baked it and turned out the cake. It was a hard mess that tasted awful. Instead of crying about it we all laughed. I threw it away and went back to the regular recipe.

Finally, we Irish share the gift of heritage. We know where we come from and we know who we are. We know our history. We learn about our contribution to the world in the arts and writing. Children learn Gaelic, the language of Ireland. At the time we hate learning it, but as we get older we appreciate the unique sense of self that it provides. In spite of being a small country, we share a big, powerful history, and we are proud of being Irish. We don't have to trace our ancestry because we already know it. That sense of ourselves, the uniqueness of Ireland that makes us different than other European countries, is what gives us our confidence. It is the backbone of our people.

Anne Martin

Emigrants leaving rural Ireland to embark on ships to America were giving up life as they knew it. Trading the often difficult and monotonous life of the Irish countryside for the chaos of New York City required a certain kind of character. It needed not only resiliency of spirit but the ability to completely reinvent their lives. Everything from how they lived, how they earned money, what they ate, and whom they associated with was different. The Irish became masters of reinvention, working in new jobs, taking on new responsibilities, and doing whatever it took to survive.

Anne Martin is a master of reinvention and is now sharing with others the formula necessary to let go of old identities and create new ones. Anne has had several careers and has spent the better part of her adult life shedding old identities and creating new ones that serve her life purpose and goals.

Anne's Story: A Grandfather's Dream

My grandfather Michael Yorke emigrated from County Cork, Ireland, to New York for a chance at a better life. He was a frustrated scholar. During my grandfather's time, education for Irish children was discouraged and in some cases even forbidden. This had a direct impact on the dreams of my grandfather. He always wanted to be a lawyer but as an immigrant with little means he was never able to achieve that goal. Instead he got as close as he could to a career in law by becoming a court reporter for the New York City court system. An avid reader, he spent his time reading each and every law. He knew more about the intricacies of law than most of the attorneys in the court.

My grandfather was the primary reason I pursued a career in law. My parents worked hard to give me and my five brothers and sisters a better life. My mother, Isabel, was one of the few women of her time with a college degree and she was also trained in shorthand and typing. When we were young, my mother went to work to help with the family finances, starting out working part-time and then working her way up to a position as the director of lawyer placement at Saint John's University.

My mother gave me two pieces of advice that she learned from her Irish upbringing: always take the road less traveled and never rely on a man for money. She encouraged me to go to law school in part because she wanted me to be a success in life and in part to fulfill the dreams of her father. So that is what I did.

In 1973 I was one of the few women admitted to Saint John's University Law School. Women were so new to the school that they had to designate one of the male bathrooms for the females. The urinals served as a reminder to the women students that this really was a place for men. The old-school professors were not too thrilled about having women in their classes so they designated "ladies' day" where the women were called on to recite law and answer questions that day. It was a tough environment and we had to be better prepared than the male students to survive the program. But I was up for the challenge.

When I graduated I was ready for my next adventure. I knew I wanted something unique that involved traveling and the sea. I took my mother's advice about pursuing the road less traveled and joined the navy, becoming a military attorney with the Judge Advocate General (JAG) Corps. Once again, I was part of a small minority of women. The navy really was an equal opportunity employer that gave women a chance to prove their own merit.

During my three and a half years as a JAG attorney I met my husband. We were married in 1980 and our only child, Lance, was born in 1982. After leaving the military I pursued a career in law and began my feminist era. I embraced the idea that no educated professional woman would ever think about wasting her hard-earned degree on housekeeping and changing diapers. I wanted it all: the high-powered career, big paycheck, perfect marriage, children, and a gorgeous home. I completely bought into the myth of "super woman." My career spanned law practice with the navy general counsel, research at Carnegie Mellon University, and finally business practice at a big law firm in Pittsburgh, Pennsylvania.

The Good Life

It wasn't until the recession of the early 1990s that I received my wake-up call. Because my legal work decreased when business transactions had fallen off, I was able to be home for dinner with my family and enjoy Saturdays at soccer games. I realized what I had been missing. Lance was growing up without me. Most days, I left for work before he woke up and got home after he was in bed. Sunday afternoons were our only family time together. While I presented an illusion of a perfect life to the world, on the inside I was numb.

I took time to examine my priorities and the legacy I was building. Although I had practiced law for fifteen years, I questioned whether I wanted to practice law for the rest of my life. To my surprise, the answer was a resounding no. I noticed that many women in my field who were considered to have "made it" had made tremendous sacrifices. Success had a big sticker price in terms of broken marriages, health issues, and missed opportunities with children. After much self-reflection I decided it was time to change and began exploring opportunities outside the legal profession. This was the first step in my reinvention.

Reinvention

I found the path to my reinvention in the most unlikely of places— at the bottom of my handbag in a tube of lipstick. I'd been a Mary Kay customer for years and I loved their products. I had heard that it offered a tremendous business opportunity to women who wanted to have a great home life and still have a career. I decided to join the Mary

Kay sales team and "test drive" this business while still working as an attorney.

This was a huge leap of faith. I did not fit the mold. I was never a beauty queen or a cheerleader and I did not have big hair or even wear a lot of makeup. Still, I was attracted to the vision of Mary Kay and how the entire culture was built around supporting and encouraging women.

After eight months of trying out the business, I decided to leave the law and work the business full-time. When my husband and I discussed the transition, we decided that quality of life was more important than all the stuff. We sold our second home in the mountains and the Porsche, and I began to build a business as a Mary Kay entrepreneur.

I was disappointed by some of my colleagues who told me point blank that I was wasting my education, but I now had a dream and a purpose and nothing could change my mind. My decision to reinvent myself was the best thing I have ever done. Once I became a sales director, I earned more money with Mary Kay than I did when I was practicing law—and I did it working half the hours.

The greatest gift I gave myself was the gift of time and flexibility. I was now able to be a hands-on mom and raise my son myself. My son, now in his twenties and a PhD student in the bioengineering department at Stanford, said it best: "Many of my friends my age do not have a relationship with their parents. Who knows what path I would have chosen during high school if my mom had not been around as much as she was."

A recent move to San Francisco from Pittsburgh has opened up another opportunity for me to reinvent myself yet again. I enrolled in several programs at Dream University®, founded by America's Dream Coach, Marcia Wieder, and began using her powerful techniques to coach my team of Mary Kay consultants.

Dreams as Power

After observing the transformative power of the Dream Coach® process in so many lives, I realized that this process could be valuable in helping others refashion their lives and careers in today's volatile economy. I decided to expand beyond my Mary Kay world and created a business that blends the lessons of my own reinvention experiences with my mentoring skills to inspire others to explore fresh new possibilities for their lives.

The dictionary defines reinvention as "to make over completely, to bring back into existence or use, to recast something familiar or old into a different form." We can reinvent in many ways—our life's work, our relationships, our lifestyles, and ourselves. However, the key element of any reinvention is a willingness to step out of our comfort zones and explore new possibilities.

That's what my Irish grandparents—and millions of other emigrants—did. They left the comfort of their homeland to explore new possibilities in a country thousands of miles across the sea. In today's turbulent economic times, we all need to be reinventors, willing to explore new possibilities and be flexible and courageous enough to take bold action to repurpose our careers, our lifestyles, and our lives to be more joyful and fulfilling.

Susan McBride Rothman

As one of only four women at the time to achieve the title of vice president in the male-dominated National Football League, Susan McBride Rothman changed this corner of the world. Susan attributes much of her success to her Irish immigrant grandmother and her first-generation Irish father.

Her grandmother was a serene, tranquil woman who taught by example. One of the most important lessons she shared with her granddaughter was her hatred of waste and her belief in a responsibility to help others. Susan was able to share this commitment to helping others within the framework of her career with the NFL. She is proud of a program she launched that is responsible for repurposing NFL licensed products with "losing team" logos. Her proposal arranged for those products to be shipped internationally to people in deep poverty in desperate need of clothing. She was able to avoid the needless destruction of thousands of garments that had previously been destroyed only because they were marked with losing team logos.

Her grandmother instilled a strong sense of respect for others in Susan's father, who shared those values with his children. Despite dying after a short illness at a relatively young age, he played an important role in shaping Susan's perspective about life. He firmly believed that all people should be considered as equals and treated with respect. Susan approached her career options with the belief that all people should be given an opportunity to succeed. Her attitude, work ethic, and skills changed the face of the NFL.

Susan's Story: Leech's Corners

My grandmother Mary Margaret Graham McBride immigrated to America from County Antrim in northern Ireland on April 16, 1904. April 16 is also my birthday so I felt as if we shared a special connection. She came to America as one of thousands of Irish immigrant maids who were seeking a better life. For reasons now lost, she traveled to a rural part of Greenville, Pennsylvania, known as Leech's Corners, where she married William McBride, also from Ireland, and had four children. My grandfather died relatively young leaving her a young widow, which she remained for the rest of her life, well into her nineties.

I spent summers visiting my grandmother, and those memories remind me of just how little we really need to be happy. When I visited Leech's Corners I was transported to another time and place, leaving my regular boring life in suburban Pennsylvania behind. Grandmother's house was out in the boonies, where all I saw was countryside and an occasional Amish family riding along in a buggy. She had no indoor plumbing, no running water except the red pump in the kitchen, and no heat other than a wood-burning stove. She was very grateful that she had electricity because many of her neighbors did not. She always appreciated her life here and, though her love of Ireland was deep, she never longed to return. Once when I mentioned that I intended to travel to Ireland to visit her old neighborhood, she asked matter-of-factly, "What for?"

Her home was a special place to me. The furniture was soft and overstuffed and the beds were covered in puffy comforters. In spite of all the fluffy covers it still got chilly at night. Grandmother turned inconveniences into adventures. We had a bedtime ritual involving a trip outside to the "Wee House." Each night I slept with my flashlight close by in case of midnight emergency visits. Without a flashlight the Wee House was impossible to find.

One of my best memories with my grandmother was playing a card game called Authors. We spent hours sitting across from each other playing cards. While most grandparents let their grandkids win, my grandmother did the opposite. I found that she actually cheated sometimes. When I caught her she'd grin and shrug to let me know it was all in good fun. Grandmother liked to win.

My grandmother had very little in the way of material things yet she was content. Grandmother accomplished what she intended when she left Ireland—she built a life, had a family, and made a home. One thing that was always emphasized was that waste was not acceptable. We were expected to always turn off lights when leaving a room, food was not to be wasted, and plates were expected to be cleaned. She lived by example and showed me that you don't have to have a lot of material things to be happy. You can be content with the simple things in life like a card game or a fluffy blanket. Appreciation of the simple things was a core value of my family, something that many Irish share. It is something that I remind myself about when my life becomes too hectic and I am dealing with the corporate pressures of today.

Fairness in America

My dad, Nathaniel Graham McBride, was a tall, slender man with Fred Astaire's looks and the intelligence and wit to go with them. He worked as an industrial engineer at Bethlehem Steel. As the first generation son born in America to Irish immigrants, my father had a strong work ethic and inflexible opinions about fairness. His parents were believers in the American dream. They came here with nothing and were able to buy land and raise a family. He grew up hearing about the "land of opportunity" where everyone was created equal and everyone deserved a chance at a future.

My father was always a hard worker and advanced within his company. When I was about thirteen my dad received a promotion and with it came a country club membership. I was thrilled. We lived in an affluent part of Pittsburgh and many of my friends were members of the club. I had always wanted to go swimming with my friends there. Before his promotion and receiving a membership, when I was invited to go to the club as a guest, my father discouraged me from going. I was always a little annoyed and could not understand why he did not want me to have fun with my friends. I thought our very own country club membership would change all that. I was wrong.

One evening my father sat me down and said, "You need to understand why I don't like it when you go with your friends to the club. Susie, that club does not allow your doctor, Dr. Selkowitz, to join. It does not allow your black friends to join. It is a restricted club and you can only go there if you are white and Christian. I can't tell you what to believe but if that club is not good enough for half your friends, then it is not good enough for you."

At that moment everything clicked. I realized what he had been trying to teach me. Dad had waited till the right moment to show me what he expected from me and what he considered to be more important than a swim at a club. I never went to the club again. My father believed in the American dream and that everyone was equal. And he lived his beliefs.

Saying Good-bye

Everyone has defining moments in their lives. When I was seventeen, my dad was diagnosed with pancreatic cancer. He was only fifty-six. Within three months he was gone. When we first received the news about his illness, Grandmother immediately came to be with her son. During her stay, she was quiet and reflective, but never outwardly emotional. Grandmother helped us all by setting an example of how to deal with the impossible—staying the course and doing what needed to be done with that gift of quiet Irish fortitude.

I was young, not familiar with the rituals of death. After Dad's death the ritual was to have a long "viewing" day for people to come and see the body and pay their respects. My mother explained this to me and I was emphatic—I did not want people lining up to stare at my dead father's face. Mom went to my grandmother and discussed my feelings with her. To have a closed casket was a radical move, one that would spark a lot of gossip, but my grandmother said, without a moment's hesitation, "If that's what Susie needs, that is what you should do." So that is what we did. My grandmother was more concerned with my well-being than with outward appearances and possible judgments.

Watching my grandmother with her quiet dignity and grace made me cherish the moments that make up each day. Though devastated, she accepted the inevitable. If this tragedy has happened to us, then we all had to learn to live with it and move on. She was so strong and such a good example. That experience made me realize how things can change in a flash of a second. Every single moment is precious.

Leave the World a Better Place

The summer after my father died, I went to work at Gimbel Brothers Department Store in Pittsburgh. It was a good distraction from my grief and turned out to set the stage for my career path in the future. With thirty other girls, I was selected to be on the store's 1969 "Teen Board." We did PR work, fashion show modeling, and worked as sales reps in the junior sportswear department. After college, I joined the Gimbel's training program. It is interesting to note that in 1974, when I joined the program, men were paid more than women. When I asked about it, I was told that they had or will have families to support. It was just expected and accepted.

After completing the program, I moved to New York City and got a job as an assistant import coordinator of several affiliated department stores. One year later I was traveling around the world developing private labels for the stores. I was very young to be traveling the world and struggled with establishing my credibility with some of the local manufacturers and agents. They were used to dealing with men and often deferred to them. Interestingly enough, my college major in anthropology and population demographics helped me to understand that this behavior was ingrained. Instead of resenting it I worked harder to prove myself and earned my stripes by proving that I could deliver. I worked the Asian market for over a decade and became very well-known and respected.

A Switch to the NFL

In 1995 I heard through friends that the NFL was hiring. Two of my friends determined that this was where I needed to go and turned my resume in for me. The NFL had just completed the reorganization of the consumer products department and had an opening. My two friends got me in the door but twelve hours of interviews with fifteen members of top management got me the job of senior director of adult products. The NFL was looking for a new direction and new ideas, both of which I was able to bring to the table. This job utilized my product development, retail, and merchandising experience—and besides, I loved football.

I never really thought about my gender so I was not consciously blazing trails or breaking down glass ceilings. In hindsight, I realize that I had no true peer group. All the other senior directors were men and most of my superiors were men. Some liked me and some did not, but I found that the key to my success was just hanging in there, working hard, doing my job, and maintaining a sense of humor. There were many times when I was the only woman in a room full of men. I had an office with a window and a title. This was unusual in the mid-nineties. My approach to being the only woman in the room was to rely on my sense of humor and pragmatic outlook, both of which I'd inherited from my Irish grandmother—as well as her unbelievable tenacity. I loved my job and was not going to quit; it was challenging at times but great fun. After all, I wasn't one of the guys, and I was trying to avoid being labeled a "bitch." So I let my creativity and work ethic speak for themselves.

During the late 1990s, the NFL started to address some of its diversity issues and things began to improve. I had been there long enough to establish some credibility and was promoted to vice president in 1999. Most important, through it all I did what it took to get the job done. If it meant getting coffee, making copies, or typing my own reports, I just did it. Of course, so did everyone else. There was always plenty of work to be done.

After some time in my position, I had the opportunity to create a women's clothing line for the NFL. I was thrilled to be able to take the NFL in a totally new direction which, considering that 40 percent of the fan base was female, was simply a good business move. Because of my gender, I was able to recognize an opportunity and develop it. Expanding on the whole concept of the importance of women football fans, I was also able to forge a deal between the NFL and the Susan B. Komen Race for the Cure. That relationship has resulted in the contribution of millions of dollars to the search for a cure for breast cancer. I remember my grandmothers' and father's words—always try to do good.

One of my proudest accomplishments involved finding a way to minimize some of the waste that had been accepted as part of the NFL's promotional practices. I found out that, because of the critical need to get promotional items out to consumers in a timely manner after an NFL event, the NFL regularly manufactured items with logos from both teams playing in a game. The winning team's merchandise had to be available for immediate sale so there could be no time delay. There was no way to predict which team might win so the NFL regularly manufactured merchandise with logos of losing teams. After each championship game, the apparel with the losing team's logo was destroyed.

Having grown up in a family that abhorred waste, I found this situation to be simply unacceptable. So I worked with an international organization that committed to getting the losing teams' products out of the United States to a country where they wouldn't show up on E-bay or anywhere else that might care about the NFL or the losing team. This program assures that the losing teams' merchandise will not be exploited and has been adopted as the industry standard. Virtually all leagues now use this process. I am proud that I was instrumental in making this change. Leave a space a better place than when you arrived.

Sometimes You Have To Suck It Up

Over the years I've encountered many young people who come out of college with high expectations of making a great income and landing stellar jobs near the top of an organization. Getting coffee, making copies, doing whatever is asked is out of the question for many. This attitude might work when jobs are plentiful and opportunities are flourishing (or it might not) but it is not a good way of getting ahead or proving your value. The problem is that the economy is cyclical and when times are tough, jobs are a rare commodity. Young women must recognize that sometimes we must make the best of a tough situation.

The reality is that people who work for others must understand that they have to play by other people's rules. They have to make the best of it. If that makes them miserable then at the right time and with the right plan they need to find something else.

I remember there was a point in my life when I was really miserable in my job. After a long period I found something else that suited me better and I finally left. After a few days at the new job my husband said, "My God, I haven't heard you laugh in I don't know how long. Welcome back."

Unhappiness at work can spread to the rest of your life. Yet people need to understand the terms of the deal that working for someone else requires. You have more security, you have insurance, and you have a steady paycheck. With that comes the requirement that you must work on their terms, not your own. It is a trade-off.

Entrepreneurs take a different approach to a career. They approach their careers similar to the way Irish immigrants approached coming to America. They recognize that they must create their own future and their own paycheck. They are willing to trade the security of the known for the freedom to work on their own terms. Either way, self-reflection and self-assessment is necessary to accept who you are. Don't forget to ask yourself what is important to you and what trade-offs you are willing to make to flourish in your life.

Sometimes It's Time for a Change

In 2009 the NFL decided it was going to facilitate reductions in staff. After working with the NFL for thirteen years, I realized it was time for a change. To encourage people to consider a career move, the NFL offered transition packages that were, at least in my case, very attractive. I had been in a serious car accident in October of 2008 and I was exhausted and needed time to heal. It was time to rest, regroup, and move on. I was fortunate that my career sacrifices were rewarded with enough financial security to give me some time to myself.

Lately, I am excited to be tackling a new challenge in my life. I am transitioning from being a corporate animal to being an entrepreneur. I am currently working with three start-up companies and helping with aspects of financing, product development, branding and introduction to the marketplace. It is exciting and rewarding. I am also working independently and calling my own shots. I love this new independent career, which I am certain my grandmother would have approved.

Chapter Seven

Irish Charm

*W*ithout a doubt, the Irish have more than their fair share of charm. With a twinkle in their eye and their fabled gift of the gab, they can convert strangers into friends in the time it takes to share a pint or a cup of tea. This willingness to share kindness and friendship makes the Irish liked everywhere they go. Wit and warmth are part of the Irish heritage.

An Irish woman can influence her family, friends, and coworkers with firm kindness sprinkled with a wee bit of wry wisdom that gets her message across. If you know an Irish woman, you have a home to go to.

In this chapter you will meet four Irish women whose stories will indeed charm you, such as Kathleen Onieal, who used her charm to succeed in a male-dominated profession after watching her mother succeed in one too. And Barbara Campbell, who uses the power of Irish storytelling to sell perfume over the non-olfactory medium of television. And Melanie Fitzpatrick, who looked Irish, felt Irish, and was as charming as any Irishwoman, but since she wasn't Irish she did the next best thing—married an Irishman. Finally, you'll meet Imelda McGratten, who left a strife-ridden city to open a pub—where success depends on the publican's charm—in one of the most charming places in Ireland: Dingle Bay.

Kathleen Onieal

Growing up in the Irish Catholic Community of Scotch Plains, New Jersey, Kathleen Hayes Onieal learned from her mother and father to honor and respect the country of Ireland and the Catholic religion. Irish immigrants to the US had two things going for them that other ethnicities did not: they spoke English and they were known for their charm and charisma. The Irish flourished because of this, as the success of the powerful and charismatic Kennedy clan shows.

Kathleen was so connected to Ireland that when it was time to go to college she decided on the University of Galway. This gave her a unique insight into America and Ireland, seen through both the Irish and American lens. She recognizes how new generations of both Americans and Irish are blending and letting go of some of the rigidity of the past.

Kathleen's parents thrived during the Kennedy era, called "Camelot," a comparison to the seat of the court of the legendary King Arthur. It came to mean a place or time of idyllic happiness. After John F. Kennedy's death, Jackie Kennedy referred to the years of her husband's presidency (1960–63) as an American Camelot, meaning a period of hope and optimism in US history.

For young Irish Americans just getting started in life the image of perfection portrayed during that time became the American dream. The Kennedys played a central role in defining the idea of Irish American success. Kathleen learned from her mother to use the good parts of an Irish Catholic upbringing to her advantage, yet to know that the trappings of the "perfect life" were often far from perfect and sometimes came at a price too big to pay. She mastered the power of discernment; as life gave her challenges she had to think for herself and never blindly follow the rules.

Kathleen's Story: First Generation Irish American

I grew up during the 1960s and 70s in New Jersey, a first generation proud Irish American. My father, John Hayes, was a Cork man and my mother, Kathleen Philomenia McCormack Hayes, hailed from the dead center of Ireland, Athlone. My father was reluctant to leave Ireland and always thought he would go back some day. My mother, on the other hand, was all about the adventure that America provided.

My parents met on an elevator in the famous Woolworth Building in Manhattan. Their Irish brogues caught each other's attention and sparked a conversation. The conversation led to a date and shortly after they married. After doing several odd jobs, my father landed a coveted job with a steady paycheck and benefits at the New York Life Insurance Company. My mother worked as the first female waitress at a lively and popular restaurant. Mom was a beautiful woman; she was tall and slim with auburn hair, green eyes, high cheekbones, and a regal sense about her. Her grade school education from Ireland was better than most high school graduates in the United States. She was well-spoken, knowledgeable, and had a sense of humor—although she could be quite serious about the idea of right and wrong.

When my mother walked into a room you would have thought the Queen of England had arrived. She had confidence and charisma and was proud of who she was. This translated well into the service industry. She was never ashamed of her career as a waitress. She looked at it as a coveted position. The best part was that my father was so proud of her. He bragged about how great Mom was and supported her 100 percent. He often would come home from work and vacuum, do laundry, and look after my sister and I while my mother worked opposite hours. They were a team. I had a great example of what marriage could be from my parents.

Mom's job gave us the means to live a comfortable lifestyle. Every summer we made the reverse commute back to Ireland. Mom's brother immigrated to England and made a name for himself building hotels.

This provided an opportunity for us to have amazing vacations at the best hotels in Ireland. Every summer was magical. I had the best of both worlds—living in America and spending summers in Ireland.

When it came time for me to go to college I chose the University of Galway. I saw my parents once a year and we spoke on the phone sporadically. This was before e-mails and cell phones. Luckily my extended Irish family was about two hours away. At seventeen, I was younger than my mother when she came to America by herself in search of a better life. I always felt so at home in Ireland that it felt easier to go across the Atlantic than to the next state in the US.

I had two big things going for me as a child. My mother never drank and neither did my father. This was a great thing for an Irish family. I never had to deal with the alcoholism that is so rampant among many Irish families. I am sure the Irish memories are very different for children of alcoholics. I was one of the lucky ones.

My parents loved America and were happy to be here, yet they had a strong sense of Ireland and my father generally limited his social life to the New York Irish community. I was very much a first generation Irish Catholic. My father went to church every morning before work and served in the Knights of Columbus. When the church bells rang at noon in his village in Ireland, everyone, my family included, got down on one knee and made the sign of the cross. Whether you were in the street or in the grocery store, you were on your knees. It was a sin to eat meat on Fridays and women wore hats and sat on one side of the church while the men sat on the other. My father continued the tradition of saying the rosary when he came to the States and it was a rule that my sister, Patricia (born on Saint Patrick's Day), and I say the rosary with him on our knees every single night before bedtime. Although this sounds a bit oppressive, it was actually a peaceful tradition to share and a lovely memory.

My childhood was comfortable and serene. I was brought up to actually think everybody was either Irish or in their hearts wanted to be Irish. This created a sense of pride and confidence because I always believed that I was a part of something special.

Never Blindly Follow—Question Everything

You can't be Irish Catholic and not acknowledge the current crisis in the Catholic Church. The Catholic Church has suffered some major setbacks, in America and particularly in Ireland. Some of the choices the Church has made in dealing with recent problems have created a mass exodus that would have been unheard-of back in my parents' day. The church has been inept in dealing with the issues of divorce, birth control, and the horrendous pedophile scandal, which has resulted in the widespread rejection of the church. The Catholic Church's wounds may never heal.

Although my mother was a devout Catholic, she was able to make her own decisions about the church. In the 1950s when my father was only thirty-nine he was diagnosed with lung cancer. The doctors told my mother that he'd have to have a lung removed but even with the operation the cancer would likely come back.

The news of the "Big C" changed my mother's perspective, particularly when it came to having children. My sister and I were the only children in the family and we were the only ones in America. My mother recognized how hard it would be for a widow to raise us on her own, and she did not want to be like many other women with a big group of kids yet little means to feed them. She made a decision that she wanted a comfortable life for herself and her kids, so she chose not to have more children. One day the Catholic priest asked my mother, "Why aren't you having more children to promulgate the faith?" As diplomatically as she could, she answered, "My husband has cancer. Maybe you should go and have them!"

Watching my mother go through this taught me a valuable lesson about faith and religion. She took the best of the Catholic Church but was pragmatic enough to recognize when something did not work for her. Having a big family with a sick husband was not a risk she was willing to take. She taught me to question—never to blindly follow.

My father did go on to live a happy and very productive life until the cancer reappeared at fifty-nine. He lived a year struggling to breathe, knowing his time had come. Fortunately, I finished school and I was able to be with him that year. My fifty-three year-old mother was devastated but not defeated. We took the time we needed together to grieve the loss of my dad. Watching her suffer that loss was one of my most difficult experiences. I decided to put my plans to go to medical school on hold so I could be with my mother as she adjusted to life as a widow. Although death is a natural part of living, it all felt unnatural for a very long time.

In the meantime, a family friend, Sister Mary Margaret Sweeney, helped me get a job at Saint Vincent Hospital in Manhattan. This job led me down the path to the pharmaceutical industry and a rewarding career that has spanned over thirty years. It was an example of the Irish community helping each other on the road to success and my mother's determination that we achieve the American dream.

Much of my success in the pharmaceutical industry is attributed to skills I learned from my mother. Mom stood for something. She knew right from wrong and she stuck up for herself and got her point across without being offensive or rude. Working in the restaurant her wages were based on the tables she was assigned. The harder she worked the better tables she got. She made an impressive amount of money in those days and her goal was to be certain my sister and I were educated and prepared to build a financially secure life. It was clear that success was the only option.

I remember as a teenager listening to her stories about the fun and politics of working. She told the story of the maitre d' at the restaurant seating one of her best customers at the table of her male coworker. She went to the maitre d' and explained calmly, "I noticed you gave my table to someone else. Just because I'm a woman do not think I did not notice or it does not matter. You know they are my regular customers and I will be handling it now." The stunned maitre d' did not respond and Mom took back her table. This was way before "women's lib." She always told me, "Being assertive does not have to be confrontational. If you want to play the hysterical female you will not make it in a man's world."

She was not afraid to show her intelligence, yet she did not steamroll over people. She had an intense drive to make money and at the same time a knack for building relationships. I saw the importance of people skills in your business life and loving what you do. She taught me that work can be fun and the key to a sense of security and independence. Somehow with the help of my father she balanced work and family life and felt both were so important in a person's life. As I was building my career she was there every day to see that my house ran smoothly in my absence. I doubt I would have been able to have the career I had without her daily commitment to her grandchildren. She believed all women should build a full life that included your own identity and ability to make your own decisions. For me, she made that possible.

Saying Good-bye to Mom

In 1999, at the age of seventy-four, Mom was living large and enjoying her retirement. Like most widows of her era, she never remarried. It never even occurred to her. I always thought that was sad because she was so attractive and certainly knew how to be a great partner in life. But her conservative upbringing made her uncomfortable with the idea of dating at that point in her life.

Being on her own did not stop her from enjoying life. She often traveled to Ireland and Australia to visit family. Her last trip was to visit the outback with her niece in Australia. She went feeling great but when she returned she did not feel well. Her appetite changed and she had trouble eating. She went back to her physician who performed a partial colonoscopy called a sigmoidoscopy that came out negative. This time she was scheduled for the full-blown colonoscopy.

I drove Mom to the hospital that morning and dropped her off for her procedure. In typical Mom fashion she did not expect me to stay—in fact she thought it would be silly for me to stay. I headed for the highway to go to work, and was about halfway to the office when a voice in my head said, *What are you thinking? Go be with Mom. Forget about work. Mom needs you.* I turned the car around and headed back.

By the time I arrived the procedure was over and Mom was in recovery waiting to meet with the doctor. The doctor came in and asked to speak with me alone.

I knew from his expression that the news was not good. He said, "Your mother has colon cancer and it has spread to her liver." I was dumbstruck. Thank God I was there to give her the news and not the doctor.

I took some time to catch my breath. As I entered her room I looked at her face and I knew she knew. I repeated what the doctor had just told me. She did not cry. She did not break down. She simply asked me to take her home and she decided at that moment there would be no chemo, no treatment, no heroics. She would spend the rest of her days on earth at home with her family.

My sister, Patricia, I, and our kids spent the next two months at my mother's house. We took turns as we both managed our families and careers but we basically spent all of our time surrounded by family. Two months later Mom went peacefully, surrounded by her family in her own home. She did it her way.

Mom's faith in God and her Irish Catholic upbringing prepared her for dying. She was never afraid. She had such a belief in being in a better place that she did not even try to fight it. One time shortly after my father died I asked her if she would be OK dying knowing that he was in heaven waiting for her. She missed him so much. She said, "My life now is beautiful but different. I will stay here as long as I am meant to be here."

I believe that Mom was never meant to get old. She was such a vibrant spirit. I have never been closer to another person and may never be. I look like her and we were similar in so many other ways. I felt a part of me died when she died.

Question Even Your Own Life

There have a few major events in my adult life where I had to deeply question the rules of the Catholic Church and how they shaped and formed some of my decisions.

The first occurred when my husband and I were ready to have kids. After trying to conceive for years, watching time pass without any sign of children, we found out that we were unable to conceive the traditional way. The doctor talked to us about in vitro fertilization. At the time it was considered a sin by the Catholic Church.

We considered the possibility of "playing God," as some people called our in vitro attempts, over living a life without children. After much thought we decided to do in vitro. My twins, John and Juliana, were born one year apart and they are the joy of my life. Two years after they were born the Catholic Church changed the doctrine related to in vitro and now it is accepted. Imagine if I had put all my eggs in the Catholic Church rule basket—I would not have my children. My mother gave me the gift of discernment when as a child I knew she chose not to have more children. I was able to apply her wisdom to my own life and make decisions that worked best for me.

Four years later I faced another major life challenge. As I entered my fifties, my life as I knew it—my own version of Camelot—began to unravel. From the outside looking in I had the perfect life. I was married to a handsome, tall, dark-haired, blue-eyed Irish American man. We had two kids in Catholic high school. We owned two Irish pubs—one in Hoboken and one in Manhattan. We had an apartment in the city where he would stay when he worked late. We had been married for nearly thirty years. I was a VP of marketing for a large pharmaceutical company. We were at the top of our game.

My husband was the kind of man whose moods were either high or low. A bit moody, maybe a bit bipolar, who self-medicated with alcohol. But out in the world he was a charmer, the life of the party, the perfect conversationalist. As the pub in the city became more popular and well-known my husband began to stay in the city more often. I also noticed he was drinking more. I turned a blind eye for quite a while until one day the truth slapped me in the face. The New York night life included wine, young Russian women, and song. That party life was now in control. Meanwhile I was home doing homework and putting kids to bed at ten, and up at six to go to a demanding corporate position. The realities of the life he was living became unacceptable, so I made the decision that if he did not change his lifestyle the marriage was over. As the kids were applying to college I would build a new life without him. The decision was obvious, but the reality of living with that decision was the most painful experience of my life.

That first year I can only describe as an out-of-body experience. All the effort I put into this man, the investments in the pubs, the mood swings, and the sacrifices all seemed so pointless. When I married thirty years earlier I never dreamed I would be divorced. My childhood Irish Catholic road map had always steered me right, yet facing this decision was excruciating. Religious expectations be damned. I knew that a relationship without trust was impossible for me. When I finally told my kids their response was, "What took you so long?" I was so worried about how it would impact them.

The events of the last few years have left me to question my faith and to doubt some of the strict interpretations of the Irish Catholic upbringing. The bottom line is that no matter what church doctrine exists stating that in vitro is a sin, or divorce is a sin, I simply do not accept these teachings as infallible. It does not fit within my interpretation and of right and wrong. I have learned that life is not black-and-white. In fact, managing the gray is the most important challenge. Like my mother, I take the best of my Irish Catholic upbringing and I make decisions that work for my life.

The idea of painting the picture of the perfect life, living up to the standard of idyllic happiness, Camelot, is a dangerous way to live. I have learned that there is no such thing as perfection. We go out in the world, we make our choices, we love unconditionally, and we live within a set of parameters of honesty, respect, and love—and we will be as close to perfection as we can get. Bad things do happen to good people and there are no set answers. Your own conscience must be your guide.

Fundamentally I am in a much better, happier place today than I was four years ago. I took the best of my Irish upbringing and heritage and kept what is relevant and what works for me. I recognize that the

Catholic Church has many wonderful things but it too is flawed. It is man-made and man-governed and as a result it could never be perfect.

The gift of a strong cultural influence gives you a road map that is helpful. However, our roads can sometimes take unexpected paths that may not be on the map. We are constantly evolving and regrouping. Being Irish gave me the confidence to know that I would be all right, although with one caveat—I had to work at being all right. Even though I identified so much with being a wife and a mother for most of my life, things shifted dramatically and I needed to shift my view from perfection to acceptance of what is. We are part of a group and we are individual, independent human beings who must take care of ourselves in our own ways.

That is what being Irish gives you: the courage to steer through the turns and know that somehow you will come out all right and even better for the journey.

Barbara Campbell

The dictionary defines charisma as "a special personal quality or power of an individual making him capable of influencing or inspiring large numbers of people." Barbara Campbell not only has charisma but she ties it to her love of her native Ireland through her work at Fragrances of Ireland.

Barbara's career in marketing took her first to Japan where she honed her business skills. A longing for home brought her back to Ireland where she found a career with Fragrances of Ireland. As a spokesperson on QVC, Barbara has an uncanny ability to use television to inspire people to try the Fragrances of Ireland line of perfumes. Through the power of storytelling, which creates a sincere connection with the audience, Barbara reaches out to uplift and make people happy. Barbara lives the core values of her company's corporate mission statement by "promoting an understanding that we are all connected by seas, by ocean, by dreams and we should all strive to make a better world." Now that is charisma.

Barbara's Story: What's In a Name?

My mother's maiden name is Sex. Really. During her childhood and well into her teenage years she had no clue whatsoever what it meant as sex was certainly not something discussed in the staunchly Catholic Ireland of the 1950s and 60s. My mum did not even know what a lesbian was until the eighties. As if that weren't bad enough, in high school my mother's best friend's name was Mary Hoare. H-O-A-R-E. They were teased relentlessly in school and berated daily by the nuns due to their surnames, although they had no idea why.

When Mom started looking for a job she used to get called for interviews all the time. After a while she figured out it was mainly because they wanted to meet this woman who said her surname was Sex.

Break the Mold

My mother was a bit of a mold breaker, and she taught me to have the courage to ask for what I wanted. When Mum married my father she was required—by law—to give up her job. Women were not allowed to work in civil service after they got married and she thought this was ridiculous. The laws began to change during my mother's time, only thirty years ago in the 1980s.

My mother was good at her job and her managing director did not want to lose her after she had children so he made some changes in how he ran his office. He allowed her to bring her baby to work packed up in a Moses basket. Like everyone else back then the boss was a heavy smoker. Mum politely told him to quit smoking when the baby was in the office. She declared, "If you want me here then you can't smoke around the baby." So the boss took to smoking by an open window.

Being the only mother in the neighborhood who worked caused quite a stir. Because she worked and had some financial independence, Mum had the means to go on trips to London to visit her sister twice a year—and she purchased her own car. This was considered scandalous in our neighborhood and the male neighbors were in an uproar.

One day the head of household from across the street rang our doorbell to speak to my dad. He said, "It is setting the wrong tone for our neighborhood to buy your wife a car. Soon all the women on the block will want one!" My dad laughed and said, "Well, I didn't buy it for her. She bought it herself. So if you want to talk to my wife and tell her she has to give it back, go ahead, but I don't fancy your chances."

Don't Be Afraid to Change the Rules

I learned from my mother that you do not have to accept the status quo. Sometimes the rules need to change for the greater good. When I became a working mother, my job required me to travel to the United States several times a year for my visits to QVC. I advised my boss that my intention was to breastfeed my daughter for one year. I declared, "If you want me to travel to America I will have to bring someone with me so that I can feed my daughter." The response from my boss was, "That will be fine!" Many of my friends were flabbergasted that I had the audacity to ask for this accommodation. But I told them that the worst that could happen is that they would say no. The best was that I could take my children with me when I travel, which I still do to this day.

When I graduated from college I was presented with an opportunity to move to Japan to work as a brand manager for Wedgwood. I jumped at the chance to go and experience the world. I lived in Japan for four years. I was dating my husband-to-be, even though he lived in Ireland. I had a wonderful job and I enjoyed living in and exploring Japan, but I realized that the long distance relationship was taking its toll. I returned home and began working for Fragrances of Ireland, which is an independent fragrance house which was looking for someone to develop its international markets. This was the perfect role for me—an opportunity to feed my travel bug while still keeping my home in Ireland.

The best part of working for a small company is the ability to try new things. We can identify opportunities or issues and act quickly; there is no bureaucracy. We work as a team to find creative solutions and develop our business. This is so rewarding because I feel likeI have been part of all the company's achievements.

Typically Ireland is not known as a player in the perfume industry. France controls the market for the industry. Many companies come out with three or four new perfumes a year. That is not Fragrances of Ireland's strategy. We have core quality products that we market strategically around the globe. One of our biggest US customers is QVC.

The first time I went on the air for QVC was unplanned. I had gone with our managing director to Pennsylvania with the intention of learning the ropes for the next show. When the time came for our product Inis to go on air the producer realized that my boss and the host were both men, and it was not going to be effective to have two men talking about Irish women's perfume. I was working behind the scenes when they approached me and told me I was going on the air. I was wearing jeans and a green sweater for Saint Patrick's Day. I had not bothered to do much with my hair that day.

I was in the makeup chair getting ready when the makeup artist told me, "We really can't do anything with your hair." My curly hair is pretty manageable when it is clean but on day two there are very few options. So I had to go on the air just the way it was. Wild curls and all.

Within forty minutes I went from being an observer to being in front of thirty million viewers on national television talking about Inis perfume. I told my own story. I spoke about what the product meant to me, that when I spray on Inis I feel like the sun is shining on me. No matter how dark the day, whether the weather is gloomy or how far from the ocean I am, my perfume Inis lifts me out of the darkness.

Be True to How You Feel

The key to being successful on QVC is being authentic and telling a story that conveys not what you think but how you feel. The stories I tell take the audience with me back to Ireland.

In spite of the lack of training, time, clothing, and hairstyle, my first attempt at selling on QVC was a great success. I received several lovely e-mails from customers telling me their stories and connecting with me personally. Afterward the buyer asked me if I had any formal training and I told him no. He said, "Well, don't change anything!" I am lucky that I work with a product that I love and that resonates with me.

Over the years the e-mails have continued to pour in and I have had the opportunity to connect with customers on a personal level. Sometimes I send out little samples for customers who have had a difficult time, such as losing a husband or losing a job. They e-mail me back and let me know how they are doing. QVC allows me to have a direct relationship with the customer. I have even had several customers come visit me during a trip to Ireland.

One of my favorite customers is an amazing woman who set up a clinic in Africa. Her mission is to provide African women with basic medical care, particularly after childbirth when the simplest of infections can be fatal. Fragrances of Ireland supports her and her organization with products not only for fund-raisers but also for patients themselves. She feels these small gifts of lotions and gels have a positive effect on women's emotional well-being as they enjoy smelling fresh and feeling energized. I feel privileged to assist in such a simple way yet support such incredible work.

Remember Your Civic Pride

One of the things I love about being Irish is that there is a sense of community. I don't know what it's like to be any other nationality but I'm proud that we fought long and hard for our independence, even as recently as just a few years ago. We respect and know what independence means to our society. My own great-grandfather lost his life when the Black and Tans put a bullet in his back. He owned a butcher shop in Dublin City Center on Moore Street. The Black and Tans were First World War veterans who were recruited to come to Ireland as a temporary police force in Ireland during the 1920s and were infamous for their cruelty. One morning the Black and Tans arrived on Moore Street, where one of my grandfather's customers had left her baby outside in a pram. My grandfather went outside to rescue the infant and was shot by a member of the Black and Tans—in the back.

It is a simple fact of Ireland's past that people gave their lives for freedom and it has continued even in recent history. As a result, rights that protect our freedom have a very different meaning to the Irish than they do to Americans. People have lost their lives for the opportunity to vote. Our history of conflict and struggle makes the right to vote a duty and responsibility. I will make every effort to work my schedule around any election day—such as the presidential elections in October 2011. I took a later flight to the US to ensure I could vote that morning.

Our community celebrates. We celebrate life and celebrate death. Whether it's a wedding or a wake, it begins around one in the afternoon and ends the next morning—or even later. At a wake everyone comes together and we tell stories about the departed for two or three days. Through the music and storytelling our people fill the holes left in their lives when someone dies, or welcome newcomers when someone marries. We unite and share in the knowledge that we'll all muddle through this and it will all be grand, again, someday.

Somehow it is.

Melanie Fitzpatrick

It's been said that a person's identity is not something one finds, but something one creates. The desire to belong—to know who we are— is something that all human beings instinctively share. For many of us, the journey is short. We naturally are drawn to the culture, the community in which we were born.

However, for some of us the road is a winding one. Growing up with red hair and freckles, Melanie Fitzpatrick was often asked if she had Irish blood. She didn't, though she longed to. Her image in the mirror reflected her own truth: that her place was among the lively, proud Irish people.

Her birth name may have been the exact opposite of Irish— Smith—but what did a name matter when she felt her blood flowed green? During her own journey, Melanie sought to forge her own identity, reflecting often on the power of name and the sense of belonging. Ultimately, through the marriage to her own Irish charmer, Melanie finally began to feel at home in her adopted culture.

Melanie's Story: Growing Up Smith

While growing up in the 1960s and 70s with the last name of Smith, I felt as common as the Cape Cod style houses that filled our suburban Connecticut neighborhood. As the most popular surname in America and England, Smith topped the charts of English surnames. You needed to look no farther than our phone book to see this exemplified. The Smiths in my town of Enfield consumed no less than six full pages of that giant residential data base that sat next to every phone in America.

With that many Smiths in town, it was routine to receive "wrong numbers" and in school we got a special chiding from fellow wisecracking students who were occasionally inclined to make fun of our last name. Though I had to draw the line in high school when my brother's friends began calling me Smitty. This was his nickname, not mine, most certainly because my uncle had named his hunting dog Smitty. I found myself exasperated in college when guys in bars would ask for my last name and then exclaim, "Yeah, right," in disbelief when I answered Smith—as if I was intentionally withholding my real name.

The teasing was something I could handle while growing up, however, what bothered me more was this cultural identity as a Smith and the lack of heritage that seemed to come with it. I wanted to belong to something that was connected to our nationality. It was apparent we were an abundant group with a long history going back thousands of years, but how did we celebrate who we were? When I asked my father what nationality we were he would proudly announce, "We're Yankees!" While I appreciated my father's pride at being a New Englander, his response did nothing to fill the sense of a cultural vacancy growing within me.

We were a part of a big Catholic population and our neighbors were mainly Polish. In spite of both parents having roots from England

and Quebec, there were not a lot of celebrations going on at their cultural crossroads. When we moved from Vermont to Connecticut during the mid-1960s, my parents latched on to our Polish neighbors and we often went to their Polish American clubs for special cultural events and celebrations. The Polish celebrations were lively, but they did not resonate with me and actually left me feeling that as a family, we were a bit culturally dysfunctional. I knew this was not my tribe yet I longed to belong somewhere.

As the only child out of six to be blessed with coppery red hair and freckles, I was often mistaken for being Irish. My mother and grandmothers enjoyed dressing me in doll-like, kelly-green dresses to emphasize this resemblance. Nicknames like Strawberry Shortcake and Carrot Top were endearments echoed by neighbors and family alike. I secretly enjoyed this attention and never denied it when mistaken for being a little Irish colleen.

I embraced this gift as a special way of being identified, because in many ways this was essential to my own need to find out who I was and what that could mean in the world outside my large first family.

My exposure to Irish ways grew when I moved away to college in western Pennsylvania. I formed a special relationship with the Dorans, who lived north of Pittsburgh and welcomed me into their family. I celebrated many holidays with them and felt the rich pride and traditions of the Irish, experiencing traditional foods and music. I began to feel a sense of connectedness to Ireland; it was an ancient country with a rich and complex history. I loved its sad stories expressed through tender ballads and raucous foot-stomping melodies, and I found the folklore enchanting. I admired the Irish fight to keep their own identity and independence under the constraints of an oppressive ruler, and I related to their attempts to prosper and develop into a first-world nation.

I understood what it meant to fight for your own destiny, your own path, because I was finding it difficult to find viable employment that was meaningful and fulfilling at the same time. I often felt like Ireland as I navigated through my own life as a performing artist during the 1980s. The constant emotional roller coaster of preparing for auditions, waiting alongside my competition, and the heartache of hoping against hope for a callback were beginning to take too much toll on me. The woman I wanted to become was in here somewhere; I had seen glimpses of her and was waiting for her to be revealed.

Life was a struggle for me in my twenties. I was determined to feel good about who I was and my acting career, but I was beginning to fear that my dream of becoming an accomplished performing artist was more of a struggle than I could withstand. Being an artist was a perfect expression of my passion and purpose but the industry was brutal and eventually the negative messages and lack of income growth drove me to put my acting ambitions aside for the moment and to take a "real world" job, as I referred to it back then.

One day while I was waitressing, a customer asked me if I had ever thought about going into sales. I had not, but her question intrigued me. I had learned how to promote myself during my endless auditions and I certainly learned about rejection, so I figured I'd give it a shot. Though this was not as glamorous as my acting career, I needed to find value in my life and create a sense of validation. The plan worked because I was good at sales and was financially successful within a few years. The feedback was positive and I began to have a new vision of my future.

Marrying Irish

As my career took off, I felt that longing surface again and this time it was for someone special to be a part of my life. I was definitely attracted to men who were tall, dark, and handsome. They were attracted to me, the small redheaded spitfire that I was, but it wasn't until my mid-thirties that I met the man of my dreams: a tall, dark, handsome . . . Irish man. A kilt-wearing Fitzpatrick to be sure. My Celtic dream was coming true.

While I was attracted to Dave's wholesome good looks, it was his Irish charisma that ultimately won me over. We also shared similar hobbies like photography and skiing. As we got to know each other better he became quite the romantic and championed most of my interests. I was an avid rock climber and Dave bought equipment and came with me. I had a mountain bike so he began coming with me on bike outings. We could talk for hours on all topics including spirituality. He was honest. He listened to me and genuinely wanted me to be happy. I knew he was special.

We were highly compatible and viewed each other as equals and most assuredly we shared the same love for Ireland. Some of our earliest dates were to the annual Irish Festival in Pittsburgh. We loved the spirited festival atmosphere and the camaraderie of folks proudly displaying their clan flags and shields. We would easily find ourselves dancing and singing to the lively bands from Ireland. My favorite thing to do was to dip under the big tent and shop amongst the multitudes of vendors selling their Irish-inspired goods.

The first Irish festival we attended after we were married, I found a lovely young woman selling handmade christening gowns. I was gifted a family christening gown from my mom, a little white dress that she used for all six of her children and most of her grandchildren's christenings. These handmade christening gowns, though, were something else. They were made out of silk shantung fabric, tinted to a soft champagne hue, with puffy cap sleeves and a broad square yoke that lay across the bodice, while delicately embroidered florets cascaded down the length of the gown. The most extraordinary feature, however, was their length; they were between 36 and 46 inches long. They were exquisite and I knew that I had to have one for the baby we were dreaming about.

I asked the vendor if they were just for baby girls and she told me a story how Irish mothers would disguise their newborn baby boys in long gowns to fool the fairies into thinking they were girls. As folklore tells it, fairies would steal baby boys without the family knowing and insert a changeling—a look-alike baby—who would either die or disappear a year later.

While this was an intriguing tale—albeit a little creepy—I found myself buying the gown and matching bonnet anyway. We set the marketplace abuzz with chatter because we were buying a christening gown and were not yet expecting. At this moment we knew we were calling in our baby boy, and we departed the festival with a smile in our hearts. Eleven months later we were blessed with a baby boy with fiery red hair and penetrating blue eyes. Another Irish dream came true with the arrival of baby Pierce, the perfect manifestation of God's love and cocreating partners. The feeling of belonging was born in my life; an identity had taken shape for me and for the direction of my life. I wondered, "What's in a name?" Can a name change your life?

Irish Visit

It wasn't until I went to Ireland in 2007 that I felt like my soul was coming home. Riding the western countryside on bicycles with my mom, sisters, and girlfriends, my heart swelled at the lush green hills and the valleys dotted with rocky outcroppings. We delighted at the sight of well-fed cattle lazing about and fluffy fat sheep bleating as we cycled past them and observed the curious colored markings on their backsides.

Rain fell every day and more than once we were completely soaked. I discovered what I was made of, cycling for miles and miles in the cold, drizzly rain. My teeth chattered and I longed to be in a warm bed. Instead I learned perseverance. I was amazed to realize that I had the drive and Zen-like focus to tough it out through being soaked and lost on the barren roads of the Burren Way. When all I could summon from my near-empty reserve was a steely focus, I became one with my bike and the road. I imagined what it must have been like for the Irish people, who for so many generations have survived much harder challenges. In the face of so much adversity, rising to the occasion and willing themselves to survive was the only thing in their power to do.

The Irish have learned to prosper despite loss of land, famine, countless battles for independence, immigrating to America, and losing their loved ones. When you meet the Irish, you notice a strong, fiery spirit so deeply connected to their faith and souls that it transcends their battles. It is this spirit, more than the beauty of their land or their incredible history that leaves the biggest impression. I am humbled by this and have used it as inspiration to complete my own journey today, soggy or not.

Ireland is known as a mythic country, a land that remains "in the mist" and "between the worlds," where fairies still inhabit the fairy circles and druids continue to practice their rituals in the remote regions of the island. Experiencing the people and music firsthand was as delicious as the brown bread, hearty soups, and beer we enjoyed every day in the pubs.

One Sunday afternoon we rode to the Half Barrel for lunch and found the place full of families enjoying time together over a meal, a pint, and watching Hurling, their favorite sporting match on the telly. I witnessed this familiar scene at another pub we ventured into on a Saturday night where families, friends and strangers sang their hearts out to traditional Irish songs performed by a local band. In Doolin, a small western coastal town that is home to many musical pubs, I was thrilled to find Fitz's Bar, where one could enjoy a pint of Smithwick's, pronounced by the locals as *Smidicks*. My girlfriends and I marveled at how uncanny it was that a Smith girl who is now a Fitzpatrick was having a Smithwick's beer at Fitz's Bar.

Here it was again, these names I am eternally connected with, revealing just how intertwined they are by forming circles around each other like a Celtic knot; continually looping and weaving a mysterious design throughout my life.

On our second night I had an exciting encounter as our group was checking into our hotel in Portumna. I met Elaine Fitzpatrick, the hotel clerk, who was elated to be meeting a Fitzpatrick from America. It was like she was welcoming me back home. She was a plain gal with dark eyes and hair and just as genuine as can be. She proceeded to educate me on the history of our shared name. I could tell this was important for her so I listened intently.

She shared that the surname Fitzpatrick is a translation from Phadraig, pronounced fa-drage. Giolla Phádraig apparently was a devoted follower of Saint Patrick. He was the King of Ossory, a kingdom in Leinster, and held reign from 976 AD until he was slain in 996 AD. When England began to rule over Ireland they anglicized Phadraig to Fitzpatrick. The Fitz prefix being of true Irish origin is a distinct source of pride for the Fitzpatricks and especially their direct association with Saint Patrick. Today the Fitzpatricks hail from the town of Kilkenny.

On our only day off from biking, we ferried to the largest of the Aran Islands, located just off the western coast of Ireland and docked on the shores of Inishmore. There the local economy is still sustained by the fishing industry and their famous handmade wool sweaters. This seemed like the perfect place to buy gifts for my boys so I set out to procure a sweater or two.

The pattern selection was vast and as a knitter myself, I wanted to understand the beauty and complexity of each pattern. At some point in history each clan had created a distinct pattern symbolizing their name. Wives and mothers knitted their clan pattern into the sweaters for their men to wear at sea. Fishing on the fierce Atlantic Ocean could be dangerous and if a fishing boat were to capsize, the sweater worn by a fisherman drowned at sea might be the only way they could identify their man. While I was not in danger of losing my man to the Atlantic Ocean, I went in search for the Fitzpatrick sweater. I was not successful in finding my husband's size, but I did take note of the Fitzpatrick pattern and meaning; vertical panels of alternating moss-filled diamond stitches and blackberry popcorn stitches. The diamonds represented wealth while the blackberry stitch symbolized the Holy Trinity.

Our trip concluded in Galway, a beautiful city displaying old world charm coupled with a thriving commerce. I found promising signs all throughout Ireland. She had changed in the last decade; grown up to make a name for herself, the economy was flourishing and a re-invention had occurred. When you cultivate a belief in yourself, you can drive the change you need for transformation. It is only by finding or reconnecting to our passion that we live a life with purpose and can actively make our dreams come true. I believe that this is possible at any age or phase in life. If you love life and are a survivor you will do it—just look at Ireland.

Something still lingers in the back of my mind, though. When my husband was courting me, we made a trip to England, Wales, and Scotland, and he had promised me that there was a Fitzpatrick castle somewhere in the Emerald Isle. I have faith that someday we will return to Ireland together and visit Kilkenny. Maybe we will even find that family castle he claims is in his family line. A girl can dream, can't she? Ah, Ireland, the land of dreams and charming dreamers.

Imelda McGratten

Vacation is a time to relax and contemplate the future. It is when we reenergize and spend time with family. For most of us vacation is when for a fleeting moment we dream of a better life. How many times have you thought to yourself, "If only I could live in this vacation paradise?"

Imelda McGratten, with her husband and five children, did just that. Turning a vacation in Dingle into a home for her family and children, Imelda left Belfast where she had raised her kids and completely changed her life for the better.

Imelda's Story: The Freedom to Choose

The most important thing in life is freedom. I came to that belief after turning my family's world upside down.

I was married at eighteen and lived with my husband and five children—Joseph, Christine, Aisling, Peter, and Grace—in Belfast until 2002. That's when we decided to go on holiday to Dingle and chose, completely on a whim, to stay there.

Where we lived in Belfast, Andersonstown, was a relatively quiet Catholic community. But in spite of the relative quiet of our neighborhood, I became used to the subtle unrest that could become volatile. Riots with the British soldiers and police in nearby neighborhoods were commonplace.

I was afraid to let my children out of my house, yet this was an everyday fact of life. I longed to live in a community where the neighbors would interact, where we could have a normal life without worrying about politics.

It is amazing what people begin to accept as "normal." I just wanted peace. My family was not interested in politics. It was only when I took the leap of faith to relocate my family to Dingle that I realized that "normal" is relative and that there are other ways to live.

Our 2002 summer vacation to Dingle changed our lives forever. The stark contrast from Belfast made us sigh with relief. My children spent the days free, roaming around the little town and swimming in the ocean. I enjoyed the seascape, clean air, the lovely view from the mountain top, and most importantly, the peace. Gone was the hidden worry that lurked in the back of my mind like an annoying gnat, coming out every time my kids were out of sight. Here we could be free.

As our vacation was coming to an end the voice inside me grew louder, saying, "Don't go back!" I trust my gut, and finally I said these words aloud to my husband. He turned to me and replied, "I think you are right."

And that was that. We didn't have jobs or a real plan. But we knew it was the right thing to do. We were moving to Dingle.

My husband returned to Belfast to sell the house. Ironically I had been cleaning and boxing up items to put in storage as my kids had grown, which made the move to Dingle a simpler transition. We sold the house.

My brother owned a lease on a bar called Barrack Heights on John Street, in Dingle. It was not working out for him. Some people are designed to be in front of the bar and some are designed to be behind it. My brother and I both knew he was the latter. I knew nothing about running a bar but I knew a lot about creating opportunity so I offered to run the bar for him. He accepted. It became a family business. Believing in the power and value of a handshake and the loyalty of family, we did not discuss or negotiate contracts or agreements. We focused on opportunity. My husband and eldest son help me run it. We created a family atmosphere and before long started turning a profit.

There is an old saying that charm is a sort of bloom on a woman. If you have it you don't have to have anything else; if you don't, it doesn't really matter what else you have. I have been told that I have it and my success running the bar proved it.

I suppose I could walk with kings and paupers and never feel out of place. Our bar became home to the people of Dingle. Our bar was not a tourist bar. It was for the farmers and the locals looking for friendly faces and conversation. I got to know everyone. I remembered what they liked and I asked about their families. I put a bit of sunshine in their day. It brought them back time after time.

The more successful the bar became, the more challenging the working relationship became with my brother and his wife. It appeared that my family's success had created jealousy and anger with them. In the forthcoming months the vision of how the business would evolve was completely different in both our heads and only through the unrest did that become apparent. Communication was difficult between us and behind the scenes became unbearable. There was too much bickering and I decided that it was time for me to walk away. I gave him back the keys and realized for the first time in my life that to walk away is not always a sign of defeat. Sometimes it is an acknowledgement that one has done all one can do.

The bar was never the same. To this day it has been handed over year after year to different managers. Yet they can't create that family atmosphere that attracts the local folks. They can't seem to find the charm that is needed to bring their customers back.

I learned so much from this experience. I recognized that there are times in life where you must walk away. Whether it's to create a safe place to raise children or to work in an environment where you are appreciated and respected, sometimes walking away is mandatory. Walking away from what no longer works for you frees up space in your life for new and better opportunities to come to you.

As luck would have it a call center moved to Dingle and I applied for a job. I got the position on the spot and thanks to my work ethic and that almighty ability to make customers feel like kings I was promoted to manager and supervised over fifty employees.

My gamble of relocating our family during a vacation has paid off. My children have achieved the dreams I had for them. Even more important is that in Dingle they learned to dream for themselves. It may not have been the case if we stayed in Belfast. They are an inspiration and through them I have learned to take bigger risks and truly live my life. I have learned that you can never turn your back on opportunities.

A Higher Level

My children are wise beyond their years. They have as much knowledge now as I have at the age of forty-five. I wonder how far they will have evolved by the time they get to be my age. Will their thinking be at a higher level? They have worked out life wisdom twenty years earlier than I did. That's what every family should be doing with each new generation—moving to a higher level, especially in communication.

My journey has taught me that if I'm not happy I need to find out what makes me happy. I'm a simple woman because I'm content with the little things in life. Especially giving—giving is what makes me happy.

One constant that brings me joy is my writing. The heart never changes. When I write something it comes from the heart. I know that I am not the only person who has walked my journey. Others have gone through my challenges and everyone has challenges of their own. My mum always told me, "It will come to pass. Don't take it too seriously, it'll all come to pass, it's just a matter of time."

When I write, I experiment with different perspectives, which helps me overcome negativity and find a balance. Finding beauty and grace in our lives is what matters most. Last year my eldest son, Joseph, took me on a trip to Asia. After coming home I wrote this poem about my home.

Dingle Bay

There's just something about going home
No matter where in the world I roam
My heart is tied to this one place
And the picture in my head I can't erase
I follow that road, the Lispole Straight
And I know when I get to Ballintaggart's gate
I cast my eyes to the left for into sight
Is the scene that fills my heart with delight
The Atlantic Ocean at the mouth of Dingle Bay
The Skelligs Hotel, Burnham, The Marina and Funghi some days
Beautiful Dingle nestled quietly by the Sea
And each time I see it, it's like the first time for me!

There are few things in life that you see every day that are so beautiful that it's like seeing it for the first time. The view of Dingle Bay is that for me. Its charm brings me back.

I'm most proud of accomplishing the little things in life. I am proud to say that I have lived my life with grace and style. I married young; I have five wonderful kids and a grandson. I always kept a peaceful home and worked most of my life, sharing all my experiences with my children.

I took a big leap of faith in moving to Dingle. That's how it is when you go through something life-changing. At the time when you're going through it, it's hard to see the light at the end of the tunnel. But at least if there's a glimpse and you know that somebody else has come through it, then that gives you hope. And that's the only thing we can have in life . . . hope.

Chapter Eight

Irish Artistry

*I*reland is a spectacularly beautiful country, full of green rolling hills, ancient gray stone castles, dramatic cliffs, and ocean vistas. Full of riotous color in some places and hauntingly serene mists in another, it is no wonder that Ireland is a land of dreamers and artists.

Being able to see beauty then recreate it in art, music, or story requires another gift that is abundant among the Irish, the gift of imagination. No one enjoys a good story more than an Irishman, and the ability to spin a good yarn seems present at birth. Ireland is world-renowned for the writers who have called it home—including W. B. Yeats, G. Bernard Shaw, Oscar Wilde, Jonathan Swift, Brendan Behan, and James Joyce, to name just a few.

The Irish artist has much to draw from when sharing Ireland's beauty with the world. In this chapter we introduce you to Regina Lowrey Adducci, who started playing piano on her kitchen table and ended by making stained glass windows, because art is art wherever it is found; Rachel Arbuckle, who made a business out of turning Irish legends into art and money; and Ann Montieth, who turned her passion for photography into a way to help other photographers succeed and preserve the beauty of Ireland for generations to come.

Regina Lowrey Adducci

Art is a connection to God and a sharing of the soul messages with the world. There is art in creating beautiful music, paintings, and even windows. There is also art in creating a beautiful life, a life that touches many with a quiet gift of acceptance, grace, and most of all, love.

Regina Lowrey Adducci brought her gifts of art and music to the world and shared them with many. Among the many outlets for her talents was a business devoted to creating spectacular stained glass windows. Regina, a masterful artist, always had a knack for creating a sanctuary of peace for everyone who knew her.

Regina's Story: A Piano for My Birthday

It was a cold winter's day in Penrose, Colorado, in 1943. I was living with my grandparents because Mom and Dad were working in Denver. There was not enough time to work and take care of me and my sisters so we stayed behind in Penrose until our family got back on our feet and they could send for us.

I lived the carefree life of a much-loved child, and like many children, I had my dreams. I wanted a piano with all my heart. I dreamed of the songs I would play and the melodies I would write that would fill our little two-bedroom farmhouse with joy.

Maybe today, my seventh birthday, will be the day, I had thought. I dressed slowly that morning in my best dress, a lovely blue dress with yellow flowers on the collar. I laced up my black Mary Janes and used my black marker to fill in the scuff marks. I brushed and braided my curly brown hair while I waited to hear something from downstairs. Maybe Grandma and Papa would accidentally bang on the piano keys as they moved it into the little nook between the kitchen and the bedroom; the perfect place for me to play and entertain the family with all my new songs. Not a sound came from the kitchen and I finally got restless and headed downstairs.

My sister Jackie greeted me with a crooked grin. "Where are you headed so spiffy this morning Sissy? Oh yeah, it is your birthday!"

I looked around the room for the piano but just as it was so many mornings before, there was no piano—just an empty space where one belonged.

When Grandma came out of her room, I saw that she had a thin package behind her back. She began singing "Happy Birthday" and my sisters Jackie and Pat joined in. Our little house was so full of people and so little space. I positioned myself at the head of the long wooden kitchen table waiting to see my lot. Maybe it would be something special after all. I was too excited to give up hope for a good birthday. As Grandma passed the package to me I slowly unwrapped the twine and brown paper to find a book inside. The title was *How to Play Piano*.

At first I thought, *What a cruel joke. How can I learn when I have nothing to play?* But remembering my manners I thanked Grandma for the book and started leafing through it.

The next morning I had an idea. If we could not afford a piano, I would just have to make one. I got out my chalk and while everyone was asleep on Saturday morning I drew the keys of the piano on the kitchen table. It looked exactly like the keys on the cover of the book. By the time everyone was awake, I had taught myself the first three songs in the book. It did not matter to me if others could hear the notes—I heard them in my head.

A few months went by. One day I went into town with my grandfather and in the window of the general store I saw an advertisement for a piano competition at the elementary school in Penrose. I begged Papa to let me join. He explained, "Sissy, you don't know how to play. You don't have a piano!"

"Yes I do," I replied, "You just can't hear it—but I can!" I am not sure why but Papa let me enter the contest. I sat at the kitchen table and practiced my music every day.

When it was time for the competition, I arrived at the auditorium early, all dressed up and ready to go. I sat at the real piano and began to play the notes. This time the audience could hear me. To the surprise and shock of my grandparents, I won first place in the competition. I was the star.

I often wonder why Papa let me enter that contest. I think it was due to his own work ethic that he learned from his immigrant parents. They had to work hard to make a life for themselves in America. They worked hard to reach their dreams. Perhaps Papa respected my passion and admired my hard work in practicing the piano I fashioned for myself. Hard work was always a part of my upbringing. Hard work and appreciation of family is what my grandparents taught me.

Move to Denver

About a year after the piano competition I moved to Denver to join my parents. My mother and father worked odd jobs in Denver and it was time for us to try to be a family there. There was only one problem. The school in Denver would not let me attend. I had a terrible case of eczema and my skin was blotchy and dry. The principal thought I was contagious and informed my parents I was not allowed to attend classes. I knew what it was like to feel isolated, different, and unaccepted. I decided that I would never let anyone feel that way in my presence.

Having nowhere else to go, I stayed every day with my Aunt Lucille "Cody" Workman. She was 100 percent Irish and she was a joy in my life. Having no children of her own, Lucille thought of me as her daughter. Lucille taught me how to cook, studied with me, and gave me the most precious gifts of all—her time and her love.

Artistic Gifts

I guess you could say I was gifted artistically. I could draw and as I grew up I found that I saw colors and shapes differently than other people. I also loved meeting new people and learning about cultures and what made people tick. I incorporated all my life experiences—the people I met, the places I went and the colors I saw—into my art. After marrying the love of my life, Joseph Adducci, and starting a family, I found an opportunity to use my artistic skills to make some extra money. I started drawing advertisements for stores. Owners of a dress shop hired me to draw ads for their dresses. My four children often sat around me with their colors and paper, drawing their own creations while I worked.

I did a little bit of anything related to art and food—decorating wedding cakes, catering parties. Eventually I was drawn to the stained glass business. I drew my own designs and I loved the process of bringing them to life in glass.

I always had a love for flowers and incorporated flowers into every design. Whether it was a religious figure, a geisha girl, or a window, flowers were always hidden in my pieces. Flowers bring beauty and grace to the world. They also teach people how to live. Shine in your beauty during your short time on earth.

Amazing Grace

My husband, Joe, and I created a loving, busy home for our kids. Joe was the rock of stability. As an accountant he was reliable and steady. I was always coming up with new ideas to work using my talents and still be home for the kids. When the kids were off in college I turned our sunroom into a stained glass studio. Joe helped me every step of the way. I never studied stained glass—or art for that matter. I just knew I could do it, just like I knew I could play the piano even though I didn't have one. I could pick up on artistic creativity pretty quickly. Joe lovingly referred to me as "Amazing Grace!"

My home was a place of refuge and comfort for many. Everyone was welcome. The more mouths to feed, the more to celebrate. When my daughter Pam went off to college she met her best friend, Tricia. Tricia was homesick for Texas and her close family. Pam and Tricia came to our house most weekends and every holiday, and Tricia became another member of our family. She even stayed with me when Pam was off doing her own things. Tricia graduated and moved to Germany and I went to visit her there during a family trip to Italy. People who need each other become family and remain connected throughout their lives. It is important to keep your own family as well as create a new one with the people God puts in your path.

One of my pet peeves was judgment of others. I had no place for it and I raised my children to be tolerant, accepting and giving. During the 1980s I had a good friend in the art business who was gay. He had a lot of trouble fitting in. The outside world judged him for his choices. The Church condemned him. I simply chose to love and embrace him. He became a lifelong confidant and friend and part of my extended family. We even went to an art class together in Arizona and shared a hotel room. Talk about scandal. My husband Joe and I just laughed about the sheer ridiculousness of some people.

Battle with Breast Cancer

When I was in my early sixties I was diagnosed with breast cancer. I knew I had it for a while and the fear of the diagnosis held me back from going to the doctor. I was having such a good life. My children were raised, my stained glass window business was thriving. Joe and I were traveling together and finally we thought we would have time for retirement. But that was not in God's plan. My time was less than I thought it would be.

Still I put up a valiant fight and I was strong for my children and my grandchildren. I wanted them to know me even if I would not be here physically. My little granddaughter, Francesca, was just three years old when my time was coming to an end. I wanted to give her a gift that would remind her of me and last a lifetime; one that she could share with her own granddaughters. I bought her the boxed set of the Shirley Temple movies from my day. Like me, she loved music, to sing and dance, and this way I would pass on my love for art, music, family and adventure down to her. It was a perfect way to say hello and good-bye at the same time.

Good-bye, Regina

On November 21, 2000, Regina Lowrey Adducci lost her battle with cancer and passed away. Her daughter Pam Adducci DeCarlo remembers the impact her mother had on everyone she met, including her granddaughter, Francesca.

Losing my mom was one of the hardest things I've ever gone through. I thought she would live forever. She was so full of life and had so much to give the world. During her illness she never complained; she never made it about her. She took her painful treatments with strength and dignity. She still traveled in between and she celebrated her grandchildren and her life by being involved with them until the very end. She taught my brother Joey the stained glass business and asked him to take it over so she could leave a legacy.

Regina was loved and celebrated throughout Colorado. Her windows grace many a church and institution in our state. More importantly, though, are the memories of her and the love and support she brought to everyone she met. To this day, my brother gets calls from people remembering our mom and her kindness and grace. He keeps her memory alive by running her business and using the skills he learned from her.

Francesca cherished the Shirley Temple movies and watched them frequently. When Francesca started first grade just a year after my mom passed, the teacher asked me if I had ever thought of putting Francesca in musical theater. He said, "She would be a natural." Francesca found a natural affinity for musical theater and has performed in eighteen musicals, nine leads and one professional show, all since she was just five years old.

I often think of my mother's story about the piano she drew on the kitchen table. She passed her love of art and music to my daughter. The gift she shared with Francesca just before she died made an impact that will last a lifetime. Every time Francesca sings a note, takes a dance step, or recites the words of a play, I think of my mother. I know she is watching over us, sketching flowers, humming a tune, and sending us love from heaven.

My mother knew the secret of being an immigrant in a new country. She embraced the best of everyone. She celebrated her children, her family, and her talents and shared them with the world. Mom learned from her Austrian grandfather and her Irish aunt that life was precious and the connection to people is what makes it worthwhile. No one ever said life would be easy. Yet keeping faith, working hard, loving all those you can, and sharing your life with others is what makes it worthwhile. That is what being Irish all is about.

Rachel Arbuckle

Ever since she was a young child, Rachel Arbuckle's active imagination created images in her mind. She found inspiration for her unique designs in Irish history and the art of the ancient Celts.

She was thrilled when she discovered she could combine her love of making art with a career. Rachel's love of art and her good business sense allowed her to create a business around her talent. Today her art is celebrated around the world.

Rachel's Story: Interest in Art

As a young girl in Dublin in the 1970s there was plenty of history and storytelling that shaped my interest in art. I had an active imagination and a fascination with Irish folklore and mythology; in school I read about Irish legends like Queen Maeve and Finn McCool. But while other kids just read the books, I'd create images and scenes for all the characters in my head. Naturally, I began to draw, paint, and record my own creations.

In 1979 Dublin Corporation began the construction of the new Dublin City Council's office in Wood Quay. As they started to dig, they found a huge archaeological site—a real Viking city was discovered in Dublin. The archeological discoveries created a big public campaign to halt the construction of the new buildings. Instead the owners granted a short window of time for the site to be excavated. All the underground treasures that could be found were given to the National Museum of Ireland. To the horror of many a historian, the rest was covered up with concrete. Although I was a young girl, I remember the protests and the people on the streets trying to protect the remnants of the Viking city.

With the discovery of an ancient Viking city right in my own home town I became more intrigued than ever with Irish mythology, and

Celtic and Viking history. My artwork was influenced by the ancient times and places, by the book of Kells, the Book of Durrow, and the ancient stories and manuscripts that bring the history of Ireland to life.

I never set out to be an artist, but from the earliest time I can remember, drawing, painting, and music were my passions. But the high school I attended in Dublin was an academic one and I was encouraged to study to become a veterinarian. Veterinarians earned a good living and it is a respected profession. It never occurred to me that I could make a career out of art. It seemed completely impractical. It was not until my final year in high school that I realized that art was actually offered as a major.

Dublin Art College

When I heard about the art college in Dublin I completely changed gears. I dropped my science subjects one by one and applied for acceptance into the art program. The admissions counselor told me that I need to submit a portfolio. I had no idea what a portfolio was; I'd never done anything like that before. I took a week off from school feigning illness and worked on my first portfolio. I sent it in and although I'd never formally studied art, I was lucky enough to be accepted to the NCAD of Dublin.

Another bit of luck occurred when I was awarded a spot with the Crescent Workshops of Kilkenny, which offers an exclusive course put on by the crafts council of Ireland. The course teaches artists and craftspeople how to set up a business. Business sense is critical for artists so we can learn how to make a living doing what we love to do. It is not enough to be passionate about art; you have to possess business sense to make it a career.

My first project for my art business was the design of a deck of playing cards based on the Irish legends. I designed all the cards and took out a hefty IR£14,000 loan from the bank to get them printed. I had some help from my cousin in the banking industry to secure the loan. I also came up with my own set of greeting cards. Every weekend, I loaded up my powder-blue Fiat 127 and drove from town to town in

Ireland flogging my creations to small gift shops along the countryside. I had a nice arrangement of products and I put together a little stand. I was only twenty-three, so I was nervous to go into the stores and ask for business. I felt like I was playing dress up and my costume was "Business Woman." In spite of my nervousness, I presented the items as a package to the shops and they sold very well.

I decided to bring my products to Showcase Ireland, Ireland's biggest creative exposition show, and I took many orders. About a year later I was approached by a distributor willing to sell my cards and greeting cards for me. In the beginning I paid the distributor a commission to sell my products. Somewhere along the way the tables turned and the distributers took over my production costs and paid me commission on the sale of my products. That's when things started to get easier.

The distributor relationship suits me well because it gives me time to paint and create my designs without the huge start-up financial investment. I have the freedom to work when I want to work and where I want to work.

I moved to a small village in Tuscany, Italy, in 1993. I have made my home there among the olive groves and vineyards and raise my three half-Italian children there. My business gives me the best of both worlds. I come to Ireland often for business. My muse is Ireland and its history and beauty. My kids get the benefit of having a stay-at-home mom who happens to paint while they are at school.

My artistic style is interweaving the history and stories of the Irish legends, such as Finn Mac Cumhaill and Queen Maeve, into a contemporary setting. One of my most popular pieces is my portrayal of the Celtic Tiger. The Celtic Tiger was the symbol of the economic boom Ireland experienced in the early 2000s. Of course now the Celtic Tiger is dead and once again Ireland is experiencing a recession. One of the best things about being of Irish descent is that we know we are strong enough to turn this around. The key is doing something about it. I meet people at trade shows who were architects and construction workers who got laid off and are now reinventing themselves or pursuing an old dream. They become painters, hat designers, writers, jewelry makers. The Irish are resilient and we are willing to evolve and try new things. The small business entrepreneurs will be the ones that get us out of the bad times and create the future.

People have a choice. You can sit at home watching the bad news on TV and moan and groan about the economy, or you can get out and do something different. I always choose to be different. Like so many Irish, I want to embrace the challenges of life and make something better. I love that I have been able to combine my love of Irish history and culture, with my love of art into an ability to make a living.

Ann Montieth

Ann Montieth began her career because of a passion for photography, but then she discovered that a love of something is not enough to make a commercial success of it. Business knowledge is critical to the success of even an art business. So after learning what it took to make her business succeed, Ann decided to help other photographers learn how to make money to remain viable.

Ann has become the industry's leading authority on photography studio business management. She has developed a program and course of instruction designed to help other photographers succeed. She is a frequent lecturer and serves as a consultant to many studios around the United States and abroad, including Ireland. In addition to authoring many books on the business of photography, Ann and her husband continue to run two popular portrait studios.

Ann's Story: Irish Connection

My connection with Ireland is unique. My father's side of the family is proudly Scots-Irish, although my parents never visited Ireland. Growing up the daughter of an army officer, we moved thirty-four times before I got married. Traveling for fun was not an option.

It was the music that first attracted me to Ireland. When I was a young child, my father taught me to harmonize on folk songs, and I later learned many of them evolved from Celtic music. I play piano by ear, and I love the simple beauty of traditional Irish music. I have an extensive collection of Irish CDs, and some of my favorite songs are about places in Ireland. Many of the lyrics were written by authors who were forced to leave Ireland because of economic hardships. Their lyrics express a longing to return to a beautiful land.

I studied English in college and developed a love for the poetry of W. B. Yeats. Eventually it occurred to me that it would be wonderful to visit the places that Yeats and others wrote about so lovingly. So in 2002 my husband and I embarked on our first trip to Ireland. I'd been there about fifteen minutes when I was hooked.

Since then we have returned to Ireland at least once a year, traveling almost the entire coastline. Because I do photography and teach about it for a living, I had never been motivated to take pictures on vacation, but Ireland changed all that. I have photographed in nearly every county, and many of my Irish photographer friends say that I have seen more of Ireland than they have. I've returned many times to those places that I heard about in songs and poetry, and I'm especially fond of the Drumcliffe, County Sligo churchyard where Yeats is buried. It is flanked by the fabulous Ben Bulben mountain, and on a sunny autumn day, it is one of the most peaceful places in the world.

No Gloom

My paternal grandmother, Julia Virginia Valentine Price, was born on Valentine's Day, 1876, the same year the Pennsylvania farmhouse in which I live was built. Her earliest memory was traveling by covered wagon from Texas to Arkansas. She and my Scots-Irish grandfather, Lemuel Kendall, homesteaded a farm miles from the "town" of Alabama, Arkansas, which consisted of four houses and a general store. It was many years before they had electricity and refrigeration, but they made ends meet by trading produce for flour and sugar at the crossroads store. They had six children, of whom my father was the youngest.

After the death of my grandfather, "Gran" Kendall divided her time among the families of her children, always asking who needed an extra hand. We were lucky to have Gran with us probably more than our fair share of her time, mainly because as a military family, we were constantly on the move, and we always needed new curtains. Gran was great at making curtains.

As an only child, I spent many hours in her company eagerly listening to her tales of life on the farm: how they worked the land, did the butchering, churned the butter, and dealt with the joys and sorrows of life. Her stories of life on the farm were like scripts from the TV series *The Walton's*. She never complained about the hard work; the stories were always about the great adventures they had. Those stories provided unforgettable glimpses into a truly rich way of life, though today it would be considered to be poverty.

Once she told me that some of her fondest memories were of events that occurred during the Great Depression. People spent more time getting together to tell stories, dance, and sing. Everyone would bring a covered dish, and "the good company was good medicine." I think of this often as we confront a difficult economy. There's no reason to be gloomy.

Speaking of good medicine, Gran had a home remedy for everything. If you cut your foot, she made a poultice of bread, milk, and herbs to make the swelling go down. If you had a cold, she gave you a comforting mixture of herbs that included peppermint.

As I was growing up, it seemed that there was nothing she couldn't do; as an adult I recognized that she had no need of a feminist movement. On the farmstead she was an equal with my grandfather. They were a team, and each day they went to bed knowing they had accomplished something important. She used her sharp mind and her common sense to take charge of what needed to be done.

My parents named me Julie Ann as a tribute to my grandmother. When Gran was ninety-two, I flew to Arkansas with my six-month-old daughter Julia so Gran could meet her latest namesake. The photograph that I took of the two of them is a family treasure.

Gran lived to be ninety-three. She enjoyed good health until the last six months of her life, keeping busy knitting booties for hospital patients. One of the qualities I admired most about her was her enjoyment in keeping up with what was new and her ability to educate herself on any subject of interest. She was fascinated with space exploration, and she knew more about the space program than I did.

She took great pride in her children's accomplishments. My father, Bruce Edward Kendall, was the only college graduate, but all her children led successful lives because she saw to it that they were educated in other ways. When it became evident that my father might be able to attend college because of his skills as a basketball player, my grandparents moved the family to a larger town so that he could attend a real high school. All his primary schooling took place in a one-room schoolhouse. After graduation from the University of Arkansas, where he captained the basketball team, he joined the military and was on General Douglas MacArthur's staff during the occupation of Japan. In 1967–68 he served as commanding general of the US Army in Japan. Not bad for a Scots-Irish lad who grew up in the backwaters of Arkansas.

My decision to become a journalism teacher was largely formed because of my grandmother's emphasis on the importance of education. Journalists always continue to learn, and it was journalism that led me into photography.

A Business Experience

Although both my husband and I benefitted from good educations, when we decided to go into business for ourselves we were entirely unprepared for the complexity of entrepreneurship. We should have known better than to borrow money without a business plan, but we just assumed that Jim's background in business and my knowledge of public relations was all we needed to propel our part-time photography business into a profitable career.

We took the advice of a local banker to finance our business on a demand loan, because at 5 percent interest it was cheaper than mortgaging our home. Our failure was that we didn't ask enough questions and we learned the hard way that interest on demand loans is variable. Less than a year later, the interest rate had ballooned to 23 percent, and we faced the definite possibility of losing everything we owned.

It took an incredible amount of hard work and self-discipline to overcome this first lesson from the "School of Hard Knocks," but there's truth to the saying, "What doesn't kill you makes you stronger." I emerged from five long years of chaos with a good understanding of what it takes to achieve financial success in a "passion business." I converted this experience into the subject matter of my classes for artists. Typically artists are frightened or repelled by the discipline that business imposes on their artistic freedom. Although I got into photography to exercise my creativity, I found that I was even more fascinated by the creative process of creating a business. It's that creativity that I enjoy sharing with my colleagues.

I also learned that life is far less stressful if you live within your means and have a rainy-day fund. My grandmother taught me self-sufficiency by her example and by passing on her philosophy: "Try as hard as you can not to be a burden to others; that way you'll be in a position to help others when they need it."

I happened to be in the "first wave" of women who kept my job during pregnancy and after we had children. Feminists of the day told us we "could it have it all." It didn't take long for that myth to die a richly deserved death. Raising a family and a business at the same time means you always feel that you are shorting one to serve the other. The elusive search for so-called balance never ends. I have a sign over my desk that says, "Once upon a time there was time."

Nonetheless, I have no regrets. Women today have opportunities and choices their grandmothers never had. So I hope they make the best of them by choosing wisely and recognizing that, as a wise woman once told me, "Life doesn't have to be perfect to be perfect."

Most of the things that annoy me are business related. By nature, I'm a planner, and I hate it when there's a glitch in a plan that I did not anticipate. In an effort to keep this character trait from driving me and others crazy, I try to keep in mind Murphy's famous laws:

> *Nothing is as easy as it looks.*
> *Everything takes longer than you expect.*
> *And if anything can go wrong,*
> *It will, at the worst possible moment.*

These axioms have been fun reminders for me to "chill" every now and then.

In spite of the demands of running a business and worrying about the many hours I spent *not* hovering over them, on a personal level I am most proud that my children turned out to be mature adults who are leading productive and satisfying lives, with the added bonus that they have chosen well-adjusted spouses. So far, the grandchildren are also doing well. There is no sign of the dreaded entitlement syndrome which would stir the ire of Gran.

Professionally, I find it satisfying to watch photographers whom I have taught become financially successful, especially those who go on to teach others. A few of them have gone on to teach me, and that is an extra-special satisfaction.

What really adds joy to my life these days are my trips to Ireland, where I get to photograph what I consider to be the most beautiful country in the world. What's more, I get to spend time with my Irish photographer friends, who two years ago honored me by making me a life member of the Irish Professional Photographers Association and a "fellow" of that body, incredible gestures that mean much to me. Every time I go to Ireland, I feel like I'm going home.

My advice to young women starting out is to find something that gives you joy, whether it is raising children, homemaking, a profession, or a hobby. People who don't find something to be passionate about usually end up unhappy, bitter, irksome, or bored.

Chapter Nine

Irish Generosity

*T*here is an Irish saying that goes: *"Make a difference in your little corner of the world."* Making a difference starts with one person having the courage to make a change, take on a project, or stand up and say, *"No more!"*

The Irish have faced numerous challenges and come back each time with a fighting spirit and a generous soul. The following stories show how just one thought can spark an action that makes a difference in a family, a community, or a country. Jane Rundle has spent her life promoting peace as a way to overcome tragedy. Diane O'Connor and her husband saw the children of Belfast being raised in strife, and by offering them a glimpse of peace changed not only Ireland but the world. Lorraine Suankum and her daughters Caliegh and Delia Fabro took their love of Irish dance to Hawaii and brought its joy to the deaf. Marianne McDonald, a world-renowned scholar, took her own personal tragedies and used them as the inspiration to found an organization that has helped thousands. And Sister Mary Anne Owens, the director of Catholic Charities in Dallas, Texas, has given her life to helping people in need.

Often it only takes one person to make a difference—one person to turn the tide, change an opinion, or touch a life.

Jane Frances Rundle

On a bright, sunny Belfast day in 1976, Anne Corrigan Maguire took her four children, including a six-week-old baby, out for a walk. Suddenly a car driven by Danny Lennon, a young republican who had just been shot dead by British soldiers, went out of control and swerved into the path of the family, killing the children and maiming the mother. Haunted by the deaths of her children, Anne committed suicide three years after the accident.

The children killed that day were the niece and nephews of Mairead Corrigan Maguire. Betty Williams was a horrified witness to the tragic accident. These two women turned their grief into action and founded the movement called "The Peace People." Their organization played a part in stopping the violence in Northern Ireland and inspired peace around the world. Later that same year, those two previously unknown women, Betty Williams and Mairead Corrigan Maguire, were awarded the Nobel Peace Prize.

Like Betty Williams and Mairead Corrigan Maguire, Jane Rundle has spent her life turning her grief into action, thus promoting peace. As a four-year-old, Jane accompanied her mother taking food to her great-aunt Kate who lived in a little room in Kenmore, New York, and thus Jane's development of social and moral conscience began.

Mairead Corrigan Maguire was the commencement speaker at Jane's college graduation from Ursuline College of New Rochelle in 1973. Already involved with integration and peace issues, Jane's heart was ready to hear Mairead's message. Jane was so touched by Mairead that she decided that if she had a daughter she would name her after this woman.

She sought and found peace when her firstborn child, Laura Mairead, was stillborn, peace when she had a brain stem stroke at thirty-four, and finally peace and hope for other stroke survivors like herself. By being in service to others, Jane found peace of heart. She knows that world peace begins in her heart—and yours.

Jane's Story: Rose of Tralee

In 1973 I was a senior at the College of New Rochelle, founded by the Ursuline nuns to educate Irish immigrants. I noticed a flier for the International Rose of Tralee Competition. Growing up extremely proud of my Irish ancestry, I knew the lyrics to the Rose of Tralee song but was not familiar with the competition. The winner of the Rose of Tralee pageant "must be of Irish heritage and have beauty, intelligence, and truth in her eyes." My friends encouraged me to enter the competition. I had the Irish background, green eyes, auburn hair, and Irish wit. I figured that the truth would surely shine through in my eyes.

The competition's focus was on intellect and social consciousness. Thank goodness there was no bathing suit competition for this beauty pageant. Instead of writing my final senior papers I worked on my Rose of Tralee application. The application was daunting and I had to really understand my Irish heritage. I wrote of the stories I heard growing up about my family and the discrimination they faced as Irish immigrants in Ontario, Canada.

For a lass with a British name like Rundle, I had a lot of Irish blood in me, not to mention a good bit of the Guinness. My mother's Irish doctor told her to drink Guinness to increase her iron during her pregnancy with me, her sixth child. My father's paternal grandmother, Elizabeth O'Neill (Wicklow), immigrated to Montreal in 1841, a few years before the major Irish immigration of 1845 to 1850. My ecumenical spirit and stubbornness must have come from her, since she married Henry Rundle, a Celt but also an Anglican from Cornwall, England, in 1858. I can only imagine how her parents felt.

I wrote essays recording the history of my Irish heritage and mailed my entry to The Rose of Tralee Competition. Soon I received a letter stating that I was one of the candidates selected for an interview in New York City—a shock indeed.

My friends who cajoled me into entering this contest shared their best clothes with me so I would look stunning. My friends at the college rallied around so much that my entry was more like a community competition. On a Sunday afternoon, I took the train into New York City. I walked a fair distance uptown from Grand Central Station to the office of the Irish consulate. A trio of young adults with Irish accents interviewed me. And I made the cut. I would be contacted for the next interview.

It was another special Sunday for my interview of a lifetime. Again my college roommates dressed me and off I went on the train to New York City. This interview was more intense, conducted by a full-blown committee. One of the questions they asked me was what I was going to do when I got out of college.

I was a fine arts fiber design major in college. I told them that I hoped to go to Ireland to continue my studies in textile design and to work as a weaver. In a stern voice, one of the interviewers asked me, "Are you aware that there are Irish weavers who are unemployed?"

I quickly responded, "Oh, that's OK, I'll pick studs—I mean, *spuds.*"

Oh my God, I really blew it, I thought. *There goes my trip to Ireland.* But after a few seconds of silence, which seemed like an eternity, the committee members burst out laughing. Yet although they laughed, I was convinced that I had kissed good-bye to being a Rose of Tralee.

Thank God for the Irish sense of humor. The committee selected me to be one of the five finalists for the Rose of Tralee competition. Now this was getting serious. There was to be one final "judgment day." As a finalist, I was invited to a dinner–dance at Tavern on the Green in Central Park. In addition to having "beauty, intelligence, and truth in my eyes," I would be judged on dancing and social grace.

This time around, instead of enlisting my friends' ideas for what to wear, I went to the top. Our college chaplain, Fr. Sean Cooney, was from Ireland. He of all persons would know what I should wear to such an occasion. I brought two gowns over to his residence. One was a stunning, sultry, 1940s black crepe gown with a subtle bustle and sequined straps. The other was a puffy-sleeved flowered gown, a bridesmaid's dress. As expected, Fr. Sean chose the flowered, unflattering dress. I thanked him and off I went with no intention of following his advice.

The all-important Tavern on the Green evening arrived. My friends helped me with my hair and makeup. Fr. Sean Cooney and other college staff came to be moral support for me. My entry had grown from a dorm room adventure to a wider college audience event. I arrived at Tavern on the Green, looking knock-out gorgeous in my black 1940s gown.

As I danced with one of the judges he told me, "I have my favorite and I have my Rose of Tralee." I politely said, "I would rather be the Rose of Tralee!"

Later in the evening, four other finalists lined up next to me and my name was not announced. I did not get to throw my hands up in surprise and smile and cry at the same time when they announced my victory. I acted my way through hugging the winner and not crying until I left the restaurant. The judge who told me he had his favorite came up to me and encouraged me to enter the following year. He should have known better. We Irish do not easily forget. I was a woman scorned.

I can still see that Rose of Tralee winner. Her dress was pale lavender chiffon with big puffy sleeves—just like that flowered gown I left in the dorm room, the one Fr. Sean suggested I wear.

In my stunning black gown, I guess I looked more like I was just arriving home at 4:00 a.m. rather than arising at 4:00 a.m. to milk the cows. I still have that 1940s gown, although it no longer fits. I am saving it to wear when I win the Giller Prize for my Irish-Canadian-American novel.

Find Peace Within Ourselves

Since the Rose of Tralee competition, my life has taken many unexpected twists and turns. I always succeeded in whatever I pursued. Whether it was my Irish stubbornness or just a strong work ethic, I never gave up.

My first overwhelming challenge was losing my firstborn child, Laura Mairead. She was a beautiful full-term baby. My partial placental previa had been missed on the ultrasound. She died trying to be born. My child died in violence. The next morning I thought about all the women who lost their children senselessly due to war and poverty. I was more committed to peace than ever before.

With Mairead's death, the happiest time of my life turned into the most tragic. I was inconsolable, yet I had to find peace. The most difficult part was never having the opportunity to hold or know Mairead. I was raised with a strong base of faith in God; however, I could not pray anymore. How could I pray to a God who had allowed my daughter's death?

God graced me through that time of bereavement by putting in my life a husband of faith, John, and Sr. Irene Farmer, a Sister of Charity of Halifax. She became my spiritual director. She helped restore my connection with God and to have the courage to dare risk another pregnancy. To bring peace to my heart, I reached out to other bereaved parents by initiating a bereaved parent's support group. I also shared my story on local cable and radio stations about what it is like to lose a child. I worked with the hospital to set up more compassionate procedures for women in my situation.

God blessed us with a son, Andrew. Life was wonderful. When Andrew was just two and half years old and I was thirty-four, I stroked. I literally had to learn how to do everything all over again. I had to relearn how to crawl, walk, master basic bodily functions, organize, work beyond grade four arithmetic, and face other challenges.

When you have a crisis impact your life, you have to get down to your core character to find the strength to go on. If there's nothing there you're in a lot of trouble. Fortunately for me, my faith in God and what I had gone through losing my daughter made me strong. To raise my son, I had to fight to get better.

At the hospital I requested that my parish priest come and give me reconciliation, communion, and sacrament of the sick. The moment after the priest administered the sacraments, it became clear to me that I was going to live. During my recovery I insisted that someone from the church bring me communion every day. I wrote "spiritual therapy" in the chart hanging over my bed. I needed Jesus' nourishment. It gave me hope.

My life became focused on learning how to walk so that I could keep up with Andrew. I still hoped to teach my son how to do the basics like ride a bike and ice skate. We achieved that and so much more.

Andrew is now a high school teacher and a wrestling coach. I still have some residual effects of the stroke though most people would not notice. Over the years I have made it my life's work to help other stroke persons. I edit and write a newsletter for the North Shore Stroke Recovery Centre, I peer counsel other stroke persons, and I have served in disability advisory and advocacy situations.

Look for Blessings in Everything

My parents raised us to be grateful to our ancestors for what they endured to keep our Catholic faith alive. I often reflect on the story of my paternal great-grandmother's terrifying trip from Ireland to Canada. In the bowels of the crowded boat, she vomited constantly while praying the rosary nonstop. She, along with my other ancestors, arrived in Quebec and Massachusetts with not much else than their rosaries in their hands and their faith in their hearts.

I receive great strength, stability, and peace from my faith and from my ancestors' courage and faith. Knowing where I come from and being grateful for what my ancestors endured strengthens my commitment to seize the opportunity to live my faith deeply, so deeply that my heart might be at peace even if I am surrounded by tragedy, chaos, or suffering.

It is my responsibility and my privilege to pass our family baton of faith to my family's next generations and to any person who seeks hope and peace. When I live my faith, I praise God. I honor my ancestors.

When asked if God were to give me a choice between enduring my daughter's death or having a stroke, I always choose the stroke. Laura Mairead's death injured my spirit; however, the crushing pain purified my heart and soul. The greater one's pain, the purer and more peaceful one's heart becomes, open to love.

My parents taught us to be proud to be Irish, to be grateful for our Catholic faith, and to be vigilant for God's blessings. Watch for blessings in everything. I cannot state that Mairead's death was a blessing; however, good did come as a result of her brief time with us and from her death. My stroke was a blessing because I have become far more compassionate and patient and far less judgmental. I take the time to simply be present to others, to listen with purpose, so as to honor their dignity. I now live in the present.

I pray that I live my life as a prayer. Every moment with my son Andrew is a treasure. Every day is a gift. Amen.

Diane O'Connor

Diane O'Connor and her husband, Rob, have spent the last twenty-five years changing the lives of the children of Belfast. It started one morning when Rob read a newspaper article about a man in California bringing children from war-torn countries to America for the summer. Rest and a reprieve from violence gave the children a much needed break and a glimpse into a life without violence.

Rob and Diane did what few people do. They took an idea and ran with it. They used their backgrounds, talents, passion and faith to create a nonprofit organization that helped the children of Northern Ireland. In the process they founded the catalogue company, Creative Irish Gifts, and found so much more than a career. Through their commitment and tenacity, their work created a rippling effect that changed the course of a country and played a part in bringing peace to Belfast.

Diane's Story: Violence

During the 1980s in Belfast, Ireland, a normal day in the life of a school-age child included potential bomb threats, segregation, and fear. Children were segregated by religion—Catholics on one side and

Protestants on the other. Summers were particularly brutal for children due to "Marching Season" when Protestants took to the streets to stage parades, often causing tensions between Catholics and Protestants to escalate into violence.

My husband and I became unlikely heroes when we decided that something had to be done to promote peace. Adult Catholics and Protestants during the time of the "Troubles" were set in their ways with their belief systems and desires for segregation. Yet the children, the eleven- and twelve-year-olds perhaps, could still be reached. Maybe there was a possibility of promoting peace among a new generation by getting kids out of harm's way and giving them a reprieve for the summer. Perhaps a chance to interact and spend time with their so-called "enemies" in a safe and peaceful place could change the conflict of Northern Ireland.

My husband, Dublin-born Rob O'Connor, and I set out to do just that. With no resources and no plan to speak of, we embarked on a new journey of promoting peace among the children of Belfast.

I met Rob on a blind date in New York City where I was attending the Fashion Institute of Technology. His Irish charm won me over and we quickly fell in love. Rob took me to Ireland for the first time shortly after our wedding and I fell in love with the country, the culture, and his family. I knew that Ireland would be a part of my life forever. I gave all my children Irish names: Aidan, Rory, Ailish, and Kira.

Rob's career took us to Chicago, where we lived for seventeen years. It was there that Rob read an article about an organization in California that made it possible for underprivileged children born overseas to come to America for the summers and live with host families. The families offered the children a reprieve from their stressful life conditions while educating them on new and different ideas on how they could improve their own lives.

This was in the early 1980s when Belfast was embroiled in the height of its troubles. The Catholics and the Protestants were in a heated fight, car bombs went off daily, unemployment was at an all-time high, and children lived in the middle of a virtual war zone.

An Idea is Born

Rob started exploring an idea: What if we brought children from Belfast to Chicago for the summer? They could live with host families and have a month of reprieve from the violence. We would bring children from both communities—half Catholic and half Protestant—and provide opportunities for communication, play, and fun, so they could see that they were all really the same. Regardless of the religion they practiced, they were, after all, human beings. Being devout Christians with the belief that we were put on this earth to make a difference, we took Rob's idea and created the Irish Children's Fund.

We decided to bring 150 twelve-year-olds—boys and girls, many from poor families—from the divided community of Belfast to spend five weeks of the summer with host families in Chicago. Chicago has a large population of Irish families so they rallied around the idea; finding host families and funding was not difficult. With just $2,000 in the bank we decided to launch. We received support from the local newspapers and started fund-raising. With God's help and guidance, and many volunteers, we raised $70,000 for the first 150 children and their ten chaperones to come to America.

Every little gift was a miracle from God. We worked with Catholic Charities Foster Care division to interview and screen the host families. Through a connection in Ireland we hired a school teacher, Gary Rocks, as our director in Ireland. This was another little miracle. Had Gary's last name been Irish like McCarthy or English like Reynolds, he never would have been successful. But his nonpartisan last name, along with his passion and experience, made him the perfect candidate to be the face of the ICF in Ireland. Gary took over connecting to the children in the communities and screening them.

The first trip was amazing. On the plane to America, the Protestant children sat on one side of the aisle, the Catholics on the other. They did not want anything to do with one another. Throughout the summer we hosted a series of activities, picnics, and fund-raisers for the children and the host families to attend. By the plane ride home the children were sitting intermingled, finding friendship and kinship that had nothing to do with religion.

Creative Irish Gifts

Bake sales and car washes are what got the Irish Children Fund off the ground, but to keep it running we had to come up with a strategy. As the popularity of the organization grew, so did the cost and responsibility of running it. We needed more than a bake sale and a grassroots fundraising scheme to keep it going. A system had to be instituted to guarantee regular and long-term financing. Because of my background in merchandising we decided that we would launch a catalogue to support the program. In 1986 we launched Creative Irish Gifts, selling Irish merchandise. It was a wholly-owned subsidiary of the Irish Children's Fund and its sole purpose was to keep the program going each summer.

With four young children at home I entered the world of working moms, only without a paycheck. Rob worked to pay the household expenses and I worked to fund ICF. I attended the Chicago Gift Show and ordered merchandise and shipped it to my house. I set up shelves in the basement and phone lines. Volunteers worked the phones from nine to five on weekdays. I staged the merchandise in the basement using sheets as backgrounds and hired a photographer who donated his services, taking pictures sometimes until dawn. The printer was so touched by our mission that he donated his printing services. We had our first catalogue ready and we mailed it to seventeen thousand households using a donated mailing list. My kids and I actually sorted and stickered zip codes on the first mailing. We were in business.

As with every company we had some early challenges but overall the catalogue was a great success. We slowly grew out of our basement. We lived in a residential neighborhood so the Fed Ex trucks and semis rolling up the street were a concern for the neighbors, but we did what we had to do.

God gave us another blessing when Rob was approached by an entrepreneur in Akron, Ohio, for a new job opportunity. Rob turned down the position and the move because of his commitment to the ICF. But his prospective boss would not take no for an answer. He offered Rob free warehouse space, shelving, furniture, computers, and utilities to run the catalogue from Akron, Ohio. Rob could not turn down the job or the offer. So my family and our catalogue business moved to Ohio.

As the catalogue business took off so did the opportunities that ICF could provide. We were able to extend the program so that when the children returned to Northern Ireland, the ICF program did not end. Both Protestant and Catholic children socialized and played games at the group's leisure center in Belfast and attended weekend outings and summer camps at a large home in the seaside town of Ballycastle, Northern Ireland, called Fellowship House. The kids could be free to explore and interact without the worry of religious affiliation.

A Lifetime of Change

The program was such a success that many of the kids wanted to come back again when they were older. We decided to create a program for the fourteen-year-olds who had come when they were eleven, to spend another summer in the United States. This program not only promoted religious tolerance but also promoted work opportunities and helped develop life skills. Unemployment in Northern Ireland in 1986 was at an all-time high of 17.2 percent. Opportunities for work were virtually nonexistent. Many of the children in the program had unemployed parents who were on the dole. The program for the older children focused on vocations. A child interested in cosmetology was able to live with a host family who operated a beauty shop. A child with an interest in business was paired with a small business owner. The children could go to work each day and learn something that would help them in their future.

These relationships between the children and the host families have lasted a lifetime. Many of the host families have gone to Ireland for weddings, graduations, and other celebrations and have stayed connected throughout the years.

A 1995 independent study by the department of psychology of The Queen's University of Belfast shows the positive impact of the ICF program on participants as compared to a control group. It shows our young people have less religious prejudice, a better self-image, and are more confident and successful in their careers and personal lives. Of course it will take another generation to really make a difference and truly change the culture. Yet we did our part and our lives are better for having opened the door to this amazing journey.

By the grace of God things have improved in Northern Ireland over the years and we brought our last group of children to the US in 2011. Over the course of thirty years, 3,655 children have gone through the program. We sold the catalogue to a business entity but I am on board as a consultant for the time being. I hate the word "retire" because I know I will always want to be involved in something. I want to stay busy and continue to make a difference every day I am here on earth.

One of our proudest moments was receiving recognition from Tony Blair, ex-prime minister of Britain, when he said, "The people of Northern Ireland don't trust words; they trust actions. Your program has brought about incalculable benefit to these youngsters by way of tolerance, hope, and exposure to a better way of life."

I thank God for the opportunity to take a small idea—a dream really—and watch it grow into an amazing, life-altering force. I am forever grateful that I was truly able to make a difference in the lives of so many children. If you change the life of a child, you change the future.

Lorraine Suankum, Caliegh and Delia Fabro (The Celtic Keiki)

Ireland's diaspora can be found on all continents and corners of the globe. No other culture has been able to replicate with such success the Irish ability to assimilate and permeate other cultures. Even in the most remote recesses of civilization you'll find a friendly son of Saint Patrick. The Irish love to mingle and mix and are known for their Irish hospitality.

The furthest place from Ireland may be the paradise of the Hawaiian island chain. Here in the tropics, the Irish found a home in the islands and in the heart of her people. Irish Hospitality mixed with the aloha spirit and brought forth the force known as The Celtic Keiki. Keiki (pronounced "kay-kee") means child in Hawaiian, and Celtic means great in Gaelic.

Twins Delia and Caleigh and their brothers Tristan-Patrick and Gavin, make up the Suankum Clan—what is better known as the Celtic Keiki School of Irish Dance, Music, and Culture. They are a family of performers led by their Thai daddy, Ahkom, and their New York Irish mother, Lorraine Suankum. Known as Hapa-Haole (Hapa meaning Asian/Pacific Islander and Haole meaning white/European), the children with their exotic looks and Irish personalities are a fusion of two great island nations and a mixture of the best of both worlds. They introduced Irish step dancing to Hawaii's Pacific Islanders and took the genre to a new generation and population. Along the way they discovered that this form of dance was especially appreciated by the deaf.

The Celtic Keiki twins are the youngest wise Irish women in this book.

Lorraine's Story: Bow Irish is Irish?

My dear mother grew up in Brooklyn and was the quintessential native New Yorker. I hailed from the tiniest town on the outskirts of New York City, College Point, which was known as an Irish breeder and feeder town that grew the boys that would swell the ranks of New York's finest and bravest. Its girls would marry out of high school and raise large families like the ones they grew up in. My bedroom window played host to the city skyline each sparkling night. We were close enough to see the city but far enough to live in peace.

I thought everyone in New York was Irish or wished they were. I knew my grandparents came from Ireland and that was the extent of my knowledge of my heritage. My parents embraced the American culture and did not really raise us in a traditional Irish household. We didn't know much about our lineage nor did they seem particularly interested. My parents were born in Greenpoint, Brooklyn, and that was Irish enough for them. My mom listened to the Ink Spots and the Temptations. The closest thing my father came to acknowledging Irish entertainment was watching Bing Crosby, James Cagney, and John Wayne movies.

The disparity between mythical Ireland and Irish history puzzled me. I thought Irish was something you did, not something you were. It seemed to skip a generation or was bred out of our line. I knew we weren't the Irish who had parents with a brogue, or came from a farm, or the ones who went "home" to Ireland each summer.

Of the five children, only I had a passing curiosity about our ancestry and the Irish jig. I took one Irish jig lesson and realized that Irish dancing was only for "reel" Irish girls as we used to call them. We were another breed, more sophisticated and twice removed from the confines of an ancient culture and mindset. Maybe even a better breed. We were the next generation of Irish: the New York Irish-Catholics— the *best* kind. To us, Irish music meant bands like U2, The Pogues, The Cranberries, and Thin Lizzy.

Irish in Hawaii

When my twin daughters, Caliegh and Delia, were born in 1994 on the island of Oahu, I thought more about my culture and Irish roots. My great-grandfather John Blake was a professional Irish dancer and performer who migrated to America in 1911. In my grandmother's family, the O'Connors, are some of Ireland's finest musicians. I found myself haunted by the memory of my grandparents' songs and odd sayings, and I heard myself parroting the old wives tales to my little babies. "Bless yourself when you leave the house or when hear an ambulance." My true Irish was coming through. "You only take with you what you give to the poor," I'd remind the girleens as we donated our coveted dollars each week at Sunday Mass. "If we give away our money won't we be poor?" they'd ask. "Not having money doesn't make you poor," I'd explain. "Not having anything to give makes you poor.

As long as you have a song or story to share you'll always be rich."
There is a world full of people who have plenty of money and nothing
to offer. The Irish are raised to give of ourselves.

As they grew, the girls and their two brothers, Tristan and Gavin,
wanted to share their happiness in the form of their music and dance.
"It runs in our family," they said. "The new face of Irish dancing is
Asian."

Hawaii and Eire share many cultural similarities. Both of these
small island nations understand the importance of self-sufficiency. We
both have a rich oral history filled with myths and legends of giants
and of the little people. While the fabled Giant's Causeway is all that
is left of Eire's large men, statues of King Kamehameha depict him
at over seven feet tall. The menehune are thought to be cousins to
leprechauns who came to these islands as stowaways on Pacific bound
ships. Hawaiians and the Irish acknowledge a spiritual life and love for
the land. They actively resisted industrialization and the exploitation
and pollution of their natural resources. Their wise men, called Druids
from Gaul, are known as Kahunas in Hawaii. They were healers and
the keepers of knowledge, genealogy, and history. They were the
holders of magic and the conduit to the forces of nature and the gods.
The similarities can also be seen in the cultural practices of tattooing,
chanting, dance, and ceremony. Each were feared and regarded as fierce
warriors. We understand the importance of preserving your indigenous
culture beneath the yoke of a dominant language, religion, and system
of government. Both peoples had their sovereignty and language
abolished and wrestled away from them. They saw their ancient beliefs
and way of life displaced. They embraced and consecrated themselves
and their kingdoms to Christianity. Both cultures have also experienced
a revival and resurgence of their outlawed languages, forbidden dances,
and unwritten music.

I wanted my girls to understand the importance of preserving,
promoting, and perpetuating their native values despite a dominant
English force, a consumer-driven mentality within a materialistic
society. I wanted them to understand their rich heritage, how a poor

people could dominate the earth with their long list of achievements. You cannot change your Irish DNA—it will surface. No matter where you reside, the Irish are tied to their land, tied to their traditions; it is through their music and dance that they are tied to their history. I taught them it is not what you have that makes you great, but what you give.

I sang the old songs to them, read them the ancient stories, and recited the classic poetry from Ireland's great writers. One day, they saw Michael Flatley dance on television and that was it for them. They could follow his moves instinctively. It was obvious they had the Irish. I bought them Irish pennywhistles and they could play them without a lesson. By seven years old my girls were dancing and choreographing their own routines.

Their cousin completed the set and brought the lilt of Irish ballads to parties and events across the island. People clamored to see the girls dance and hear them sing. Their thirteen-year-old cousin Kiana Ahovelo just left the troupe and the island to pursue her professional solo singing career on the mainland. "Kiana's *Danny Boy* is so haunting," brags Caleigh, "that I saw grown men cry and women hand over their jewelry—a diamond and emerald ring!" "What about the time when those musicians gave you that handmade harp?" Kiana recounts wistfully. "A man from Newfoundland sent me a handmade mandolin with mother of pearl inlay!" Delia adds joyfully.

It's what you give that counts. The girls are known for their giving and donate their time and talents to provide free music and dance lessons to the Children of Deaf Adults (CODA) each Saturday morning beneath the sheltering stones of the Central Union Church Choir room. Their private lessons, beginner group lessons, and hard shoe classes allow them to offer free classes to Hawaii's deaf and disabled children. They teach the classes using American Sign Language and find it helpful when they perform at large venues like their upcoming show at the Hawaii Shell.

The girls also lend their dance and signing talents to other up-and-coming performers. They have been training with a young deaf woman and helping her perfect her hip-hop routine for the Hawaii Stars competition and $10,000 prize for charity.

The girls study American Sign Language at Saint Francis School in Manoa and have been signing since they were small. The deaf love the hula and Irish dance. One is a story told by the hands and the other by the feet. Being a very visually stimulated dance, the deaf can see the distinct repetitive patterns and complicated footwork and equate them with the similarity of our Celtic knots. The deaf community seems drawn to the Irish music and culture. The deaf also find one hundred thousand welcomes (*cead mile failte*) as they gather for a monthly dance and social in the Celtic Room adjacent to O'Toole's Pub. Daddy Ahkom "Art" Suankum takes the stage with his guitar and plays an old Beatle tune while Caleigh and Delia take the microphone and sing along. "The Beatles were Irish, ya'know," one listener swears. "I never miss a Celtic Keiki show—and I'm not even Irish!"

The Celtic Keiki School of Dance, Music, and Culture opened in the summer of 2005, after the girls returned home from their whirlwind tour of Ireland. We explored our traditions, met our cousins, and saw where our people came from and lived for the past four hundred years. Ireland welcomed us as ambassadors of aloha. Irish hospitality was met with an aloha spirit and East met West in the form of little twin girls.

When the girls returned to Hawaii they brought with them a burning desire to awaken the Irish spirit in the islands. They brought home authentic instruments: fiddle, bodhran, bones and whistles, among other things. Each child plays more than five instruments and Caleigh can play eleven. Hawaii welcomed the Celtic Keiki back with open arms, eager to learn of the land beyond the waves. It is believed that three-quarters of the Hawaiian population share Irish ancestry. The girls discovered that Hawaii's last Monarch Prince, Kuhio, so loved his Irish friends that they celebrated his birthday on March 17 in grand Irish style—with a Saint Patrick's Day parade. The girls resurrected this royal tradition and celebrate by leading the Saint Patrick's Day Parade through Waikiki each year.

The Celtic Keiki were instrumental in bringing the first Feis (a traditional Gaelic arts and culture festival) to the Pacific and stole the show and first place medals from the larger and more experienced dance schools. The Celtic Keiki were unorthodox—dancing and smiling, whooping it up, flipping their forty-five inches of long, straight, black hair, competing in homemade dresses that came down past their knees. We sewed them ourselves for only twenty-five dollars. The girls took first place and stole the hearts of the dance judges. "That's how it should be done," remarked one judge, referring to the girls' smiling and shiny faces, without makeup, without wigs, without the pageantry, and without the stern looks.

When the girls were featured in *Irish Dance* magazine they knew they had put Hawaii on the dance map. They were invited to play, sing, and, of course, dance at Irish festivals across the country and shared the stage with such living legends as Paddy Noonan and Derek Warfield and his Young Wolfe Tones. They had reached the pinnacle of their young careers when they received a telephone call from Derek Warfield saying he was coming to Hawaii to see them. We accompanied him on stage in concert. Together they sang the very first song they had ever learned, an Irish song, The Wolfe Tone's famous *Streets of New York*.

Caleigh and Delia: The Force

Our Irish mother is our secret weapon. She is the force behind us. She taught us that the Irish are pioneers and we should expect greatness. "Bring something to the table," our mom always says. Having something to contribute to the conversation and to society at large is a prerequisite for success. As Irish Catholics we are defenders of the faith and beholden to the poor and desolate.

Catholicism is to Ireland what Judaism is to Israel—a part of our identity. On a small island like Hawaii we consider everyone our aunty and uncle and call all our neighbors and friends cousins. This sense of ohana or kalabash family is evident in the multiculturalism of our organizations. The Celtic Keiki and Hawaii's other Irish groups, like the Wild Shamrocks and Friends of Saint Patrick, achieve a measure of true brotherhood that couldn't be peacefully reached in Ireland itself or understood on the mainland. We are a rainbow coalition of brotherly love that includes Irish from all denominations: Roman Catholics, Protestants, Christians, Mormons, Jews, Buddhists, atheists, pagans, and even modern day Druids.

At a typical Saturday morning dance class at Central Union Church we begin, barefoot, poised amidst a sea of Asian children with lineages like Tonga Irish, Palau Irish, Chinese Irish, Maori Irish, Tahitian Irish, Filipino Irish, Hawaiian Irish, Thai Irish, Marshallese Irish, Japanese Irish, and African Irish. These Hapa children are joined by others who have no Irish but a love for the music, dance, and culture.

We all work together to ease the suffering of those less fortunate. Last Christmas, Central Union Church and The Celtic Keiki distributed one thousand gifts of shoes, clothes, books, toiletries, goodies, blankets, and toys to Oahu's homeless veterans, homeless children, Hawaii School for the Deaf and Blind, the MaryJane Home for Unwed Mothers, and a prison rehabilitation program known as "Celtic House" run by eighty-year-old Anglican Father Ruby. We feed recovering addicts on Thanksgiving, entertain the elderly at Easter and Christmas, and tend to the homeless on New Year's Eve.

Generate Aloha

Our advice on generating aloha in your life: start each day with a prayer of thanks, start each week in thankful worship, and start each year grateful that you can do more than the last.

We all inherit gifts and can manifest strength. Our great-grandmother could read tea leaves, our grandmother could read people, our mother interprets dreams, and some of us have the healing touch. And of course we all have the Irish gift of the gab—or the blarney. We advise other young ladies to cultivate their own gifts and uncover their strong suits. A body follows where the mind leads. Keep your mind fixed on your goals and strengths. Where your mind is your soul will be too.

You don't have to be Irish to love our music, dance, and culture. When people wonder how girls from Hawaii learned Irish dancing, we tell them, "It's the amount of Irish in your soul, not in your blood, that makes you a true Irish." The Celtic Keiki are *reel* Irish. *Slainte.*

Marianne McDonald

Nestled in the foothills outside of San Diego is the large, rambling sanctuary that Marianne McDonald calls home. The ranch style structure, a historical landmark, is located at the end of a private drive and guarded by a gate and stucco walls and six ragamuffin dogs—all rescued from shelters—who dart out to welcome and inspect any visitors. A world-renowned professor of theatre and classics in the department of theatre at the University of California, San Diego and a member of the Royal Irish Academy, she is a popular professor who commands long waiting lists for a place in her classes.

Her love for the classics began early with her introduction to Latin in the first grade at the Convent of the Sacred Heart in Chicago. The Convent school provided a sanctuary from a home life that was challenging at times due to the turbulent relationship of her parents. She completed her secondary education at the Chicago Latin School, which introduced her to Greek and cemented her love of the classics. After obtaining a bachelor of arts in classics and music from Bryn Mawr College, she earned a master's in classics from the University of Chicago and a doctorate in classics from the University of California, Irvine.

In addition to being a world-renowned scholar, professor, author, and playwright, Dr. McDonald has lived an exciting and active life. She has embraced adventure and enjoyed snow skiing and scuba diving and even completed a trek to Mount Everest. In pursuit of her studies, she lived in several countries and was honored for her contributions to the preservation of classical and historical works in both Ireland (*Thesaurus Linguarum Hiberniae*) and Greece (*Thesaurus Linguae Graecae*). Her passion for teaching and philanthropy has allowed her to support worthy projects that have resulted in the sharing of access to some of the greatest scholarly works.

Born in 1937 to Eugene Francis McDonald and Inez Riddle McDonald, Marianne's life has been a study in contrasts. Though blessed with access to tremendous wealth, this did not protect her from being touched by tragedy on more than one occasion. It did, however, allow her to take those experiences and turn them into opportunities for helping others.

Marianne McDonald has been honored by and presented with dozens of awards that recognize her many gifts of philanthropy, the most significant of which was the founding of the Scripps McDonald Center in 1983 to combat drug and alcohol dependency. What is most apparent after a short time in Marianne's presence is her tremendous compassion and empathy for those who are struggling, particularly with alcoholism and drug addiction and the consequences of these diseases.

While sitting in a cozy room surrounded by awards and certificates, mementoes and family photographs, she spoke freely about her life. When asked which accomplishment she was most proud of, this modest woman paused and smiled before answering, "Rescuing my dogs."

Marianne's Story: A Father's Influence

My father grew up in what was essentially an Irish slum in Syracuse, New York. His grandparents came over from Ireland during the potato famine and like so many others, settled in America seeking a better life.

He ended up supporting his entire family when he was only fifteen after his father died, followed shortly by his brother's death. He had several sisters and his mother to support so he went to work earning money any way he could—delivering newspapers at first, then becoming a used car salesman.

Although not able to graduate from high school, he cultivated his talents and creative genius. Taking his earnings from the car business, he bought out an inventor who was selling the technology behind radios. While working on a car engine one day, it exploded and destroyed his hearing in one ear. This tragedy became an opportunity when he applied his imagination to the problem and invented the Zenith hearing aid, which was the best and cheapest hearing aid available at that time. He was most proud that it didn't just help him, it helped others as well. His example of compassion and philanthropy is one of the reasons that I have always felt a responsibility to reach out to others. He took his investment in radio technology and founded the Zenith Radio Corporation, which later manufactured televisions. This company gave him—and ultimately me—the freedom to reach out and help others.

A Family in Chaos

My family life was colored by my parents' dysfunctional and volatile relationship. My father had married a "trophy wife," a woman who was much younger. I felt sorry for my mother, "someone who marries for money and pays for it." She was a nationally known concert pianist and was fluent in five languages. My love of music is one of her legacies to me.

Unfortunately, my parents were substance abusers; my father was an alcoholic and my mother preferred prescription drugs; these addictions placed a heavy burden on my shoulders. They divorced when I was twelve and I remained with my father. I admired his tremendous work ethic and respected his solid sense of morality. He had a strong sense of right and wrong and was passionate about maintaining the highest standards of quality and ethics in his business.

I was very proud of my father. I was torn between a wonderful life of excitement and opportunity and a reality that required me to serve drinks to him from the minute he came home. Still, I treasured the opportunities I had. I met people like Admiral McMillan, who went to the Arctic. My father went with him and installed a short wave radio that allowed the Inuits to broadcast to Australia. His genius and his work with radio changed the entire industry and the way people communicate today, touching so many and making their lives better.

He embraced a variety of causes and projects. For example, he funded *Ebony,* the first magazine that celebrated black culture. He had known prejudice and hated it. He was compassionate and honorable and lived life with passion. His compassion for the victims of prejudice and injustice was a constant in my life and a trait I have embraced as my own.

As complicated as my family life was, I was empowered by my father's example. He was a firm believer that you can do anything if you believe you can do it and want it hard enough. Motivation is everything. The only thing we cannot be is immortal. But as Plato said, we can be immortal when we touch other people and make a difference.

So I am grateful to my parents for what they gave me. No matter how bad certain things were in my childhood, I give them credit for the good they taught me. The old thing was to blame your parents; the new modern thing is to blame yourself. Each of us is given the tools to learn and fulfill our destiny. You can survive anything coming from an Irish Catholic background, and you can even make it into a joke. The Irish sense of humor helps you cope (I kissed the Blarney stone, literally)—it saves the Irish because sometimes you have to laugh or otherwise you'd go insane. I like to think that I share a bit of the Irish wit and wisdom in my own character. Perhaps this is how I find happiness despite my troubles.

Alcoholism as a Legacy

Alcoholism and substance abuse have left deep and painful scars on my life. As a child of alcoholic parents, I survived a childhood marred by conflict and turbulence. I lost my only brother to suicide in 1965 when he was high on marijuana and under the influence of alcohol. I had spoken to him on the phone a short time before he took his life and I had no idea what he was going to do. The memory of his death is still painful today.

My experience with him made me very sensitive to anyone who is feeling so much pain. I believe that you must take such outcries seriously. Perhaps trying to fulfill a need to provide an alternative to a drug and alcohol addicted life, I looked for a way to help prevent such tragedies.

The McDonald Center was a tribute to my father and ironically a benefit to my own family: its program helped my mother and several of my children. It has helped thousands of people and it gives me a sense of joy to know that I have helped those who have gone through the hell of a life lost to alcoholism and emerged from a tunnel of darkness to see the light of sobriety. In this program people learn to love themselves enough to be honest and committed to choosing a fulfilled life over a living death.

But as many people know, the existence of a program is not always enough to save someone. I suffered the excruciating heartbreak of losing a child to drugs and alcohol. My fifteen-year-old daughter Kirstie was high on LSD and drinking with friends when she played Russian roulette with a loaded gun and lost. The pain was unimaginable. I was lost myself for a year as I struggled to come to terms with my grief. I fled to Ireland and immersed myself in my work. Eventually I realized that I had responsibilities to many other people so I pulled myself together. But not a day goes by that I do not think of her. It will be like an open wound for the rest of my life. The McDonald Center became an act of contrition for what I felt was my role in this wasteful death.

Less obvious but equally damaging is how alcoholism impacted my relationships. When you are a child of an alcoholic, you replicate the chaos. I fell into relationships again and again. I was multi-married. Because of my own issues with commitment and my struggles with relationships, I loved passionately but not wisely. I am grateful that I was blessed with six wonderful children—a virtual UN portrait including an Irish redhead, blonds, brunettes, and my half-Japanese son. My father would have been proud, with his love of all types of people and his hatred of prejudice or injustice. My family is unconventional and has been tested by challenges, but each of my children is well-loved. Sadly, alcoholism touched many of them as well. But now all are living good, sober lives and pursuing their own dreams.

Lessons Learned

I have learned many hard lessons when it comes to my children and their struggles. You have to listen to them, love them, and let them be who they want to be. Empower them to learn in their own way with their own skills—tell them to be the best that they can be. Just don't expect the impossible.

I tried to give them the gift of an education, or at least the opportunity for one. But the most important thing I hope I have taught them is compassion. Compassion is love. The Greeks have a beautiful way of describing love. They have three words for love. *Eros,* which is erotic love, a nice big explosion that can die like a firecracker; *philia,* which is affectionate love, like the love you feel for a friend; and finally, *agape,* or selfless love—"love thy neighbor as thyself."

I was the firstborn, my father's "son" in a way. He taught me to shoot and fish and empowered me to stretch myself and to believe that no woman should be limited by her sex. He also provided me with financial independence such that I could pursue my dreams and try to make a difference in this world.

I embraced my love of the classics and have been blessed with the opportunity to share that passion with my students. I believe that education is absolutely the one gift that no one can take away. It is more important than money because it will always belong to you. It is a life-long legacy to yourself that you share with your children and the world.

As a professor, I have been able to touch many students—people I saw as gifted and talented but who were struggling to reach their potential. It has been immensely gratifying to see them overcome their fears or insecurities and succeed. Of course, success varies from person to person. I get tremendous pleasure from knowing one of my students is in turn spreading a love of learning. I have also been able to use my scholarship to preserve some of the language and culture of Ireland through my sponsorship of various projects and work at Irish universities.

I also hope I have touched many in my published works as well as my teaching, besides my many translations of Greek drama and my own prize-winning plays, which are performed throughout the world. In all these works I try to convey the value of compassion and a sense of justice.

Everyone, every woman, should define success on her own terms. Being a great mom is success, and I envy those who have succeeded with their families—kept them alive and kept them happy. I think they are the most successful. Still, I won't say "happiest of all" because everybody should define their own happiness. People must follow their own conscience.

I think that is ultimately what the Irish have: conscience. Finally, what counts is knowing that you have satisfied yourself with what you believe is right. I like the idea of trying to give with one hand so that the other hand doesn't know what you are doing. Do good daily. A person who helps his or her fellow man is richest at the end of all.

Sister Mary Anne Owens

Sr. Mary Anne, who has served as executive director of Dallas Catholic Charities for the last fourteen years, is described by colleagues, parishioners, and friends as formidable, tenacious, and a visionary. She has been called a warrior for the working poor in Dallas for her inability to take no for an answer.

It's a reputation that is just fine with her. Having served as a sister in the School Sisters of Notre Dame for the past forty years, Sr. Mary Anne has chosen a life of service and education.

It's a commitment that she describes as having been written into her bones by her parents Andrew Owens and Mary Anne (Minnie) Hanlon Owens, who immigrated to the United States in 1922 from Cavan and Kilkenny, Ireland. The couple had four children: Jimmy, Thomas, John, and Sr. Mary Anne.

Her parents' message of service and faith resonated with Sr. Mary Anne. She was especially inspired by her mother, Minnie, who was often said to have "never met a stranger who did not become a friend."

Matthew 25:31–40 tells us that to live a life of faith means to act with loving care for people in need: to feed the hungry, clothe the naked, and welcome the stranger. It was taught early and often to the Owens children, and they were expected to be their "brothers' and sisters' keepers."

It should come as no small surprise, then, that most of their children lived lives of service. Sr. Mary Anne went on to head one of the largest human service organizations in North Texas.

When Minnie passed away in November 2010, just shy of her 105th birthday, Sr. Mary Anne said it was with a joyous and open heart that her stories, messages, and vision would live on in her family.

In June of 2011 Sr. Mary Anne will take on a new role as provincial (an official in charge of an ecclesiastical province acting under the superior general of the religious order) for a new province in her congregation of the School Sisters of Notre Dame.

Sister Mary Anne's Story: Immigrant Links—Do What You Can

For the last fourteen years I have devoted my life to Catholic Charities of Dallas. With over sixty-seven thousand clients each year I have heard many a story of the plight of the immigrant. Each story, each person reminds me of my parents, Andrew and Mary Anne Owens, and their own journey to America from Ireland. They arrived in 1922 with less than twenty-five dollars in their pockets and big hopes of a better life.

Nowadays immigrants to America may come from different countries but the experience is the same. Looking into the faces of clients I see proud yet desperate fathers and mothers looking for a little help and a friendly face. The requests are simple but necessary: a mother in need of a box of diapers, a father asking for rental assistance, a grandmother requesting school supplies for the granddaughter she is raising. I see my mother in their faces.

Each immigrant has a link to the past, the family and culture they left behind. Each time I serve it is a call to share justice instilled deep within me by my parents. In New York in the 1950s, when my parents were raising us, the kind of support Catholic Charities provides did not exist. Families had to make it on their own, pinching pennies and often going without.

My mother never forgot those early years—and made sure her four children didn't forget them either. We heard about those first difficult years as an immigrant and how my mother cleaned other people's homes. Yet my parents were always looking for ways to help others with whatever bit they had as soon as they could. We often packed up boxes of clothes and toys for our cousins in Ireland. It was our responsibility to improve our community and make things better.

Moving from a little farm in Ireland to a Manhattan apartment is like going to another planet. In Ireland the economy of the family was tied to the land. Farmers relied on crops and slaughtered pigs to eat and earn a living. In Manhattan my mother prayed for a job making beds in a hotel. She worked long hours in hopes of one day working her way up to be a cook or a server. Refugees and immigrants of today experience the same situation. They are still struggling. They do the jobs that no one else wants to do. They'll do anything to earn money because they have to put food on the table. It is all about creating a better life for their children.

And yet, they always ask how they can give back. In my family it was part of the culture. My parents believed in the philosophy of "pay it forward." They never used that saying but they lived the principle. My mother always said, "You are your brother's keeper or your sister's keeper."

This is one reason I love the immigrant culture so much. In our community—and definitely in our family—there was an understanding that you have to come to America to be financially secure, but you're also here to contribute to the common good of your community. My parents worked with all their neighbors, so they knew what their needs were. There was never a sense that you're entitled to anything. You had to contribute in some way or other.

My mother always said, "Saint Patrick's Cathedral in New York City was built on the dimes of the domestic workers." The working poor and the immigrant communities contributed what they could at whatever level they were able. My mother believed she owned the cathedral.

Catholic Charities

That's how I feel about Catholic Charities. It belongs to the people of the diocese, regardless of religion. It's not my agency. It's the people's agency. Therefore, the responsibility to sustain it is theirs as well.

My mantra with volunteers is, "You will benefit much more than the people you serve." Volunteers come to us thinking they will make a difference—and they do—but in fact the volunteers are blessed by getting something even better in return. Many people in America have so much more than they need. Our culture has become one based on wants and desires. No sooner do people obtain a possession than they tire of it and it is discarded and forgotten. Ultimately the poor benefit when people embrace the service and grace of passing it on.

The Gospel message "Don't waste the bread," is alive and well at Catholic Charities. Nothing is ever wasted. When you see that embodied in real life, it is incredibly powerful. Sharing the smallest thing creates gratitude in the heart of a refugee.

This spirit of giving continued throughout my mother's whole life. When she was in her eighties, she volunteered for a New York women's homeless shelter that was run by the Catholic Church. She often spent the night at the shelter with the women. Her friends asked her why she stayed there and she answered, "I'm not sleeping anyway."

Folks could not wrap their minds around it. Friends worried the women at the shelter would harm her. My mother was never afraid. On the contrary she formed a bond with many of the women and grew to love them. She admired their ability to survive on the streets. She listened to their stories and gave the best gift of all—the gift of her time. She called it "chatting them up" and she found out all there was to know about them.

Just like anywhere else, an office, a school, or a women's shelter, some of the women were selfish and some of them were generous. Some of them had very deep-rooted issues. She could see herself in some of those women. She told me, "It could have been me. I was just one step ahead of them. I am not sure what made the difference. Maybe it was my hard work. Maybe it was fate. Maybe it was grace mixed with a little luck. It takes very little to distinguish between making it and homelessness. It could have been me. Now it was my job to help them."

Bringing Unity

During my time at Catholic Charities I strived to promote unity. Unity is belief in faith and in our community, faith that we are all part of God and belief that we are here to serve. It is one of the gifts of the Holy Spirit. By bringing the people of the dioceses and the poor together we created unity and everybody is the richer for it, including me. Through the many programs to help the poor, whether it is housing, medical, or childcare, I witnessed the blessing of unity and the evolution of the Dallas community.

I've learned that change happens much slower than you would hope, but it comes. Everybody has some talent that they are willing to share, and sometimes they don't know it when they come in but they may learn it going out the door. And if they find their passion, that's all anyone really needs in life.

Has running Catholic Charities been easy? Definitely not. At times I've had to make difficult decisions as head of Charities. But I had to ask myself, *What is the most loving thing to do in this situation?* Sometimes the most loving thing to do is the most painful thing to do. And I think I draw those decisions from my own faith life, career life, and advice from people that I respect.

My future contains an opportunity to transition to a new role. After fourteen years of serving as executive director, I will be leaving to be provincial for a new province in the congregation of the School of Sisters of Notre Dame.

I'll be taking with me so much but especially the experience and influence of the poor in my life. They have become the lens through which I see things. I've been seriously blessed, and I take a commitment to share what I've learned and see where God leads me next.

Afterword

Becoming a Dreamer
by Marcia Wieder

During our journey to seek out words of wisdom from Irish women around the world, we became aware that this project is much more relevant than we had imagined. Though we knew that women everywhere are responsible for shaping our lives and the lives of so many others, we did not truly appreciate the role of the powerful matriarch until we began this project.

We found that successful, accomplished, and happy women often gain strength from their families, particularly their mothers and grandmothers. This trait appears to be universal and cross-cultural. Hence we know that another book or maybe even two or ten more must be written, celebrating the wise words of women from other cultures, religions, or ethnic groups.

While networking and interviewing women, we became aware of a universal truth. Women everywhere are seeking ways to be more fulfilled as professionals and mothers, wives and daughters, and even friends. Women strive to do it all and seek perfection—whatever that is—as a goal. Women are often burdened with unreasonable expectations created by their own self-imposed rules and goals.

We feel we can learn from each other, share our triumphs and our struggles as we travel through life, hoping to reach a place of balance and contentment. Each woman in this book had big dreams and the courage to live in pursuit of them to create a unique, inspiring life experience. Each faced challenges yet managed to change their lives for the better.

Now that you have experienced a bit of Irish wisdom, the next step is to take action to attain your own dreams. But how do you find the courage to go after your dreams?

We met a woman who, though not Irish, has wise words to share, so we have included her as a taste of what is to come. The creator and founder of Dream University®, Marcia Wieder made it her lifelong mission to inspire people to "believe in your dreams simply because they matter to you." Marcia's commitment to helping people around the world qualifies her as Irish in spirit.

Here is Marcia's story and proven strategy for making your own dreams come true.

Marcia Wieder, Honorary Wise Irish Woman

In the late 1990s I had my very own "B List." I was dissatisfied with my body, my boyfriend, my bank account, my building, and my business. Basically I was dissatisfied with my life. I began to realize that complaining was not getting me anywhere and I needed a different approach. I had a marketing-in-media agency in the National Press Building and it was pretty prestigious; I was president of the National Association of Women Business Owners. I had a list of credentials and "things" that said I should have been happy, but I wasn't. It was not about being ungrateful, because I felt a lot of gratitude for my life, including the ups and the downs and the successes and the losses. At the end of the day, I needed to answer the most important question: How do I want my life to be and what am I willing to do about it?

I closed my marketing-in-media agency. I moved to San Francisco and began a passionate quest to discover who I really was and what I really wanted. Often what we want in our thirties and forties is quite different from what we want in our fifties and sixties. The only way to recognize the difference is to give yourself some time to explore and contemplate the question.

One day, I heard a radio commercial for the Make-a-Wish Foundation and decided to attend the meeting. That night I found myself sitting around a small table with five other people talking about how we were going to help children. The goal was to do what we could to make a sick child's dream come true. I was deeply touched and inspired that evening. Here I was in "Nonprofit Land." The paint was peeling off the walls and the little room had a bulb hanging over the table we worked at. Yet I felt happier than I had in a long time. I left the meeting in an emotional state and got in my car to head home. Before I turned the key in the ignition I began to sob. That moment changed everything for me. I finally began to wake up. This was the moment I realized, *Oh, I love helping people make dreams come true.*

That night my "vision" became even clearer. Helping sick children was important but I wanted to create a message for adults around the world also. I wanted a message that would change the world I knew best—Corporate America. My message would heal people's hearts and fulfill my soul. I created Dream University®, the only university in the world dedicated entirely to helping people achieve their personal and professional dreams.

For over twenty-five years I have spent my life doing just that, helping people all over the world achieve their dreams. When I announced to my family and friends that I was closing my business to start a company that was going to help people make dreams come true, they said I would starve. Luckily, they were wrong.

The number one way we sabotage our dreams is by bringing our fears and doubts into them. This happens when we utter three little words: "But what if?" But what if I go for my dream and I fail? But what if everybody is right? But what if I can't make a living? But what if? And if you're projecting your worst fears into the dream, then every time you move toward the dream you're moving toward your worst nightmare.

I teach people to separate. There's the dream. What is it you want? What does it look like? Put some meat on the bones. Write it out in detail before talking about it. And that usually dredges up the doubt. So I call them the Dreamer and the Doubter. And about that Doubter: people think it's the enemy, but really, the Doubter or the doubting part of ourselves will give us our list of obstacles. Wherever there's an obstacle, you can design a strategy to manage it. Obstacles are either something you believe about yourself, life, or your dream, or something that requires a strategy or a plan.

People realize that what's stopping them from pursuing their dream is usually some small lingering belief that they don't even necessarily believe anymore. You recognize that your lingering beliefs are either moving you forward or holding you back. The problem is that you have forgotten that you can control what you choose to believe. So my tenet is, "Can you believe in yourself or your dream or whatever it is you want to create simply because it matters to you?" Not because there are promises, guarantees, or assurances, but because it really matters to you. And then prove that you believe in it by taking action on it.

That's where the transformation actually occurs; with one step you're in action. You're no longer just thinking about it and talking about it. People relate to you differently because *you're* relating to *you* differently. You're actually doing something about it. Take that next step to show that you're serious about your dream, and then once you take that one, take the next one. That's really it. Making a commitment to an action step and then actually taking the action step, that's putting your stake in the ground. One surefire way to activate the Doubter is to say what you want, then do something else.

The ability to say "no more" to what's no longer true, is powerful. You may no longer be passionate about it, the window of opportunity has passed or you just keep talking about it and not doing anything about it. To be able to say "no more" to what's no longer true opens up the space to say, "Now what? Now what do I really want? Now what will really matter to me? Now what will feed my heart and my soul?"

It takes courage to take a stand for your dream. On the other hand, the cost of *not* doing can kill your soul. The choice is between surviving in a status quo existence or embracing your future. Say to yourself, *Wait a minute, this is my life and I do have some say about it.*

I'm not saying that all dreams need to be Mother Theresa "change the world" dreams. Your dream may be of quality time with your family, losing weight, or taking a class. It may be doing something meaningful. Unfortunately most people never even stop to ask the question, "What are my dreams?"

Women often ask me, "Isn't it selfish to focus on my dreams?" Research shows that people who live their dreams live ten years longer, have a better quality of life, and are happier and fulfilled. They feel like they have made a difference. Pursuing your dreams is actually an act of generosity for yourself and your loved ones.

I believe that at a spiritual level we were created to create; joy, love, and abundance are our birthrights. Life is not about survival and problem solving and putting out fires. It's supposed to be filled with happiness, purpose, and abundance.

Then the question becomes, "Well, what is it that I love and how can I get paid well for doing what I love?" A lot of us stifle our dreams before we even explore the possibility. We're living in dynamic times and a lot of the old structures are breaking down. There's never been a better time to pursue your dreams. Don't believe the press. Don't look in your checkbook or on the news or in the newspaper to decide whether or not you want to pursue your dreams. Don't listen to well-meaning friends and family who tell you can't do something. Get in touch with what you love and what makes you happy—and do it.

The advantage of living in these times is that you can change. You can change your mind again and again and you can chart your own course. When I had the opportunity to be on the *Oprah Winfrey Show* the topic was empowering women to start their own businesses. I boldly asked Oprah what her dream was. She explained, "My dream is to create a company where people could have fun. A place where people come together, make a contribution, and give back to the world." I thought, *This is really important because this is the richest self-made woman in the world and she had the courage to act on what was real and true for her.* Then Oprah asked me, "What's your dream?" I explained, "My dream is for people to have dreams again. My dream is for people to have courage to schedule the date to start working on their dreams so they have a chance of bringing them to life instead of just living filled with nice ideas."

Every guest who had "made it" on the show said the same thing. "If you don't love it, don't do it!" There will always be days that you hate your business and there will be failures and setbacks but if you inherently love what you are doing, your passion will get you through the dark days.

People often ask me, "How can I get on *Oprah?*" I say, "Just be your own Oprah. Be the bright light. Be the revolutionary. Be the lone voice that speaks up for what's important to you."

To view a full list of all the contributors in *Wise Irish Women*, please go to www.WiseIrishWomen.com.

About the Authors

Patricia "Tricia" Connorton Kagerer

Serving as vice president of risk, safety, and process improvement for one of the country's most elite construction companies, Tricia learned what it meant to be the only woman in the boardroom—and how to exceed expectations in a tough, male-dominated world. An expert in risk management, process improvement, conflict resolution, and business culture, Tricia climbed to the top of the corporate ladder and transformed the culture of the organization.

Tricia attributes her success to her strong Irish Catholic upbringing and what she learned from her two role models: her mother, Pat Connorton, and her grandmother, Peggy Prendergast. Both women dedicated their lives to hard work, tenacity, and faith, serving to accomplish one goal—to give their children a better start in life.

Tricia was born in the Bronx, New York, and was raised in El Paso, Texas. She has visited Ireland several times, where she spent time on the family farm, Clanevan, in County Wexford, Ireland.

After suddenly losing her mom in 2007, Tricia decided to channel her grief into her book, *Wise Irish Women*. Tricia is an author, keynote speaker, and recipient of numerous awards, including the *Dallas Business Journal*'s "Women to Watch" and the *Business Insurance Magazine*'s "Top 25 Women to Watch."

Tricia has a master's degree in education and human development: conflict resolution from Southern Methodist University. She holds a business and public relations degree from Regis University in Denver, Colorado.

Tricia is married to Markus and they have two children: Tommy and Anneliese. They currently reside in Plano, Texas.

Laura Prendergast Gordon

Laura Prendergast Gordon is presently serving as one of two deputy city attorneys for the City of El Paso. Born and raised in El Paso, Texas, she graduated from Bryn Mawr College in Bryn Mawr, Pennsylvania, and then received her JD degree from Texas Tech University in Lubbock, Texas. After graduating from law school, she returned to El Paso and has spent the bulk of her career as a public servant working for the City of El Paso in the office of the city attorney.

A fifth generation El Pasoan on her mother's side, she has always cherished the strong influence of her Irish father's family. Growing up in a close-knit family that enjoyed just being together made her value the gift of time spent with loved ones. Many of her most treasured memories involved sitting around the table at her grandmother's house enjoying a strong pot of tea and hearing family stories.

After losing her father to a sudden illness in May 2007, she began to reexamine her Irish roots and felt a desire to explore the strong values and wisdom of her Irish family connection. The *Wise Irish Women* project was a way of paying tribute to the women in her life who inspired her to strive for success and happiness.

Laura is married to Patrick R. Gordon and has two children, a son, Patrick Thomas, and a daughter, Aidan.